Revolutionary Women

Revolutionary Women

A Lauren Gunderson Play Collection

Emilie: La Marquise du Châtelet Defends Her Life Tonight
The Revolutionists
Ada and the Engine
Silent Sky
Natural Shocks

LAUREN GUNDERSON

methuen | drama

LONDON · NEW YORK · OXFORD · NEW DELHI · SYDNEY

METHUEN DRAMA
Bloomsbury Publishing Plc
50 Bedford Square, London, WC1B 3DP, UK
1385 Broadway, New York, NY 10018, USA
29 Earlsfort Terrace, Dublin 2, Ireland

BLOOMSBURY, METHUEN DRAMA and the Methuen Drama logo are trademarks of
Bloomsbury Publishing Plc

First published in Great Britain 2024

Cover design: Rebecca Heselton
Bust © lambada/Getty Images. Flowers © Evie S/Ananthu Selvam/Christie Kim/
Ryunosuke Kikuno/Samuel Bryngelsson/Unspash

A catalogue record for this book is available from the British Library.

A catalog record for this book is available from the Library of Congress.

ISBN: PB: 978-1-3504-0158-7
       ePDF: 978-1-3504-0160-0
       eBook: 978-1-4081-0159-4

Series: Methuen Drama Play Collections

Typeset by RefineCatch Limited, Bungay, Suffolk
Printed and bound in Great Britain

To find out more about our authors and books visit
www.bloomsbury.com and sign up for our newsletters.

Contents

Emilie: La Marquise du Châtelet Defends Her Life Tonight

Commissioned and first produced by South Coast Repertory

with support from the Elizabeth George Foundation

The Revolutionists

Commissioned and first produced by Cincinnati Playhouse in the Park

Ada and the Engine

A Central Works Method Play

Commissioned and Premiered by Central Works

At the Berkeley City Club on October 17, 2016

Silent Sky

Commissioned and first produced by South Coast Repertory

with support from the Elizabeth George Foundation

Natural Shocks

The World Premiere of Natural Shocks was presented in October 2018

by WP Theater

Lisa McNulty, Producing Artistic Director   Michael Sag, Managing Director

Preface

The women in my plays are revolutionaries outward and in. The *outward* comes from the historical significance of many of my subjects: the sexist norms they defied, the glass ceilings they shattered, the brazenness with which they fought for their passions.

But the *in* matters most to me. Their interior battles, discoveries, and revolutions that push them to contend with and ultimately define themselves. The internal cauldron of their own minds, the personal reckoning that happens only in the heart where revolution becomes evolution. Great characters define themselves as such by toppling their internal obstacles, and the motivation of my two-decade-long playwriting career so far is just that: women *are* great characters.

What makes a character great? Self discovery born out of struggle, drive, passion, and the costly but necessary evolution mentioned above. Great characters require a journey fueled by urgency, risk, need, and struggle. Great characters need a resilient, flawed but unflappable heart that is tested again and again. Finally, great characters demand an internal world complex enough for secrets and desires that cannot stay quiet or kept.

Most of my young life in Decatur, GA, I absorbed that the characters capable of those great stories were men: Hamlet, Willy Loman, Tom in *The Glass Menagerie*. The women were always on the sidelines, or if they were the main character (Nora for example) they were almost entirely alone in a world of men. This I couldn't stand. I loved theatre too much to settle for women being written into only the supporting subplots of someone else's journey or isolated from other women. I knew that we were worth the whole damn story.

Thank goodness that I started to see something new to me when I was in my teens: Sarah Ruhl, Lynn Nottage, and Paula Vogel's plays started to be performed on more and more stages. This spurred me to seek out more women playwrights and I started reading Carol Churchill, María Irene Fornés, Marsha Norma, Tina Howe, Sarah Kane, and Lorraine Hansberry. These women thrilled and challenged me with writing that was clever, poetic, fully emotional, decidedly feminist, and from a woman's perspective. I saw their plays and said "yes!", then said "more!", then said . . . "me?" Might I amplify, add to, and perhaps even join the canon of feminist playwrights? If I didn't see enough plays that spoke to and for me, perhaps I should write them myself.

So I did. I wrote what I wanted and needed, knowing that if I wanted and needed it others would too. I didn't want just one or two women onstage in a single play, I wanted ten—no!—I wanted entire casts of women. I wanted women who were funny, righteous, broken, ruthless, brilliant, and sexual. I wanted the cresting thrill and hollowing shock of deep, forceful emotion as well as the highest-minded intellectual, scientific, and political subjects all tackled by women. I wanted mothers, sisters, lovers, leaders, friends, and enemies; all femme, all unforgettable. I wanted women of depth, feeling, ambition, and emotion, and I wanted to root for them up until the end. I wanted love stories, loss stories, political stories, friend stories, family stories, existential stories, comedies, tragedies, and histories. And I wanted great men who were also feminists; men who lived and loved fiercely alongside these irrepressible women. I wanted to write plays with endings that were not always triumphant for my characters but were always true, not always happy endings but hopeful ones. I began writing because I wanted women and girls at the center of every story, not because of politics but because of the utter and unique power they bring when they are centered. I wrote the heroes I needed, because I needed them to embody and inspire people like me.

You will find in these plays a lack of one thing: personified antagonists. This is a feature I've only recently realized about my plays and is perhaps one of the more significant elements of my version of feminist writing. Why? Because the twin antagonists in every play in this collection are not people, they are patriarchy and time. Both are ever present, both uncompromising, both a threat to everything my characters need, want and strive for. Sexism needs no introduction, and needs no walking-talking villain to show up and give our characters the struggle of a lifetime. Time is the universal antagonist ceaselessly challenging my ambitious protagonists to do enough, be enough, love enough, prove enough, know enough before their last breaths. I don't write villains because I don't need to. For my characters the world as it is proves enough of an antagonist. Simply by wanting to be an astronomer, a physicist, an engineer, a rebel writer, or a woman in charge of her future my characters are revolutionaries on arrival.

This collection is an honor like few others. It represents half a lifetime of writing, each play an experiment in storytelling, theatrical craftsmanship, and feminism. Because, of course, a revolution has also taken place in myself. Writing these plays, working with theatre makers across the world, learning from each and every process has deepened my love for theatre, amplified my confidence in the necessity of our artform, and given me the greatest gift of lifetime in the arts: an evolution of one's own. These plays have changed me, challenged me, and taught me. They have given me a life similar to my protagonists: one that insists that women are worthy of the greatest theatrical stories that we dare to write.

Lauren Gunderson, March 10, 2023

Lauren's thanks

Thanks to twenty years of advocates, mentors, collaborators and co-creators. Thank you to some of my earliest advocates—Margaret Edson, Meghan Monaghan, Steve Yockey, and John Glore Emory University Theatre and Creative Writing Department, and Essential Theatre. Thank you to honest, collaborative, and fierce agents—Corinne, Kate, and Leah. To the many directors, dramaturgs, actors, designers, and Artistic Directors who have pushed the plays deeper with their thoughtful questions. To my family—my mom, dad and sister who are always the best opening night dates, and to my husband and boys who have given them a run for their money. Thank you to Dom, Julie, and the Bloomsbury Methuen team for your work and support. And thanks to audiences all over the world, for your time, your laughter, your gasps, your understanding, and your resilient hunger for live theatre.

Introduction: Time and Space

Over the past few years, time seems to have worked differently. In the pandemic shutdowns we seemed to have been stuck in a strange, lingering, semipermanent present tense. Having become familiar with Lauren Gunderson's work in the decade leading up to the calamity, it's been a great privilege to revisit them for this collection.

Lauren's plays are about women making choices to try to be their authentic and full selves. Her interest in history is clear, but her use of science and poetry, math and philosophy set her work apart. Lauren refuses to accept that assumption that scientists and mathematicians were always men, or that those fields are at all wholly separate from poetry and philosophy.

In a larger sense, though, Lauren's plays are about time, and about how time functions for and treats women differently than it does men. We are forced to consider if women perceive time differently and more acutely than men, that time may be crueler for us, at least in the plays. Time is always so present, and it is a ravager. So many of the women Lauren concerns herself with have been forgotten as time passed, and she pulls them into a theatrical present so that we can share the moments together for a bit, as she asks us to ponder our future. Will we see a future where the women with revolutionary ideas will be able to easily share space with others? In what ways will we use our time?

Each of the remarkable women under consideration in these five plays are aware of time passing in their lives. They are aware that they have fallen out of their own time and into some kind of relationship with people in the audience, who are not in quite the same moment. The ultimate concern about the passage of time—mortality—affects every woman under consideration in Lauren's plays assembled here. For each of them, there is never enough time to finish their work, to make their marks, to tell us their stories. They work fast, they talk fast—they know they have to, because in a way they are all seeking to achieve immortality by being in communion with us. If we carry their stories forward, then death and time can be cheated. Lauren gives them, and us, the gift of more time with them, their ideas, their humor, a version of their full selves. Sometimes she even gives them more time to step into the future; something the physicists would perhaps find questionable, but Lauren invites us to the land of poets and philosophers, with different possibilities.

Emilie: La Marquise du Châtelet Defends Her Life Tonight

Emilie: La Marquise du Châtelet Defends Her Life Tonight was my introduction to Lauren Gunderson's world just shortly before it premiered in 2009. I was working in a literary office at a large American regional theatre. The conversation about the underrepresentation of women's plays on our stages was just beginning in earnest. I brought the play to my artistic director and was symbolically patted on the head. He said that it felt slight. And I couldn't understand that. There were several plays floating around then, as there often are, that were investigating the relationships between philosophy and art science. And this one centered on a woman almost lost to history made it more important to me.

The play crackles with life even as Emilie reckons with her death and her life, and the things left undone and unsaid. The theatrical device of Emilie not being able to touch the people who lived life with her, the people she loved, is painful to watch, but it also forces us to think about the incredible amount of "life" she is not ready to let go of—that she will defend to her actual death. She is passionate and brilliant and selfish and loving, so very fully human even as a theatrical construction.

Lauren walks us through science and math which might be daunting to most people. She does this with an assurance and deftness that lets us feel as smart as our heroine. It's quite an accomplishment that the fights between the brilliant Marquise and her genius lover Voltaire are the vehicle for our understanding of Newtonian physics, but that's the gift Lauren gives us. We are comfortable with the big ideas as they come, because this is a play about the Marquise, and for her big ideas were her life. To understand her, we can grapple with the concerns of whether fire has weight or whether Sir Isaac Newton was right about everything, or we can see the foundation laid in the eighteenth century for the discoveries that will define the twentieth. We struggle with her to find the formula for measuring love vs. philosophy. The power of *Force Vive*.

And we will also grapple with the concerns that any woman, any human, might— have I been a good enough parent? Or partner? Have people been good enough to me? Have I been good enough to myself? Is the work ever done? No, the work is never done. Emilie already knows how her story ends; she has told us so. We know that this last pregnancy will bring about her death, and she will run out of time for the great works of math and physics she is still figuring out.

There is a scene in *Emilie* towards the end of the first act—as called in the play: "The scene in which the daughter is finally seen and heard." Emilie and her daughter Gabrielle confront each other just before Gabrielle is to be married off to a prince. Her mother has been able to live life on her own terms compared to so many women of this time and place, and the daughter challenges her as to why her mother thinks she could be nothing more than a wife. Why doesn't her mother see her as exceptional, why would she think that her daughter would want things to be easy instead of interesting? Emilie realizes that she herself missed the opportunity to support another woman, in this case her own daughter. She has missed a certain kind of chance to secure her legacy.

The Revolutionists

The need for women to support other women circles back to us in *The Revolutionists*.

(*Wait. You should know that we're either tangling or untangling time a little in this collection, depending on how you view reality. On the historical timeline, it's about fifty years after Emilie's death, in real (that might not be the right word) time, it's been six years between the two plays.* Emilie *comes first because* Emilie *came first.* Ada and the Engine *will have a premiere the next year in 2017 just as Ada Lovelace comes next in time in the nineteenth century. Then Henrietta Leavitt and her friends will join us in the early twentieth century but Lauren's* Silent Sky *actually already happened in 2011.*

Natural Shocks *happens today and it happened in 2018 and it is not history at all yet. OK—back to* The Revolutionists.)

Like *Emilie, The Revolutionists* is filled with concerns and ideas that are not slight: freedom, motherhood, love, friendship . . . all playing out for us with the highest of stakes as the guillotine is raised. The four women perhaps exist in Lauren's mind, or perhaps in the mind of the woman at the nominal center, Olympe de Gouges. De Gouges was a playwright and human rights advocate. Unfortunately, her time was smack in the middle of the French Revolution. Joining her on stage is Marianne Angelle, a woman made up of many women from this moment, arriving to us as a free Black woman from Saint-Domingue, a friend of Olympe's seeking her aid in creating abolitionist pamphlets. They are joined by Charlotte Corday, the teenager who assassinated Jacobin leader Jean Paul Marat. And then, of course, why not, they are joined by deposed Queen Marie Antoinette herself.

In six years and also in fifty years, much can change. While Emilie and her contemporaries may have realized they were at a crossroads in history (indeed Voltaire spent a bit of time in prison for his dangerous ideas), the culmination comes with the French Revolution and then the implosion of the Revolution and then how the Revolution turned into the Reign of Terror, and how the Enlightenment and the age of revolutions continue to echo.

Although this is another play concerning historical women, the tone of *The Revolutionists* is a leap from *Emilie*. Emilie is certainly aware of the audience, but she holds a fixed point on stage and in relation to the people she lived her life among. The women in *The Revolutionists* exist together only in this play. This play exists for them to be together. They are just as sexy and smart as Emilie (and later Ada and Henrietta), but they are not concerned as much with being representative of history so much as they are representative of women in danger. Yet again, women are running out of time.

Although one might expect the much-maligned queen to be the one who has the hardest time seeing beyond her personal situation, Lauren surprises us by making the artist Olympe the one who has the most trouble in summoning courage to face reality and doing what needs to be done. She is great on the grand stage presenting her Declaration on the Rights of Women and pursuing immortality with her writing and speaking, but she struggles in the personal relationships and being the kind of friend that her friends need. Marianne needs a pamphlet, Charlotte needs last words, Marie needs a rewrite. We know, and they know, that they are all headed to the scaffold, and the artist must learn she has to be there. She shouldn't look away.

The theatrical gestures in this play are more subtle than in *Emilie*. The women here are trying to create the play that will hold them in history—"Hi, story." The performance demands a level of meta-awareness, which will then turn around and break your heart. It will demand you feel something, as is Lauren's real signature as a playwright. In the hands of the right actors and directors, the moments of connection between Marie and Marianne are simply gorgeous and smart. The Austrian cake-loving queen and the Black woman fighting to free the enslaved people of what will become Haiti don't seem to have much in common. Indeed, you might initially wonder why Marie is in this play at all. This is where Lauren challenges us—is she asking us to see all women as inherently revolutionary if they speak at all? If they demand to be remembered? If they choose to be the heroes in their own stories? Yes. Marie and Marianne form a strange friendship as they talk about their husbands and children, as they become people for each other and the audience instead of symbols. Women who understand that teacup bows are really the best.

We witness Charlotte's death and then Marie's. And then finally, it is for us to witness Olympe's walk to the scaffold. This walk is where we have really been for the course of the play, with Olympe, about to reach the end. The historical de Gouges was writing a play in which the queen was a sympathetic character, and that was one of the "crimes" for which she was sentenced to death. Lauren has humanized these women in this play about a play about a revolution about a group of women who probably never met but are here together and for each other. *The Revolutionists* is a play about women who are in a moment of time which must end for them, but it restores them to us.

Ada and the Engine

With *Ada and the Engine* we return to a more contained story of one woman. Ada Lovelace remains a little more in the contemporary consciousness, remembered as the first computer programmer. In her notes on Charles Babbage's work, in addition to proposing algorithmic processes, she seems to have seen beyond the numbers and calculating possibilities and into the ideas of computers for analyzing and maybe even creating complex "thoughts." Lauren takes us into a version of her life, again making us feel very smart for understanding computer science, and diving deep into Ada's own self-description of herself as a poetical scientist.

That poetical part can't be dismissed, for Ada was the only legitimate child of Lord Byron, and in imagining the shadow in which she spent her life, we know that Ada could never have lived the expectedly quiet life of a mid-nineteenth-century English lady. In an almost reversal of Emilie's relationship with her daughter, here we are called upon to consider Ada's relationship with her mother, Lady Byron. Her mother, like Emilie, has misunderstood her daughter deeply, in this case fearing that her father's sins will appear in her and ruin her. She miscalculates saving her daughter from her father's perceived or real insanity by letting her study mathematics. However, Ada's mind is wild for ideas ranging from poetry to engineering and more. And she is powerfully charming and straightforwardly delightful.

In Lauren's play, Ada's relationship with Babbage is dangerous. He is older, he is unsuitable as a husband, and yet he is a soulmate. For Ada, the time between their ages is less important than the synergy of their minds, yet she acquiesces to marry the man her mother chooses for her. The tension that pulls her between her mother, Babbage, her husband, her children, and her work is untenable and dramatic, and she, too, runs out of time. Unlike with Emilie, Olympe, Marianne, Charlotte, or Marie, we are a bit taken by surprise by Ada's short life. The play runs in a mostly linear fashion, there is not the limbo aspect of *Emilie* nor the looming guillotine of *The Revolutionists*. Just, in the end, a quiet end and a question as to whether the bird that Ada was, ever really got to fly. Unlike Emilie or Olympe, Ada seems less concerned with her legacy or future fame, even as she fights Babbage about how her notes should be presented. She is a perpetual student, chronically interested in everything.

The engine at the heart of the story can, as Ada notes, "hold the past, the present, and the future, all at once, all together in its beating metal heart." This is an amazingly poetic and even Romantic thought considering how the computer age has turned out for us. And it is impossible to think about Ada's dream of a computer that could write music in a pure way, but that lack of purity is part of what Lauren is pondering with this play. There is so much beauty, but there is not a tidiness to it. Ada's mind and life are messy. And so many roads lead back to her father.

For the historical Ada Lovelace there are some mysteries that Lauren has mined: Why did she ask to be buried with her father? And, what did she say to her husband when she was ill that made him abandon her on her deathbed? Lauren gives us a poetically and scientifically sound investigation of those mysteries. Structurally, Ada stays in her play more than the previously discussed ladies. The nod to theatricality comes mostly at the end, in another gesture that will become part of Lauren's signature— time collapses in the last several pages as Ada enters immortality and we see her in our own world, everywhere.

Silent Sky

Silent Sky is about another kind of computer entirely—the real women who calculated the parameters of space and the stars. The Henrietta Leavitt that history gave us was a brilliant astronomer whose discoveries provided a key for defining the size, the vastness, of the universe. In *Emilie*, we meet the woman whose work paved the way for Einstein's famous equation defining energy and mass and light. In *Silent Sky* we meet the contemporaneous scholar whose work undergirds relativity. The study of light and heat come together here, and, again, depending on how you measure time, this play is next to *Emilie*.

As with Ada, Lauren's Henrietta is imagined as a full person, despite the things we don't know. This play is the leap after *Emilie*. Emilie is in an after-life, beyond time. In *Silent Sky*, Henrietta and the people who surround her stay mostly tethered to a reality of time, compressed and speeding up, as they come to understand the vastness of time and space. Emilie lives her passion in defiance to the norms of her era, while Henrietta is suppressing much of hers. She is a well-behaved American woman of the early twentieth century, for the most part. She goes home when her father is dying, she is chaste and shy with the man she falls for, she is scandalized by women wearing pants. But she would still like to know what our place is in the universe and why we are here.

And yet, in her own way, she pushes and challenges the time in which she lives. She leaves home, and then leaves home again, to pursue work as a computer at Harvard, even though it's not exactly what she hoped. Henrietta and her friends, clever suffragette Annie and sharp Scottish Williamina are tasked with studying photographic plates of stars created with the powerful telescopes to which they are denied access. The mysteries of the universe are explained, but as in her other plays, Lauren uses these scientific inquiries to study women in their moment. What is important is that Henrietta sees something no one else notices and it creates a puzzle in her mind, one that can only be solved by relying on her relationships with the women in her life. Annie and Williamina are supportive of Henrietta's work, indeed they are responsible for some major discoveries of their own. But it is in her conversations with her sister Margaret about music that the universe comes into focus. The Cepheids of the Magellanic

Clouds, their blinking is musical. The sustaining and pulsing of light and the universe are tonal. It's music. There is no hard line between science and art. The skies are not subject to silence.

The relationships between the women are so beautifully centered in this play. Emilie is mostly separate from other women. The revolutionists are reliant on theatrical constructs. Ada is in a simmering war with her mother, and her mentor does not support where her heart is leading her. But here, with *Silent Sky*, we have a true communion of women who understand each other and help each other understand. The deep friendship that Henrietta, Annie, and Williamina share is inspiring—they support each other, root for each other, they take care of each other. And Henrietta and Margaret have a bond that transcends the challenges they have in seeing the other clearly and fully. None of the women in Lauren's plays are sniping or competitive with each other as a trope might have you believe, but in this play the women get each other. They are not as alone as the others sometimes feel.

"Time is . . . persistent," Annie says to her as Henrietta is facing her death. "But light, its speed, is a constant—one of the few in the universe. Just so you know, I choose to measure you in light." Like Emilie and Ada, Henrietta falls ill, and her time runs out. Like Ada, Lauren gives her the opportunity to step out at the end and be timeless, immortal, as her ideas get translated in our time, in this case to travel the universe.

Natural Shocks

There will be spoilers here, so feel free to go read the play or all the plays and come back later.

This last play is a sharp turn from the others. Angela is not a person from history, a heroine from the past that Lauren is bringing into a new focus for us. The other women have been rescued from time, but Angela is from our time. A time that is not the French Revolution but is as dangerous and deadly for the woman Lauren has invited us to know.

Like the other plays, *Natural Shocks* considers mothers and daughters, women and men, love, math, what it is to find and be yourself as a woman in the world. The world in this one is small, though. Angela is a former roulette croupier who has become a top-tier insurance agent and she is hiding in her basement as a tornado bears down on her house. She is a woman with a deep understanding of risk, but everything she knows about statistics and probability are colliding in the moment in which we meet her.

And it is a moment—as an audience, we are trapped in time with her, just her. This is a monologue, just us and Angela. We are trapped in a long, few minutes of Angela's life as we spend about seventy-five minutes with her in the theatre. As the story unfolds and we come to trust, distrust, and trust our narrator again and we learn, that like the other women Lauren writes for, she has dared to try to make her own way in the world and she has run out of time. Instead of a guillotine, it's the peculiarly American scourge of gun violence. The tornado Angela is being terrorized by is the husband she is trying to leave for another woman.

On Valentine's Day of 2018, a young man walked into Marjory Stoneham Douglas High School in Florida and in a matter of moments shot seventeen people dead, leaving the Parkland community and many more traumatized, heartbroken, and angry. What made this time different from so many other school shootings was that many of the surviving students organized for action. There had been other movements for gun control before, most notably Moms Demand Action which came into being after the 2012 Sandy Hook Elementary School shooting in Connecticut. The Parkland kids were just kids though, and so quickly they pulled together with other young people around the country for March for Our Lives events just a little over a month later. In April of that year, there was a call for actions and events to take place to protest gun violence and commemorate the nineteenth anniversary of the Columbine High School shooting in Colorado, not the first school shooting and certainly not the first incident of gun violence, but one that burned into the memories of Americans who watched it unfold on television.

Lauren contributed *Natural Shocks* to that effort. We were in the wake of #MeToo, and this play takes a hard look at the sad truth guns play in domestic violence and the murder of women. More than 100 groups signed on to produce the play.

This play functions as a poignant finale to this collection. You'll find all the themes and touches that define Lauren's work: women at the center, the relationships that define and confine women, smart women in perilous situations, considerations of our place in a larger whole, math and science. It would be remiss to not highlight one more flourish: Angela and all of these women are funny and alive. These women have passion and joy and dreams. These are big plays with heart, even the one with only one person on the stage.

Lauren's plays often contain a touch of Walt Whitman (in *Silent Sky*, his book is a gift from Henrietta's father), and in thinking about her plays I often think about the closing of the exuberant "Song of the Open Road":

Will you give me yourself? will you come travel with me?
Shall we stick by each other as long as we live?

How long we each have is the greatest mystery we live with as we float through time, relative and persistent time. In rereading these plays, I found myself returning and returning to the question another American poet, Mary Oliver, asked of us in "Summer Day":

Tell me, what else should I have done?
Doesn't everything die at last, and too soon?
Tell me, what is it you plan to do
With your one wild and precious life?

Lauren has given these women another wild life for us to spend with them in the theatre—time well spent.

Julie Felise Dubiner
Princeton, New Jersey, USA
2023

Emilie
La Marquise du Châtelet
Defends Her Life

Tonight

"Mon royaume de Cirey n'est pas de ce monde"

(My kingdom at Cirey is not of this world.)

—Emilie du Châtelet

Characters

Emilie du Châtelet, *40 dressed in no particular era, confident and curious*
Voltaire (V), *50, dressed immaculately in eighteenth-century fashion, charming, boyish*
Players:

Soubrette	*A young woman, mid-20s, plays Emilie and others*
	Mary-Louise, *simple and stupid*
	Daughter, *direct and strong*
Gentleman	*A handsome man, 30s, plays Jean-François and others*
	Jean-François, *young and doting, sincere*
	The Marquis, *serious but warm, very formal*
	Maupertuis, *sexy and academic*
	Marain, *snide and proud*
Madam	*A slightly older woman, 50s, plays Mother and others*
	Mother, *serious and wounded*
	Madam Graffigny, *obnoxious and rich*

Setting

A theatre space with moveable everything.

Written on/in this space at the beginning: **LOVE**, **PHILOSOPHY**, and **F=mv**.

Eventually: a doorframe, two desks, chairs, and a bed—all of these are mobile.

Notes

Tableau—Any choreographed tableau or scene without specific dialogue should be presented with music of the era or in the style of, say, Lully or Rameau.

Tally—Emilie will be keeping a tally between **LOVE** and **PHILOSOPHY**.*

Touch/Presence—Emilie can't touch anyone ever and she can't leave the stage.

Lights—Lights go out when Emilie touches someone. When Emilie returns from the blackout, she is always breathless. She goes back to that dark place again, and resurfaces. It shouldn't look pleasant or easy.

Writing—Emilie must also have the capability to write on the walls with chalk or something more inventive. By the end of the play the space should be full.

---

* Far into the 1700s *science* was known as "natural philosophy."

Pronunciation

Leibniz = LIE-bnitz
Cirey = Sear-EE
Maupertuis = MAW-pear-TWEE
Marain = MAR-AH

Marquis = MAR-KEY
Marquise = MAR-KEYZ

A Brief Definition of *Force Vive* and Squaring

Force Vive ($F = mv^2$) is a scientific concept that was hotly debated in the seventeenth and eighteenth centuries. Proposed by Gottfried Leibniz over the period 1676–89, the theory was controversial as it seemed to oppose the theory ($F=mv$) advocated by Sir Isaac Newton. In Leibniz's view, Newton's equation of was incorrect because it eventually becomes zero, meaning that the force stops and is "dead." Newton explained that God would come along and add more energy. Leibniz's squaring of velocity meant that energy keeps going and doesn't need outside replenishment of energy; i.e. it was "alive". During the French debates on the subject, Newton's equation became known as "Force Morte," while Leibniz's equation was called "Force Vive". However, Leibniz's theory was not clearly explicated and lacked a detailed experimental finding.

By advocating for Leibniz's squaring of Force, Emilie du Châtelet translated Leibniz's idea in a way that was easily understood and added the decisive evidence of a Dutch researcher. Today, due in part to du Châtelet's work, we understand that the two equations are describing different things—Newton's equation describes the Conservation of Momentum ($F = ma$—Force equal Mass times Acceleration), while Leibniz's equation became what is understood as Kinetic Energy ($E=mv^2$)—Energy equals Mass times Velocity squared).

Scholars see du Châtelet's legacy including both her championing of Leibniz's squaring, and her French translation of Newton's *Principia*. Her analysis and writings prompted scientists of the following centuries to regard energy as being proportional to mv^2 and can be traced to Einstein's development of $E=mc^2$.

**** Thank you to Dr. Judith Zinsser, whose mentorship and book, *Emilie Du Chatelet: Daring Genius of the Enlightenment*, gave me so much of the world of this play.

Act One

Blackness. Then a single light. **Emilie** *is in this light. She is a little stunned to be here. She breathes—also stunning.*

Emilie Breath.

She flexes her hands, testing, getting her bearings.

Body.

Again.

She steps out of her spotlight, then steps back in.

Space.

And Time.

Again?

Life again?

But I'm dead. I'm here. You're here. You're dead? No. Poor logic. Back to facts.

She starts with the basics . . .

There are things called *living* and things called *dead* that exist as people. Hearts and the squaring of hearts.

She draws a simple heart. Then squares it: ♥²

She is finds **F=mv** *is written.*

Then there are things called "living" and things called "dead" that exist as *Force* and the squaring of Force. Motion, mass. Squared.

She squares it: **F=mv²** *remembers this now . . .*

Force Vive, it's called. *The Living Force.* "Living" because of that little 2.

She erases the 2: **F=mv**.

Now it's "dead".

She squares it again: **F=mv²**.

And alive again. Mathematically speaking.

A thought forms.

Because when you square it, you give it "life."

A new energy into . . .

I died thinking two things: One—I'm not done. Two?

She points to the ².

Two. A number that seems the symbol of a double. But made small and set on high? Is an imperative to expand, extend exponentially—a life-like dynamic—*yes!* Squaring adds *life*—that's why we called it Living Force—that's what I fought for. *That* number in *that* equation was my life's work—

No, my life's *question*. And I died without an answer.

I died thinking: Living and the Living Force . . . so what?

She gets it now . . .

And that's the impossible question that brought me here:

She touches the ².

What do we mean?

Sees that **LOVE** *and* **PHILOSOPHY** *are written.*

And I realize it's a bold attempt to quantify such things . . .

But Time and Space are generous tonight.

So I ask . . .

Of all my loving—

She marks under **LOVE**.

and all my knowing—

She marks under **PHILOSOPHY**.

What matters, what lasts? If lasting even matters. What's the point?

Asking tricky questions is what I do best.

Tonight, I may finally know and finally, finally rest.

Music and lights flood the space revealing the remnants of an eighteenth-century stage, small but splendid though a little dilapidated. **Voltaire** *and the Players are in a tableau that would be titled: "Love and Philosophy".*

Emilie   My name is Emilie.

She points to **Soubrette**.

I think that one's me, too.

The trio rushes into another tableau where **Voltaire** *is voraciously kissing* **Soubrette**.

Definitely me.

A moment, glancing at the audience.

Let me see if I can set this stage.

Points to herself.

Emilie.

Points to **Soubrette**.

Also me. Somehow.

Points to **Gentleman**.

Perhaps my husband. Or Newton.

Points to **Madam**.

One of the many courtiers that find me generally intolerable. Or my mother.

Points to **Voltaire**.

And this one. You'll know his name. François-Marie Arouet. Voltaire.

The tableau shifts into an adoration of **Voltaire**, *the genius.*

I love this man. And lucky for you we fight in English so you'll be sure not to miss a thing.

Emilie *turns to* **Voltaire**, *starts to speak. The Players hand* **Emilie** *and* **V** *scripts from which they read right now.*

Voltaire   "The Life and Love of Emilie La Marquise du Châtelet." By me. Voltaire.

Turns to her, in character.

What happened to my life before you? I'd hunted for love, but found only mirages.

Emilie (*not "on script"*)   Wait. Why are we starting here?

Voltaire   A scene in which Voltaire declares his love.

In character.

"I love you."

Emilie (*not "on script"*)   This isn't the—Start at the beginning.

Voltaire (*continuing anyway*)   "And when love stares you down it is the only thing in the heavens with light."

Emilie (*on script*)   "Love is science, then."

Voltaire   "Love is *magic*."

Emilie   "One should be able to tell the difference."

Off script.

Who wrote this?

Voltaire   *Hey.*

Emilie (*reads unenthusiastically*)   "You distract me, handsome hero."

Voltaire   "A distraction is just an opportunity arising, goddess of the mind."

Emilie   Goddess of the—?

Voltaire   "Athena and Aphrodite would bow to your feet—"

Emilie (*off script*)   OK—*Stop*. Stop. This isn't right.

Realizes as she looks at her script.

Because *this* isn't *my* story.

To **V**.

This is *yours*.

She tosses the script. **V** *is insulted.*

And tonight is *mine*.

From now on? My story. My life. Because Time and Space have obliged tonight, and they really don't do that very often, and you never know how much of them you're going to get, and I'm *going* to get an answer tonight even if I die trying—*again*—so we need to start at the *beginning*, and start *now*!

Music—something big.

The scene with the father.

Gentleman *enters, as Emilie's Father.*

My father was a hero to me. Very simply he allowed me: myself. One of the larger gifts one can be given.

She marks under **LOVE**.

I learned that he'd loved a woman at court.

Soubrette *enters as this woman.*

And shunned all others at Versailles to hear her talk about the stars. But. He was a fool, cheated on her with a richer woman, lost her to another man, and cracked his own heart for good.

Soubrette *exits.*

He married my mother out of convenience—a fact not lost on her.

Madam *enters as Mother.*

My mother sees my education as a waste of time. She thinks my father is rewarding everything she is not.

Emilie *marks under* **PHILOSOPHY,** *which irritates* **Madam,** *who exits.*

Soubrette *enters now as* **Emilie. Gentleman** *leaves.*

Which is true. I steal my brother's tutor, learn English, Latin, celestial mechanics, all the math there is. My tutors can't keep up.

Emilie *puts a mark under* **PHILOSOPHY.**

I host the best minds in France and my husband pays for them. Did I mention I was married? We're skipping ahead.

Gentleman *enters as* **Marquis du Châtelet**.

My husband. A good man. And just. And calm, thank god. I mean the highest compliment when I call ours a true and unique . . . friendship.

Emilie *almost marks under* **LOVE** *but doesn't.* **Gentleman** *kisses* **Soubrette***'s hand and exits.*

But he has wars to manage. And I have a name to uphold. And the children. Did I mention I had children? Three. Fascinating creatures raised by the nursemaid which leaves me free to study . . .

Gentleman, *as* **Maupertuis**, *and* **Soubrette** *study.*

With my mentor, Maupertuis. The first man outside my family that respects me, challenges me . . .

They kiss all over the books.

An academic relationship. Not without its own distinctive benefits.

Soubrette *stops groping—she's had a thought and abandons* **Gentleman** *to check her books.*

Gentleman *is a little perturbed.*

Maupertuis is my only vein into the heart of academia. I need him, but he doesn't need me.

Gentleman *distances himself from* **Soubrette**.

As a lady I'm in no position to run out to cafés and mingle with these minds, or god help me, *think out loud* . . .

A doorframe appears. **Gentleman** *goes through the café's door without* **Soubrette**.

Emilie *changes* **Soubrette** *into man's clothes . . .*

But I want to go where science is *done*—which is not in courts or academies, but in The Café Gradot—an all-male, all-night establishment wherein my sex is restricted to various services unbecoming of my class. And my patience.

So we do what we must.

Emilie *sends* **Soubrette** *through the doors.*

Emilie *marks under* **PHILOSOPHY**.

Women determine the fate of great nations, of the human race itself, but for us there is no place where we are trained to think, much less to think for ourselves. And if we insist, we are mocked, scorned—

Just as **Soubrette** *is kicked out again* **Soubrette** *exits.* **Emilie** *erases the mark under* **PHILOSOPHY**.

Gentleman *appears through the door.*

The men of letters laugh, the men of court frown.

Madam *appears.*

And the women . . . oh they of much gossip and little substance. They are the vipers and hate me because I dare to ask "why" and, more dangerously, "why not?"

But court is essential. So I spend all of my time pleasing those whom I don't even like. I am rich, secure, and . . . *painfully bored.* And court couldn't care less.

Madam, **Gentleman** *scoff at her and exit.*

Then. I meet V. Who cares.

Enter **Voltaire**. *She underlines the* **v** *in* $F=mv^2$.

V for velocity. That sounds about right. Monsieur Velocity.

His reputation hits first. Bard. Bastard. Rebel poet twice locked in the Bastille, almost always exiled somewhere, and *still* the toast of Paris.

V *sees* **Emilie**, *likes what he sees.*

A chance meeting, but these things are always chance. Until they aren't.

I see him at a salon discussing Newton, the opera a few times, at court a few more, ballet, gardens, the pâtisserie near my house. It was after we met at Mass that I knew for certain chance had become choice.

The scene at the opera.

At the opera. Some crackling music/vocals. **Voltaire** *moves to her and they sit. They both know that they're being watched.*

Soubrette *joins* **Gentleman**, **Madam**, *as audience.*

Voltaire   Madam Marquise. It is a pleasure to see you. And quite the honor to be seen with you.

Emilie   We seem to be making a habit of it.

Voltaire   I do love that pâtisserie. How was your éclair?

Emilie   Much like you I'm afraid: too sweet, not quite filling. How was your tarte?

Voltaire   Couldn't stop myself. Speaking of which, you're not bored by my growing infatuation with you?

Emilie   On the contrary. I think it's good for your health.

Voltaire   My health? You barely know me, Madam.

Emilie   I know your reputation. And your work, Monsieur.

Voltaire   You do?

Emilie   Of course I do.

Voltaire Of course you do.

Emilie Most of your operas by heart. Though I thought that last one was a bit wordy.

Voltaire Now you tease.

Emilie If honesty is game-play.

Voltaire Everything's a move, my dear.

Emilie A dear perhaps, but not yours yet.

Voltaire I hear a "yet."

Emilie And missed the "not."

Voltaire My god . . .

Emilie You have one?

Voltaire Only muses.

Emilie They're a fickle bunch.

Voltaire (*falling for her*) Madam, you are . . .

Emilie Speak, poet. The anticipation tortures the air—

Voltaire (*sincere*) Goddess.

Unstoppable.

I fear—

Emilie What's to fear?

Voltaire A dangerous thing.

Emilie For you or me?

Voltaire We may be in this one together.

Emilie You presume too much.

Voltaire I do.

Emilie Well stop it. I am not that easily deduced.

Voltaire I *know* that you're a devastating force at cards, you're married to a military creature, and you scare off any allies at court by overindulging in the excruciating habit of reading.

Emilie You're not scared then?

Voltaire I don't plan on playing you in cards. And don't tell anyone but . . . I read too.

Emilie Well then, perhaps we do have . . . like minds, mutual interests.

Voltaire Very mutual, very interesting. And I'm a quick study.

Emilie   Not too quick—that'd be disappointing.

Voltaire   Well, we can discuss your varied preferences over wine tonight?

Emilie   Monsieur, you're very charming, but you don't get to know my preferences until I know yours. What do you think of Descartes?

Voltaire   A . . . revolutionary mind.

Emilie   Leibniz?

Voltaire   Metaphysical mind and unfortunately German.

Emilie   Newton?

Voltaire   Genius. The world is complete.

Emilie   And me?

Voltaire   Genius. The world is complete.

Emilie *grabs* **V**'s *knee suggestively—.*

Immediately upon their first physical contact, the lights, music, and all breath in the space are gone with a crackle and a spark. Blackness.

One light turns on. **Emilie** *is alone, baffled, scared.*

Emilie   I'm sorry. I didn't realize . . .

She looks at her hands.

With another crackle the lights and music and players return. **Voltaire** *calmly walks to his previous position.*

Voltaire   Genius. The world is complete.

Emilie *goes to touch him—****she gets one hand on him and the lights go out more violently***.

One light comes on again. **Emilie** *is alone, breathless.*

Emilie   Descartes was right: mind and body are distinct. In this case profoundly so.

I understand now. No touch.

Touching life is like having it. And I realize that I don't.

This time, my life is not *really* life or mine.

She erases the^2 *from* **F=mv**.

But I'll take it anyway!

With another crackle the lights, **V** *and Players return.* **Emilie** *guides* **Soubrette** *to replace her in the scene.*

Emilie and **Soubrette**   And me?

Voltaire   Genius. The world is complete.

Soubrette *touches* **V** *successfully. The Players are scandalized.*

Emilie *marks under* **LOVE**. *Thinks about it. Then marks under* **PHILOSOPHY**, *too.*

Emilie   And with a new variable in this glorious equation, the world takes off. Which always makes such a mess.

Voltaire   A scene in which Voltaire woos the unconvinced Marquise.

Emilie *and* **Voltaire**, *as well as* **Gentleman** *and* **Madam**, *are playing cards in Emilie's house.* **Gentleman** *and* **Madam** *eavesdrop avidly.*

I love you—

Emilie   My husband is a general—

Voltaire   —in a thousand ways.

Emilie   —directly under the King.

Voltaire   I'm blushing—I don't blush.

Emilie   I'm required at Versailles.

Voltaire   When you say "orbit", I can't control myself.

Emilie   Really. Orbit.

Voltaire   God help me.

Emilie   You're ridiculous.

Voltaire   It's a lovely way to live. Come away with me.

Emilie   I can't.

Voltaire   Teach me.

Emilie   You are a most thrilling wreck but I can't, and you know I can't.

Voltaire   You toy with me. I'm just a puppet to you.

Emilie   You're a playwright. An *actor*. What can I say?

Voltaire   That you've met your match.

Emilie   You shouldn't waste your time.

Voltaire   Not a moment wasted with you. Your very breath fuels my *fire*.

Emilie   That's nice. I win.

She wins the card game and takes his money. **Gentleman** *and* **Madam** *exit.*

Voltaire   You don't care for me at all.

Emilie   V.

Voltaire   You'll crush me and I'll die, and you don't care at all.

Emilie   V.

Voltaire   Yes, Siren?

He pouts.

Emilie   Look at me.

Voltaire   It will set me on fire to do so, but I'll risk it.

Emilie   I'll explain my hesitation.

Voltaire   You reject of my noble intentions?

Emilie   I'm married. What's noble?

Voltaire   They're *sincere* intentions. I can't help it.

Emilie   That would be your reputation.

Voltaire   I can't help the urge to bite every corner of your frame . . .

Emilie   V . . .

Voltaire   And read every thought in your head . . .

Emilie   And if I give you any sign of my true feelings . . . I'm afraid you'd tackle me.

*A moment. A smile. Then he tackles her with a kiss. **The lights plunge her into darkness**.*

The single light points out **Emilie**. *She makes another mark under* **LOVE**.

As the lights crackle back on, we see **Voltaire** *and* **Soubrette**, *as* **Emilie**, *with much fewer clothes on, grinning, grinning, grinning.*

During this, they dress each other. It should be the picture of affection.

Emilie and **Soubrette**   I'd like to have a rule.

Voltaire   A rule?

Soubrette   For you and I. *Just* for you and I.

Voltaire   I'm not good with rules. I find them insistent.

Soubrette   This one's easy. Well. It's simple.

Voltaire   Those are not identical meanings.

Soubrette   One rule.

Voltaire   To what simplicity shall I swear?

Emilie and **Soubrette**   Honesty.

Pause.

Voltaire   So cruel.

Soubrette   Not punishment. Freedom. Say only what we mean, and mean everything we say.

Voltaire   But . . . I'm an actor.

Soubrette   To everyone else you are.

Voltaire   We don't have to be honest with everyone else?

Soubrette   God no. We have to survive at court.

But when it's us . . . love me, mean it, and say it. Or else damn the whole thing.

Voltaire   A daunting experiment.

Emilie and **Soubrette**   A worthy one.

Voltaire   You might get hurt.

Soubrette   So might you. All for the deepest kind of knowing.

Voltaire   The deepest kind, the kindest cruelty of the heart and mind—

Soubrette   No poetry. Everyone else gets the show. I get the truth.

Emilie   The truth.

Voltaire   And that's what we want.

Emilie and **Soubrette**   That's what we want.

Voltaire   And we want that badly.

Emilie and **Soubrette**   Yes we do.

Voltaire   Then we'll have it. For you.

Soubrette   And you.

Emilie   And you.

Soubrette *and* **Voltaire** *are now dressed, kiss, exit.*

Emilie *puts a few marks under* **LOVE**.

Emilie   And though tame for a moment, the laws of the heart are based in such violence. They are starved and overwhelmed and just destructive to good behavior. The laws of the universe are clean and *predictable*. To know the universe? Be diligent. To know the heart? Be brave.

And so we brave each other. But we're still learning.

Voltaire *enters with books, upset.*

Voltaire   I'm a child with all this.

Emilie   You can't be the best at everything.

Voltaire   Yes I can.

Emilie   Fine. You know Newton couldn't write a sonnet worth a damn.

Voltaire   You're dismissing this.

Emilie   You're being a baby.

Voltaire   Kiss me.

Emilie   V.

Voltaire   Fuck me.

Emilie   Would you stop. I'm your colleague one minute, then your—what—whore?

Next time you enter a room be kind enough to let me know which way you currently see me.

Voltaire   Currently? Crusty.

I'm going out.

Emilie   I know the Calculus is hard, and that translation is awful. Just go back to the Latin.

Voltaire   I don't like Latin.

Emilie   You understand it. Just review the equations. On that sheet.

He goes to the sheet. She doesn't.

Voltaire   Emilie.

Emilie   I laid it out for you.

Voltaire   *Emilie.*

Emilie   I'm writing, what?

Voltaire   To whom are you writing?

Emilie   Maupertuis.

Voltaire   About what?

Emilie   Orbit of Venus.

Voltaire   Just. Fine.

He starts to walk out.

Emilie   V.

Voltaire   I'm ill.

Emilie   You're not ill.

Voltaire   Felt it all week.

Emilie   You're frustrated, not sick.

Voltaire   Don't bother.

Emilie   Are you jealous that I'm sharing orbits with another man.

Voltaire   Do not mock me, woman. You'll have plenty of time to write to your better, younger, meatier friends about all the things I'm too daft to understand, when I die from being sick. Which I am. If this kills me, which it might, at least I'll get a statue.

Pause.

Emilie   Sit.

He nearly "faints." **Madam** *enters.*

Some very hot tea and lemon. Warm towels.

Madam   Is he all right?

Emilie   Oh, I think he'll pull through.

Madam (*with complete lack of verve*)   Saints be praised.

Madam *leaves.* **V** *smiles and tries to kiss her.*

Emilie   Too sick for math, to sick for that.

V *settles.* **Emilie** *picks up a book. In her own thoughts.*

Voltaire   I just forget that you care. And that I care that you care. It's quite insidious this cycle we're in. I just need time.

Emilie (*thinking out loud re: her book*)   Time and space are absolute.

Voltaire   I can't force you to love me.

Emilie   But force is not, in Newton's equation.

Voltaire   But you really should.

Emilie   Newton *multiplies* speed by mass—so all force eventually cancels out—so there's *no more* energy.

Voltaire   I'm so tired.

Emilie   So the cosmos stops.

Voltaire   You wear me out.

Emilie   Which *isn't true.*

Voltaire   It's true!

Emilie   So Newton thinks *God* intervenes just to keep us going? That's ridiculous.

Voltaire   And I know it's ridiculous for a celebrity to admit, but I *need* you.

Emilie   God doesn't need to *intervene*—why bother making the cosmos if you have to keep it *tuned.*

Leibniz wrote about this—*Force Vive*. Energy that's not a *multiple* of speed, but speed *squared*—which means energy is exponential—which means it doesn't run out—which means God doesn't need to wind us up!

He notices that she's not listening.

Voltaire   I talk about myself for one minute . . .

Emilie *looks to the* $F=mv^2$.

Emilie   Maybe God's in the squaring.

Voltaire   God? We were doing Calculus.

Emilie   It's all connected.

Voltaire   Connected to what?

Emilie   To each other!

Voltaire   To whom?

Emilie   To the universe!

Voltaire   The universe?

Emilie   The universe!

Voltaire   I don't care about the universe if you don't love me!

Just tell me you do so I can get some rest.

She gestures for **Soubrette** *to take over.*

Emilie and **Soubrette**   I love you!

Emilie   Now shut up so I can think.

V *grabs* **Soubrette** *(as* **Emilie***) into a hug.*

Emilie *marks under* **LOVE** *and* **PHILOSOPHY**.

Emilie   And I start to think that both love and energy are surprisingly exponential. It would be easier to rest, to release, to stop like Newton's equation expects us to. But even complicated love doesn't give up that easily . . .

Gentleman *appears as the* **Marquis du Châtelet**, *Emilie's husband.*

Gentleman (*to us, not entirely sincere about this . . .*)   The scene in which Emilie's husband returns and is . . . happy for her.

He bows, she courtesies, they stand as friends.

You're happy then?

Emilie   I am. Are you? I never ask that.

Gentleman   Property, children, the king's favor. A wife I'm proud of. That's a good life by all accounts.

Emilie   And you look so handsome. Wars aren't all that bad are they? You're fooling all of us ladies with all that talk of battles and bravery, aren't you.

Gentleman   Of course not. Very serious. The campaign—

Emilie   A joke, dear. Joking.

Gentleman   Oh. Well.

You look—healthy. I mean lovely. Sturdy, well-fed.

Emilie   You're making me feel a bit bovine, dear, but thank you.

Gentleman   Sorry. Soldier talk.

Emilie   Which doesn't require much flattery, I see.

Gentleman   Yes. No. Well.

The children are growing up into willful creatures like their mother.

Emilie   And kind like their father. Gabrielle is pretty enough. I think she'll marry well.

Gentleman   I'll certainly see to that. And Florent is proving his skill in military language?

Emilie   And mathematics. He could be a scholar.

Gentleman   No. Doesn't have it in him.

Emilie   If he kept studying he could be something.

Gentleman   He may have your mind, but he's got my name. That makes him a general. Stop the tutor at sixteen. I'll take it from there.

Emilie   As you see fit.

Small pause.

Gentleman   Will Voltaire be joining us at the opera tonight?

Emilie   Seeing as how he wrote it, I expect he'll be there.

Small pause.

Gentleman   Is he . . . treating you well?

Emilie   He's good . . . for me. Not like your kind of good. You are the earth, he's more of the . . . elements. Thunder and lightning and . . . well.

Gentleman   I'm glad you're sufficiently captivated. I know you're hard to entertain.

Emilie   I am not. I'm quite agreeable. With decent books. And competent card players. And—you're right, I must be exhausting.

Gentleman   And I miss it.

That.

You.

They don't know what to say. **Soubrette** *(as* **Emilie***) enters replacing her again.*

Gentleman   Off we go?

Emilie and **Soubrette**   Off we go.

Gentleman *takes* **Soubrette***'s arm and exits.*

Emilie *watches him go. Turns to us.*

Emilie   This is where it gets confusing, because *that*'s Love too.

She makes another mark under **LOVE***.*

Not the fire kind, but the *bread* kind, the comfort kind. We have nothing in common but our offspring, but he is a *good* man and he loves me. Quietly and sure.

She makes another mark under **LOVE***.*

And it's ludicrous that safety bores us so.

Voltaire *enters in a flurry.*

Voltaire *(to us)*   The scene in which Voltaire is almost imprisoned in the Bastille . . . again.

To **Emilie***, rushed.*

They're on their way. Here to arrest me. Right now.

Emilie   My god, V. What did you do?

Voltaire   The markedly brilliant letters I wrote praising the English. Now the king is furious that I'm so stunningly *right*, that he wants me killed. Which is so French, that the irony is completely lost on him.

Emilie   You weren't supposed to publish those.

Voltaire   *They* weren't supposed to publish. I hate printers.

Emilie   You can't humiliate a king like that.

Voltaire   I hate kings.

Emilie   All of Paris is probably reading it.

Voltaire   And I really hate Paris.

Emilie   You *knew* you were playing with fire. Stop playing with fire! Don't you learn?

Voltaire   Only makes me smarter.

Emilie   Where will you go?

Voltaire   I don't know.

Emilie   They're coming *now* and you don't *know*?!

Voltaire   Come with me.

Emilie   Come with you *where?*

Voltaire   ANYWHERE. NOT here! Come!

Emilie   No!

Voltaire   Now!

Emilie   GO, V! Before you can't. GO now GO!

Looks at her.

Voltaire   And so I go. Not knowing when I'll see you again. I go.

She stops him with . . .

Emilie   *Wait.* Wait. I have a château in Cirey. A family estate. It's a wreck. Barely habitable.

Voltaire   Still waiting for how this helps me.

Emilie   It's a place outside of Paris. You'd be safe.

Voltaire   And you'd be there? I want you there. I need you there.

Emilie   Stop wooing. I can't think.

Voltaire   Your resident poet? Harmless, literary.

Emilie   My husband could be convinced.

Voltaire   I'll pay anything.

Emilie   That might help.

Voltaire   And you'll come?

Emilie   I don't know.

Voltaire   You're coming.

Emilie   *They're* coming! You GO!

Voltaire   Say you'll come!

Emilie   I won't SAY anything to you EVER AGAIN—Which is what happens when you go to the Bastille!

Voltaire   Meet me at Cirey.

Emilie   GO.

Voltaire   Come.

Emilie   NOW!

He goes, comes back for a passionate kiss.

The lights go out in a vicious crack. *They come back on.* **Voltaire** *is gone.*

Emilie   The scene in which he tries every method of roping me in . . . to my *own* house.

Voltaire *appears. These are their letters.*

Voltaire   Dearest Emilie, I am safe at your château. Thank you. It's a dump. Come to me.

Emilie   I am a lady of stature. I can't.

Voltaire   Did I mention that you are my heart beating? Also, your husband likes me and/or my money. Come.

Emilie   I can't run off to the country.

Voltaire   The renovations are majestic!

Emilie   How will I work? The books I need.

Voltaire   I know all the booksellers.

Emilie   The equipment I need.

Voltaire   I've already had it shipped.

Emilie   The spine of the thinking elite is here—

Voltaire   We'll invite them.

Emilie   —and the court—

Voltaire   Not them.

Emilie   —and the gossip if I left, my daughter's suitors, my family name, and—and the world doesn't work like that!

Voltaire   That's why we make our own. Love and Philosophy await.

Beat.

Emilie   You are an irritating man. I'm on my way.

Voltaire   You are?

Emilie   It seems I love you desperately.

Voltaire   Desperation can be quite enjoyable. Be my muse.

Emilie   If you'll be mine.

Voltaire   Genius. The world is . . .

Emilie and **Voltaire**   Complete.

She breathes and turns to us.

Emilie   The moment I leave Paris to live in the country and *study* . . . with *him?* That's when I switch from eccentric to rebel overnight.

Emilie *walks to* **Voltaire**, *who turns to her.*

The scene in which I come home.

They are at Cirey—and it's abuzz! The Players are busy servants in the house.

Voltaire   Now. The house is in a good state. The grounds are fertile, the orchards ripe, and the peasants generally pleased. I've stocked the stables, imported an Italian gardener and garden, and built a new wing.

Emilie   A new wing?

Voltaire   Everything painted as you like.

Emilie   Blue and yellow?

Voltaire   Green and white. We'll adjust.

Madam, *as a servant, runs off with these new orders.*

My room is connected to yours, as is the library.

Emilie   I brought a carriage-full of books.

Voltaire   I brought three.

Emilie   Luxury!

Voltaire   And I threw in a chapel for good measure.

Emilie   Can't hurt.

Voltaire   The entire East Wing is for experiments, and I've already sent for a barrage of tools and measures.

Emilie   Air pump?

Voltaire   Yes.

Emilie   Thermometers?

Voltaire   Of course.

Emilie   Calibrated Vacuum Bell.

Voltaire   I'll find out what that is then make sure it's on the next shipment.

Emilie   This is a kingdom.

Voltaire   Ready for a queen.

Emilie   My king?

Voltaire   Jester at best.

Emilie   You are not that humble.

Voltaire   Then King it is.

Emilie   And your plays? You can't perform in the hallways. Where will you work?

Voltaire   I'm glad you asked. With full permission from your generous husband to transform his attic, I present . . .

He reveals a small stage where the unprepared servants are in some happy tableau.

Le Petit Théâtre.

Emilie   V . . .

Voltaire   Isn't it charming?

Emilie   It's perfect.

Voltaire   I'll write, you'll star, we'll grab servants for the bit parts.

Emilie   It's Paris without Parisians.

The servants relax the tableau—back to drudgery.

Voltaire   You like it?

Emilie   Yes.

Voltaire   You're happy?

Emilie   Yes.

Voltaire   And you think you have a chance of staying that way?

Emilie   Yes.

Voltaire   Then. Queen of the House, Lady of the Library, may I acquaint you with the intimate details of my personal chamber. There are a few things that need a thorough going over . . . and over . . .

Emilie *gestures to* **Soubrette**, *who enters and replaces* **Emilie**, *as* **Voltaire** *carries her off.*

Emilie   This place is not of the world.

Emilie *makes a few marks under* **LOVE** *and* **PHILOSOPHY**.

Music.

*The servants [***Gentleman** *and* **Madam***] get to work arranging and hauling books and equipment into the space.* **Emilie** *supervises.*

We build the perfect home, laboratory, palace, circus . . .

V *emerges with fresh pages of a new opera. Guides* **Soubrette**, *as* **Emilie**, *to the stage, snatches* **Gentleman** *from work and starts directing them.*

We build the largest library in Europe . . . and live in it.

V *and* **Soubrette** *read books, trade books, write, and ramble—their desks face each other.* **Gentleman** *tries to enter with a message but instead becomes a shelf for all the books they use which they pile on top of him.*

The best minds in science and art fight for a seat at our table.

*Soon **Gentleman** has so many books in his arms that he is unable to see . . . **V** places a final book to cover **Gentleman**'s eyes so that he can successfully smooch **Soubrette** (as **Emilie**). The smooching takes **V** and **Soubrette** off, as **Gentleman** leaves with the books.*

And for the first time in my life I think that happiness may not be *having* all the answers . . . it may be having time and space to wonder.

V *enters buttoning up some piece of clothing, snatching a book from **Gentleman** as he passes. **Emilie** and **V** study separately.*

Emilie   I wonder . . . You wouldn't want . . .?

She stops herself, which stops him.

Voltaire   Want what?

Emilie   Nothing. Ridiculous thought.

Voltaire   I tend to like those. What?

Emilie   No no no. I was in someone else's life for a moment.

Voltaire   What were you thinking?

Emilie   No.

Voltaire   What what what?

Emilie   A baby. A baby.

Pause.

Voltaire   What kind?

Emilie   Of baby? With me.

Pause.

Voltaire   Oh. Why?

Emilie   There's a reason I didn't actually ask you.

Voltaire   I think you just did.

Emilie   You pressed me.

Voltaire   I did not. You were bursting.

V *is now giggling.*

Emilie   I was in the middle of my retraction. Stop it. I was trying to—stop laughing. It was a thought experiment. Not a real thought.

And I know it's impossible. I couldn't pull off legitimacy with my husband at war. The rumors would be mortifying, and the theatrics to fool the neighbors—it'd be Olympic.

Voltaire   You thought this through.

Emilie   Well . . . yes. I thought, and to my credit quickly *re*thought with much better judgment, that if we were to do such a ridiculous thing, it would be . . . generally unstoppable.

V *is quiet.* **Emilie** *picks up his mood.*

Voltaire   But . . . our progeny is thought and theatre.

Emilie   It is.

V *sees her disappointment. Time for a gift. He claps his hands and the Players rush into a tableau.* **Madam** *presents* **Emilie** *with a brand new book.*

Voltaire   Goddess. Because I cannot think without you. Because our legacy is built in books . . . I present this engraving for the front piece of my new book—*The Elements of Newton*—which without your consummate help I would have had neither the knowledge nor patience to complete.

A tableau of Newton, see Appendix 1. Newton (**Gentleman**), **Emilie** (**Soubrette**), *and* **Voltaire** (*himself*)*.* **V** *shows* **Emilie** *his creation.*

V *takes his place in the tableau.*

Newton shines the light to you, who then reflects it to me. I am the scribe of your dictation. And the world will know it.

Emilie   V . . . It's gorgeous.

Voltaire   It's you. And it's true. You gave me the world.

Emilie (*turned on by all this*)   Well you better give it back. Now.

Take me upstairs.

Voltaire   And ye shall receive.

The tableau disbands as **V** *and* **Emilie** *can't wait.* **Madam**, *as Madame Graffigny, enters. She is stuffy and rude, but always smiling.*

Madam   Good evening.

Voltaire (*not pleased*)   It used to be.

Emilie   Madame Graffigny. I hope you're enjoying your stay with us.

Madam   Oh, we're all talking again. How nice.

Emilie   I'm sorry?

Madam   I think it's fine manners to lock yourselves up all day talking about planets, while your guest wanders this place alone. I didn't get my café till noon.

Voltaire   The height of misfortune.

Madam   And the post is so slow I haven't gotten any of my letters.

Voltaire   Travesties abound.

Madam   And though the food is marvelous—

Voltaire   Triumph!

Madam   I can't stand eating by myself. A lady of my stature deserves—

Voltaire   A nice long walk?

Madam   Monsieur.

Voltaire   A horse ride, far away?

Madam   Good god.

Voltaire   A part in my opera. That's it.

Madam   Oh, no. I can't sing.

Voltaire   Then you'll defy our expectations.

Gentleman *enters with the post.*

I'll send up the script, rehearsals tonight, and you must, *must* go practice your lines.

Voltaire *takes the mail from* **Gentleman** *and shoves him toward* **Madam**. **V** *reads a letter.*

Madam *is escorted off by* **Gentleman**.

Emilie   You *have* a new opera?

Voltaire   There're not that hard to come by. Upstairs?

Emilie   What's that?

Voltaire *shows her the letter.*

Voltaire   The Academy posted a contest. Upstairs?

Emilie   A contest?

Voltaire   Which we can discuss later.

Emilie (*reading the letter*)   A prize from the Academy of Science on the nature and propagation of fire . . .

We'll submit.

Voltaire   Of course we will.

Emilie   This could be our chance to really collaborate.

Voltaire (*re: sex not science*)   It really could.

Emilie   This is it!

Voltaire   *Upstairs*!

Emilie   Missed your window. Time to think.

Voltaire   Yes, thinking is much more fun.

Emilie   The nature of fire.

Our basic questions?

Fire is . . . a substance itself? Or a reaction?

Voltaire   Fire is made of . . .

Emilie   Light, obviously.

Voltaire   Heat, of course. Mass? Weight?

Emilie   Can we weigh fire?

Voltaire   We must.

Emilie   We'll test it.

Voltaire   Measure it.

Emilie   In order to prove—

Voltaire   What shall we prove?

Emilie   Whatever we find to be true. Through *experiment*.

Voltaire   Through experiment.

Emilie   We'll need lots of metal.

Voltaire   Weigh it, melt it, weigh it again.

Emilie   And keep meticulous records.

Voltaire   Meticulous.

Emilie   And then we could be the first people ever to calculate the weight of fire!

Voltaire   I'll start with the dedication. Something somber but uplifting, I'm thinking couplets.

Emilie   V.

Voltaire   Prose?

Emilie   We don't have anything to dedicate. First we work, then we . . . art.

Voltaire   Right.

Emilie   Right.

Voltaire   Fire.

Emilie   Fire.

Voltaire   An essay on the nature and propagation of fire by Voltaire and La Marquise . . .

Madam, *as Graffigny, enters with a theatrical mask.*

Madam   Packed one just in case. For the opera!

Voltaire   Play's canceled.

V *exits.* **Madam** *storms off.*

Emilie (*to us*)   We spend all night, every night setting things ablaze. And though gorgeous and warm for a moment . . . there's a reason you don't play with this stuff.

It's not going as planned so he's bending the data. The experiments are lazy, the results are unclear, and he's seeing only what he wants to see. That's not science, that's drama.

A breath.

The scene in which I tell him he's wrong. Also drama.

V *enters with his notes.*

Emilie   It doesn't work, V.

Voltaire   Yes it does. Of course it does.

Emilie   When we melted lead there was no weight change. When we melted iron it was heavier than when we started. There's no consistency.

Voltaire   We already know what we're looking for. It's just bad equipment.

Emilie   Then it's bad work. We have to redo it.

Voltaire   Start over?

Emilie   Start over.

Voltaire   Because our equipment fails us?

Emilie   Because our premise is wrong.

Voltaire   It's Newton's premise.

Emilie   Then Newton is wrong.

Voltaire   He can't be wrong.

Emilie   Fire is *not* material. It has no weight. Newton is wrong.

Voltaire   When did you decide this? We are supposed to be collaborating.

Emilie   Then listen to me. Read Leibniz.

Voltaire   I'm not using that German. Newton is the pinnacle of our age, and if he says fire has weight then it has, and I'm going to prove it.

Emilie   And if Newton was looking at our data he'd agree with me. I won't submit that.

Voltaire   Then you won't.

Emilie   Good. I've been drafting alternative ideas and—

Voltaire   *I'll* submit it.

She stops.

Emilie   Oh, V. Don't.

Voltaire   I've worked on it for months, the deadline is in two weeks. I'll submit it. With credit to you, of course.

Emilie   I don't want credit for that.

Voltaire   I'm not starting over.

Emilie   The method is wrong. The results are, therefore and without a doubt, *wrong*.

Voltaire   I can come to my own conclusions.

Emilie   For *once* just consider the idea that you *could* be mistaken, that you *could* be fallible in this *one* scenario, lonely as it may be in the immensity of your usual correctness. Science isn't theatre, you can't pick the ending because it sounds nice. Listen to me.

Voltaire   Listen to *me*. You think The Academy would ever *ever* give this prize to a woman? If you want to do this work you've got to do it with me. You're nothing to them. A rich courtier with no reputation except as a card shark and a. . . tramp. Who are they going to validate, you or me? A saloniste or a—

Emilie   A minstrel? A hypochondriac sycophant? They don't care about you either. They humor you. They manage you. Stick to fiction.

Voltaire   Admit to fact.

Emilie   You first.

Voltaire   You really won't submit with me?

Emilie   Most certainly not.

Voltaire   Then we've come to an impasse.

Emilie   Most certainly.

A moment.

Voltaire   Fine. What are you going to do?

Emilie   Oh, you know. Practice cards and, what was it, tramping?

Voltaire   As a favor, as an amicable gesture showing no bitterness between friends and colleagues, I can give you a mention in my dedication. For your work.

Emilie   Please, *please*, don't bother.

Voltaire   You could use the recognition.

Emilie   And you could use a failure. *Goodnight.*

Pause. **V** *moves away, preparing to speak to us.*

Emilie *nods to* **Soubrette** *who begins writing as* **Emilie**.

And so without a plan, enough time, or a moment's hesitation, I begin to write. All night, every night, by myself, just a candle and a quill, and soon I learn the biggest lesson of my life . . . that a candle and a quill is all I'll ever need.

Emilie and **Soubrette**   Certainly all I can ever count on.

V *turns to us and presents his paper loudly.*

Voltaire   "An Essay on Fire" by Me. Voltaire.

As I have proven, Newton explains that fire is mass . . .

Emilie *turns to us, quietly at first.*

Emilie   Fire is not mass. It has no weight, therefore does not—*cannot*— respond to gravity.

Voltaire   Fire *does* respond to gravity just not . . . obviously.

Emilie   Anyone can see that a candle's flame stays tall even as it goes out. Fire is the very opposite of gravity.

Voltaire   As for Light and Heat . . .

Emilie   Fire *is* Light and Heat, is friction, is reaction, is . . .

A hint at the invisible breath of life that God scattered on his work without which the Universe could not subsist a moment more.

Voltaire   Everything else is in my *next* essay.

Soubrette *stands.* **V** *gathers his work carefully into an envelope and hands the package to* **Gentleman** (*a postman*).

V *remains onstage, confident, obstinate, unaware.*

Soubrette *hands* **Gentleman** *her essay. He exits with both pieces of mail.* **Soubrette** *exits.*

Emilie *marks under* **PHILOSOPHY** *and looks at* **V**.

Emilie   And I start to see what he can't: that he may not be my true half. And then I think . . . perhaps no one is. Or worse, perhaps someone is and I'll never know whom. And that's a cold thought. And, as we've discussed, he tends to escort a certain heat. So I forgive him over and over again. Like Newton's God resetting the planets. An imperfect equation . . . that works for now.

Gentleman *enters with a letter, hands it to* **V**.

Voltaire   The Academy's announced the winner.

Emilie   The winner? Who is it? Who won?

Voltaire   I did.

She's disappointed.

And you.

She's stunned, thrilled.

Actually some hack took the top prize. But it seems that *we both* received honorable mentions.

"We" being the new concept here.

Pause.

When did you write it?

Emilie   Nights. Till sunrise.

Voltaire   Alone?

Emilie   Yes.

Voltaire   And experiment?

Emilie   Candles.

Voltaire   Who knew?

Emilie   The maid.

Voltaire   The maid and not me.

Madam, *as the maid, leaves quickly.*

Voltaire   What was your thesis?

Emilie   Theoretical. Light and heat are related, might be the same.

Voltaire   Light and heat are the same?

Emilie   Don't be angry. I spared us a fight.

Voltaire   Then let's not argue. We're both right . . . or wrong. I can't tell anymore.

Now will you please explain your theory, or must I wait and read it like everyone else.

Emilie   Read it like what?

She grabs the letter from him. Reads.

Voltaire   They'll publish us both.

Emilie   They're going to publish it? Mine too? The Academy will publish *mine*?

Voltaire   I convinced them to print *all* the honored essays along with the winning bit of futility. I didn't know it would be such a direct favor, but . . .

Soubrette *runs on as* **Emilie** *to hug* **V** *very sincerely, no sex in this hug, just friendship.*

Emilie and **Soubrette**   Thank you.

Soubrette *exits.*

Voltaire   I didn't do much.

Emilie   You did. For your own benefit, granted, but in the end it was quite generous.

Voltaire   You deserve it. You are a stunning woman. And an impressive man. Better than me . . . on occasion.

V *exits.* **Emilie** *turns to us.*

Emilie   I take the compliment. Then think, why is manliness the compliment?

The mind, the earth, the stars, all of the things I care about are sexless.

And those sexless secrets of the cosmos only come to those who fight to know. I fight. And it's the *fighting* that's the compliment.

Then I ponder my daughter. Who does not fight.

Soubrette *enters as her daughter. Young but regal.*

She is all woman, and will have a much easier life for it. She is loyal, demure, and . . . entertainable. She is marrying a prince today.

The scene in which—

Soubrette   The scene in which the daughter is seen and finally heard. On her wedding day.

Soubrette, *as Gabrielle, Emilie's daughter.*

Soubrette   I wanted to be like you. I still do.

Emilie   No you don't. Your life will be much better than mine. Marrying royalty makes you—

Soubrette   Just another wife.

Emilie   No. It makes you queen. And everyone wants to be queen.

Soubrette   No. Everyone wants to choose to be queen. Why don't I get a choice?

Emilie   Because you don't need one.

Soubrette   You got one.

Emilie   I'm an exception. And being exceptional is exhausting. You don't want that.

Soubrette   How do you know?

Emilie   Didn't those nuns teach you to respect your mother?

Soubrette   My mother is a picture in my locket. I don't know you. You shipped me off to a convent. Now you marry me off to a prince. I don't have a mother, and I don't have a life that's mine, and that's your fault.

Emilie   My *fault* that you have a future? You should be grateful that your father and I *arranged* for such a—

Soubrette   *Bargained.* You bargained *me* for such a life.

Emilie   Gabrielle, there are so many other girls who would've begged—

Soubrette   But I'm not other girls. I'm your girl. Your girl.

Emilie   And that makes you lucky. So live your lucky life. It will be easier, by far—

Soubrette   You keep saying *easier.* I don't want easier. You didn't care what was easy, you wanted what you wanted, and you gave me up for it.

Emilie   I didn't. I didn't give you up.

Soubrette   You chose books over me. I want a choice. *Your* choice.

Emilie   You don't want—

Soubrette   *I do.*

Emilie   You don't want my life.

Soubrette   You never gave—

Emilie   You want an easy life.

Soubrette   Never gave me—

Emilie   A good life.

Soubrette   A chance. Instead. You gave me what every other *kept* woman would have given her stupid daughter. Instead of what you know, here's what I know . . .

Soubrette *changes her tone.*

A girl does not slouch. Does not speak in excess. Does not question or laugh loudly. She marries rich. She obeys. She submits. And she—

Emilie   I'm sorry.

Soubrette   She has—

Emilie   I'm sorry.

Soubrette   And she has an easy life. Good luck with yours.

Soubrette *starts to leave, then comes back for a harsh hug.* **The lights crackle and plummet out to blackness.**

Immediately the lights rise. **Soubrette** *is gone.* **Emilie** *is alone.*

Emilie   And I see what I missed: myself in her.

What have I done? What any thoughtless *man* would do. I assumed . . . and missed a woman of my own . . . element.

Nothing. She breathes.

What do I give her to give her . . . a chance?

A book. Foundations of science for anyone, for all, for . . . her.

Regroup.

The scene in which I write my first book. The silent scene that takes back the world. For my daughter. Force Vive, Space Time, fire and life, love and philosophy, this is it—this is purpose, is progeny, is *living force.*

She claps—a writing desk and chair appear.

She looks at us.

This could take a while.

She claps and the house lights turn on. She shoos us into . . .

End of Act.

Intermission

During the intermission **Emilie** *writes and writes.* ***She never leaves the stage—****or appears not to. She stretches, paces, works out an equation or two. Perhaps* **Madam** *brings her some water.*

As the intermission ends **Emilie** *is satisfied with her work. As the house lights dim and Act Two begins,* **Emilie** *gently closes the cover to her finished book and waits for us to sit . . .*

Act Two

Emilie *is ready to begin.*

Emilie   The scene in which the book is done, printed, read all over France, then all over Europe.

V *enters with Emilie's book.*

Voltaire   The scene in which a science text, *by a woman,* captivates the thinking world.

Gentleman, *as Mairan, enters reading Emilie's book.*

Emilie   And the world . . .

Madam *and* **Soubrette**, *as Emilie's daughter, enter reading the book as well.*

. . . finally realizes with whom they are dealing.

Reading the cover:

Foundations of Physics

By La Marquise

"The study of physics is made for all of us. And It's the key to all discoveries. Never stop learning."

The Players read from Emilie's book.

Soubrette   "Our most sacred duty is to give our children an education that prevents them from regretting their youth."

Emilie *flips to a later chapter, as do the Players.*

Madam   "Because we can *all* rise to the truth, like those giants who climbed up to the skies by standing on shoulders. Leibniz learned from Huygens. Newton from Kepler."

Emilie *flips to a later chapter, as do the Players.*

Emilie   "But sometimes truth is snuffed out by bombast. Like the essay by Monsieur Mairan, current secretary of the Academy, denouncing *Force Vive* with unfounded proofs."

Voltaire   *Emilie . . .*

V *tries to stop her from saying this last bit, but . . .*

Emilie   "Use his as a course in how *not* to proceed through your studies."

Voltaire   That's a mistake.

Emilie   What?

Voltaire   That last part? You just insulted the secretary of the Academy.

Emilie   He's an idiot.

Voltaire   And the *secretary* of the Academy. He's very powerful.

Emilie   It's done now. Oh, he'll understand it's just friendly critical discourse.

As **Emilie** *goes to put a mark under* **PHILOSOPHY** . . . **Gentleman**, *still as Mairan and quite upset, turns to us.* **Madam, Soubrette, V** *watch.*

Gentleman   Madame Marquise,

Though you somehow found yourself published on the topic of Force Vive, you rush to judgment like any woman confronted with ideas beyond her skill. My dear, you simply did not understand my mathematics disproving Force Vive, nor did you properly read my own writing as you misquote me throughout. I would be happy to guide you through my reasoning, if you would permit me at your little Leibniz academy in the fields. But as my equations prove there is no need to square force: Newton is right, Leibniz is wrong, and you, my dear, are out of your element. In the end, all you need to do, Madam, is to read, and reread, and perhaps you could bring us something worth our time.

A moment for his own satisfaction.

Emilie (*to us*)   It is an honor just to merit a response. But I'll break him anyway.

Emilie and **Madam**   Response to Secretary Mairan, from La Marquise.

Madam (*like reading juicy tabloid*)   I am sorry to play the mother to your wandering child, but it is, after all, the instinct of my sex to correct a failure in order to educate.

Emilie   I have been waiting for this chance.

Madam   On the point of my misquoting your work. I have included a table listing exact references, so you can stop misquoting *me*.

Emilie   A public battle . . .

Madam   On the point of my mathematical skills, I attached complete solutions to all aforementioned problems. I can walk you through the difficult bits.

Emilie   That I can win in my sleep.

Madam   Force Vive is the only theory that explains the latest findings from the Dutch experiments on velocity. So I suggest that *you* keep reading for you've obviously got some catching up to do. Yours humbly . . .

Gentleman *is outraged and starts to speak—*

Emilie (*to* **Gentleman**)   Don't even try.

Madam   La Marquise.

Madam *yanks the book from* **Gentleman**.

Emilie *makes a solid mark under* **PHILOSOPHY**. **Madam, Soubrette,** *and* **Gentleman** *leave.*

Emilie   I think I won.

Voltaire   You did.

Emilie   I did? I did.

Voltaire   And everyone will know. You won.

Emilie   Leibniz won. But I'll take the credit. This is what it feels like. Glory.

She does some cheer for herself.

V *starts to leave.*

Emilie   Where are you going?

Voltaire   Work to do.

Emilie   Celebrate with me. This is a major battle won. A victory! And everyone's talking about it. Progeny, V.

Voltaire   Not mine.

V *leaves. To us . . .*

Emilie   An odd thing when triumph over rivals matches the jealousy of friends. But. I am not apologizing. I know who I am.

Damn the heart; long live the mind.

Emilie *marks under* **PHILOSOPHY**.

So we damn them both. Cirey is quiet now—no dinner debates, or even dinners. Our fire is fading though neither of us will admit it—so we both grow colder and colder alone.

Madam *brings* **Emilie** *a pamphlet.* **V** *enters.*

V?

Voltaire   Yes.

Emilie   Did you send a letter to the Academy refuting my book?

Voltaire   Yes.

Emilie   Did you know that they published it? This letter dismissing Force Vive. You wrote that about me and then published it?

Voltaire   I did.

Emilie   And you don't tell me?

Voltaire   I thought that's what we did; submit in private and surprise each other.

Emilie   This isn't a joke.

Voltaire   Not laughing.

Emilie   You attack my work, my competence?

Voltaire   You rejected Newton; and that's irresponsible.

Emilie   I haven't rejected Newton. It's inquiry. I'm studying.

Voltaire   You've publicly adopted this Leibniz absurdity. Force Vive is a joke, it's nonsense. That little 2 is presumptive and overreaching and—

Emilie   Oh you're squaring *me* now?

Voltaire   I have to defend the truth!

Emilie   And you do that in a public letter?

Voltaire   They respect my opinion.

Emilie   I gave you your opinion.

Voltaire   And then turned your back on it.

Emilie   On *you*. It's not the little 2, it's not Newton, it's *you* I've betrayed, correct?

Voltaire   This isn't ego, it's fact. My ideas match the entire continent's.

Emilie   Which makes you popular not right! You're as bad as the monarchy— anyone who doesn't agree with you should be skewered.

Voltaire   Leibniz is incorrect, and what's worse, *obviously* so.

Emilie   Newton squares distance in the force of gravity—why not square velocity in Force Vive?

Voltaire   Because gravity isn't energy!

Emilie   You oversimplified the argument.

Voltaire   You've chosen a ridiculous argument!

Emilie   You wouldn't know if it was or not!

Voltaire   You can't prove Force Vive!

Emilie   *I already did* —but *still* you fire off your mouth to impress some Academy dogs, and make *me* sound like a—

Voltaire   What? Like a stubborn *woman*?

Emilie   Like a poet dressed up as a scholar.

Beat.

You may want to change the dedication in your next book. I wouldn't want people to mistake us for equals or friends.

Voltaire   All this for a little 2.

Emilie   All this for truth, you jackass. No man can know all.

Voltaire   But a woman can?

Emilie   Not Newton. Not you.

Voltaire   And certainly not you.

Emilie   Next time, let me know when you trash my work in public. I'd be happy to correct your manuscript before you embarrass yourself. You misspelled "Leibniz." *Twelve times.*

Pause. **Emilie** *starts to leave.*

Voltaire   I have something to say.

Emilie   Put it in a novel.

Voltaire   I can't have sex anymore.

Pause.

I'm old. Sick. Near death. I don't want to disappoint.

Emilie   "Disappoint." Don't flatter.

Voltaire   I just wanted to inform you of the malfunction of my . . . machine.

Emilie   Good thing we are very much past fucking as delicacy.

Voltaire   You don't need me for *anything* then.

Emilie   Stop acting like a wounded cat —you betrayed *me*!

Voltaire   You betrayed me first! Leibniz is a betrayal of everything I stand for!

Emilie   Then stand up to this. You want Newton? I'll translate.

Voltaire   Translate what?

Emilie   *The Principia.* The whole of it.

Voltaire   You aren't.

Emilie   I am.

Voltaire   Since when?

Emilie   About ten seconds ago.

Voltaire   Translating the whole thing?

Emilie   And *revising.*

Knows this stings **V**.

There are bits that need it.

Voltaire   What bits?!

Emilie   Force Vive.

Voltaire   NO.

Emilie   Force Vive belongs in Newton's universe and I'm gonna put it there.

Voltaire   You can't just DO that!

Emilie   I'll work on the cosmos; you focus on your pants.

Voltaire   Don't throw that around. I don't deserve that.

Emilie   What do you deserve then, a dirge for your manliness. *I* deserve better than this. I deserve more than this insult to everything I was for you.

Voltaire   Emilie.

Emilie   If I'm so awful, so useless to you, say it so I hear you say it, so we can be *done*!

A pause.

Voltaire   It seems we are growing apart.

Emilie   That'd be the trend.

Voltaire   I'm sorry.

Emilie   Of course you are.

Voltaire   I care for you deeply.

Emilie   Of course you do.

Voltaire   And I always will.

Emilie   Of course. "Always." But for now? For now, nothing, V. You give me nothing.

V *takes the cue and leaves.* **Emilie** *attempts to be calm though she is hurting and angry.*

And *nothing,* as a concept, is a larger conversation than one would think. Nothing is a definition of everything. How do we *feel* nothing? And why does absence weigh so heavy on the heart?

Stopping her emotions.

No. That's not the point.

Realizing what she just agreed to do . . .

The point is . . . that I just committed to translating the most important book in the modern world to prove I'm right . . . and piss him off.

She breathes.

Give me Newton!

Gentleman *enters as Newton with trepidation—these are big shoes to fill. He hands her a large notebook,* The Principia.

Emilie   *Philosophiae Naturalis Principia Mathematica.*

re: the book in her hands.

Newton's Laws. And once you understand them, you can understand *almost* everything. And though he and I disagree on a few minor points, Newton is the most complete understanding of the cosmos created by a human mind. But I know Force Vive is fundamental to Newton's cosmos too.

Emilie *opens the book.*

And so I translate from his Latin:

Newton's Laws of Motion.

Soubrette *enters, she is* not *Emilie, but someone new and cute.*

Voltaire *enters and sets* **Soubrette** *moving/dancing—all an exhibition of the following laws . . .*

One. That all bodies persist in the same state of rest or uniform motion in a straight line.

Voltaire *contacts* **Soubrette** *in some way that changes her trajectory/dance.*

Two. That change in movement is always proportional to and in the direction of force.

Soubrette *and* **Voltaire** *dance together dropping a letter as they spin.*

Three. That action and reaction are always equal and opposite.

Emilie *sees the letter, picks it up, and reads as* **Voltaire** *and* **Soubrette** *continue until . . .*

Emilie   "My dearest uncle."

At this **Soubrette** *and* **Voltaire** *stop. They are caught.* **Soubrette** *reads the letter too, all smiles.*

Emilie and **Soubrette**   "You flatter me beyond compare. I can't wait to be in your arms again. As always, my ass is yours."

Emilie   Her ass is what?

Voltaire   Oh dear.

Emilie   Shall I go on?

Voltaire   I know the rest.

Emilie   I'll just catch up.

Emilie and **Soubrette**   "When last you wrote me, I was given over to those special shivers"

Voltaire   Emilie.

Emilie   I swear to God if you don't let me finish, I will castrate you right here.

Voltaire   Continue.

Soubrette   "That only a lover can impart. I long for you, dear uncle."

Emilie and **Soubrette**   "Let the gossips be damned. Yours in all love,"

Soubrette   Marie-Louise.

Emilie   Your niece Marie-Louise? Your niece.

Voltaire   That sounds worse than it is.

Emilie   I'm so glad your machine's working again. It just took the right greasing.

Voltaire   I am capable of explaining if you'd let me.

Emilie   Explain.

Pause.

Voltaire   I am a man.

Emilie   Better be more than that.

Voltaire   I don't need an excuse! I don't need to be excused. I don't need permission. I don't need to be judged by you.

Emilie   Because nothing matters that's not directly related to you.

Voltaire   Oh god.

Emilie   Or your reputation

Voltaire   Fine.

Emilie   Or your little ass, you stupid, awful man.

Voltaire   I'm sorry you found that.

Emilie   You're sorry I found *out*?

Voltaire   I was going to tell you.

Emilie   Oh well, thank you for being such a gentleman.

Voltaire   For everything I did for myself, that I *needed* for myself, I'm sorry. I'm sorry I ruined *your* version of how *my* life would happen. I'm sorry!

Emilie   You betray me, in my own house, twice?! You trash my work, you lie to me, you ruin everything we built, everything that mattered, wrecked it, ripped it up, ripped it, ravaged it—everything that made sense—GONE!

She realized she has just ripped Newton's Principia, *pages scatter on the floor.*

Voltaire   I just . . . forgot that you care—

Emilie   *Stop talking.*

Emilie *whistles to* **Madam** *who charges* **V** *and slaps him hard.* **Madam** *nods to* **Emilie** *and leaves.*

I would suggest, if you wish to retain my friendship and the immediate privileges that arrangement entails, not least of which is keeping you out of jail on an alarming number of occasions, that you refrain from any form of literary bribery until I am quite out of range. You have betrayed me and broken my heart. Get the hell out of my house.

Voltaire *leaves. A moment to pick up the pages, salvage the precious book.*

Emilie *wipes through all the marks under* **LOVE**—*as well as the* ² *of the* ♥.

One must study throughout.

Voltaire *and* **Soubrette**, *as Marie-Louise, enter and she lets him have his way.*

Emilie *senses their behavior but won't acknowledge them.*

Study not only affords women a chance at the glory denied them in so many other pursuits—

They knock something over, challenging Emilie's focus as **Emilie** *make a few marks under* **PHILOSOPHY**.

—but you study *alone*. And who else do you have? Candles and quills and . . . Newton.

Gentleman *as Newton enters, not sure if this was his cue or not. It's not.* **Emilie** *waves him away, he exits apologetically. Pause.* **Emilie** *tries to continue with forced confidence.*

A scene in which Emilie translates three major proofs of the essential laws of attraction as presented by Sir Isaac Newton. Alone.

Voltaire *and* **Soubrette** *hold hands facing each other.*

One. Gravity affects the shape of the earth, flattening at its poles.

Voltaire *and* **Soubrette** *lean out creating a dome with their outstretched arms. They are a flattened globe.*

Two. The three-body problem. Or how the gravity of every object in the same system affects every other.

Voltaire (*the Earth*) *and* **Soubrette** (*the moon*) *start orbiting and revolving. They make* **Emilie** *the Sun.*

Three. The behavior of comets.

Soubrette *is now a comet who soars by* **Emilie**—*not amused.*

No matter how long their tenure in the depths of space. Gravity brings them back. Always.

Emilie *is left alone as* **Voltaire** *and* **Soubrette** *go.*

But "always" is not as comforting as it once was.

Pause.

We are a mess of trajectories. Tangled and unfeeling.

And I wish I could unfeel.

I'm smarter than this. It shouldn't be so hard.

Madam *enters as Emilie's Mother.*

And then I think of my mother. A safe, exacting woman, who had an easier life for it. And I think . . . is easy so bad?

Madam   The scene with the mother.

Emilie   These rules will make you happy, she'd say.

Madam   A girl does not slouch, does not speak in excess, or laugh loudly attracting negative attention. Do not look your betters in the eye. Do not read in public.

Emilie   How do I *know* when I'm happy? I'd say.

Madam   Take a man's right arm, not left.

Emilie   Are you happy?

Madam   When introduced to him, smile, bow, and repeat his name. In that order.

Emilie   Shouldn't happiness be easier to remember.

Madam   Do not take cheese at dinner parties. Powder your wig persistently. Display your bust enthusiastically. Be demure.

Emilie   Then I'm happy?

Madam   Do not *question.* Comment, only.

Emilie   Fine. This is not *real.*

Madam   This is how things are.

Emilie   This is extensive artifice. Rules for sitting, rules for eating, rules for talking, rules for *not* talking, rules for hair, for hands, for shoes, for fans.

Madam   The proper technique of fanning! Hold away from one's face, snap the wrist, raise the arm, and flap like a bird.

Emilie   So I play peacock?

Madam   *Emilie.*

Emilie   You just said!

Madam   You'll never marry.

Emilie   Then I can stop learning all this.

Madam   The *mouth* should be kept closed when . . . *thinking.*

Emilie   Why?!

Madam   Do not question, Emilie.

Emilie   Then what's the point? The world is bigger than this!

Madam   Not for you. So follow the damn rules.

Everything's easier. And *easy* makes us happy.

Madam *exits.*

Emilie *turns to us, furious.*

Emilie   *But it doesn't.* Easy is ignorance. Easy is a myth. That the greatest thinkers were ever remotely, even for a second *satisfied*, is mythology. Newton was not content, he was ravenous, he was wracked, he was *not done*, and I'm sure he was furious on his deathbed because of it.

Because the only thing that lasts—the only thing that you can count on to be there for you? Not people, not love . . . Physics.

And that's the only thing that works like God is supposed to: Fair and constant.

Let's move on.

Pause. Nothing happens.

Please?

Nothing. She looks around. More asking that telling . . .

The scene in which Emilie gets a break? Or a friend?

V *approaches her cautiously. She sighs, to us . . .*

Of course, physics often promotes *circular* behavior . . . here I go again.

Voltaire   Marquise. It's been too, too long. Months without a word . . .

Emilie *(totally lying)*   Has it been? Hadn't noticed. So busy with the Newton.

Voltaire *(trying to apologize sincerely)*   Yes. Well. Emilie. I came here to—to tell you—to *ask* you if you could—*we* could . . . *have* each other again.

Emilie   Oh, V, I'm done with "having."

Voltaire   I don't mean—I mean that I still need you. Extensively.

And I know that I was, on occasion, in the past, unthinking. But I'm broken open, empty without you. You are my . . . buoyancy. Without you I sink.

Emilie   You sank yourself.

Voltaire   I know I did. And it wrecked me. Please. Always you, only you. Take me back.

Emilie   The world can't go back, it'd be rude if *we* did.

Voltaire   Then forward. As friends.

Emilie *(scoffs)*   Friends?

Voltaire   *Eventual* friends?

Beat.

Emilie   How have we known each other for fifteen years and I still let you talk me into things I don't trust.

Voltaire   Because you love me.

She glares.

Eventually?

Beat.

Emilie   The Marquis and I have been invited to Luneville.

Voltaire   Luneville? Ugh. Dreadful.

Emilie   The Duke's a fan of your work.

Voltaire   —with surprisingly good taste.

Emilie   My husband will come later, but you're welcome to join me. If you won't be a pain.

Voltaire   I suppose I could summon up my best behavior.

Emilie   That won't be any fun.

Voltaire   There's my girl.

Emilie   Not yours. But glad to be back.

To us.

And part of me thinks that Physics has some heart after all.

Voltaire *smiles, ushers her into . . .*

The scene at a new court, with old friends made new.

The royal court of Luneville. **Madam**, **Soubrette**, **Gentleman** (*as Saint-Lambert*), *create a tableau of the court.*

Voltaire *and* **Emilie** *are greeted with applause and they each are separated for conversation—***Emilie** *with* **Soubrette** *and* **Madam**, *and* **Voltaire** *with* **Gentleman**.

Madam   It is very special of you to join us, Marquise.

Soubrette   We've all heard of you, it's true.

Emilie   And we're so honored to be your guests.

Gentleman   The court is complete with its geniuses. We're thrilled to have you.

Voltaire   Glad to know I'm still able to thrill someone.

Madam   I hear you're very skilled, Madame.

Soubrette   In the arts of natural philosophy?

Emilie   It is both habit and passion.

Gentleman   It won't be long before the Duke will demand a play. You are the best in the country.

Voltaire   The country?

Gentleman   The world surely.

Madam   I couldn't help but notice your carriage.

Soubrette   Full of books?

Emilie   I'm working while visiting, yes.

Madam   And your husband?

Emilie   Still called to the front. Excuse me . . .

Emilie *points to* **Gentleman**, *trying to overhear* . . .

Gentleman   I'm a poet myself. And it would be the pride of my days were you to peruse my work at some point in your tenure.

Voltaire   And you are?

Gentleman   Jean-François de Saint-Lambert. Poet, soldier. At your service.

Voltaire   Well. Good to have you floating around.

Emilie *and* **Gentleman** *finally lock eyes.*

Gentleman (*to* **Emilie**)   The scene when we meet.   **Emilie** (*to* **Gentleman**)   The scene when we meet.

Voltaire   Soldier-Poet, have you met La Marquise du Châtelet?

Gentleman   Madame Marquise, it is a very rare honor to meet you.

Emilie   My pleasure.

Voltaire   He's a poet, Emilie.

Emilie   I heard.

Gentleman   A poet only humbly.

Emilie   I haven't met a humble poet yet.

Voltaire   She's talking about me.

Gentleman   If I may say, your work elucidating the great thinkers of our age is a monument to your sex and country.

Emilie   Sex and country? My goodness.

Gentleman   I've read your books.

Emilie   Have you?

Gentleman   *Foundations of Physics.* Enlightening.

Voltaire   That'd be the point.

Emilie   I'm glad you enjoyed it.

Gentleman   More than enjoy, Marquise. It was inspiring to see a clear review of Leibniz's philosophies, and your amazing argument for Force Vive. The squaring of force—

Voltaire   Oh god.

Gentleman   —was a revelation to me. Time and space and . . . all that.

Emilie   Time and space?

Voltaire   Time and space.

Emilie   Well.

Gentleman   Well.

Voltaire   *Well.* He liked the book, Emilie.

Emilie   He did.

Gentleman   Your beauty was also mentioned, though not nearly well enough detailed. I am quite . . .

Voltaire   Let me guess. Speechless?

Gentleman   On the contrary, you inspire.

To **V**.

I'm sure you've experienced a similar urge to compose, Monsieur.

Voltaire   A *real* urge? It must be literature.

Emilie   Monsieur Voltaire has had a long trip. Excuse his entire nature.

Gentleman   Genius should never be excused.

Emilie   But it could be pleasant.

Voltaire   Why don't we go rest, Emilie.

Gentleman   Certainly I'm sure I'm exhausting. I should have quieted my . . .

Voltaire   Urge?

Gentleman   I've overwhelmed the already fatigued.

Emilie   Neither, in fact. I'd like to hear your work.

Gentleman   You would?

Voltaire   You would?

Emilie   I'll need some company before my husband arrives, and I love poetry.

Voltaire   She's talking about me.

Emilie   No I'm not.

Soubrette *replaces* **Emilie** *again.*

Emilie and **Soubrette**   Indulge me, Monsieur.

Soubrette *takes* **Gentleman**'s *arm.* **Madam** *and* **V** *exit.*

Emilie   And like the most natural thing in the world . . . we start a life together.

Not many words work to explain it.

Soubrette*, as Emilie, and* **Gentleman** *walk and talk together.*

Force.

Soubrette *points to the sky explaining the travels of the sun and the stars.*

Acting on Mass.

They turn to one another. **Soubrette** *rushes to him, a very clear kiss.*

Acting on each other. Everything on everything. Love, again, anew, *all* new, and almost—dare I say it, with apologies to my mother -*easy.*

V *walks on, interrupting the kiss.* **Soubrette** *and* **Gentleman** *break apart but are not embarrassed.* **Emilie** *takes over as* **Soubrette** *steps aside.*

Voltaire   How's the book coming?

Emilie   Excellent. How's the play?

Voltaire   Marvelous.

Emilie   Good.

Voltaire   I just love it here.

Don't you just love it, Monsieur?

Gentleman   Oh. Yes. Quite.

Voltaire   Good boy. Heel.

Emilie   Coming to cards?

Voltaire   I look forward to losing.

Emilie   Maybe you'll get lucky.

Voltaire   Maybe I will.

The Duke calls you, boy. Wouldn't dally.

V *exits.*

Gentleman   So we're clear. I adore you.

Emilie   I can tell.

Gentleman   This is the most astonishing—

Emilie   Astounding—

Gentleman   Complete surprise.

Emilie   I know. I didn't expect.

Gentleman   I can't resist.

Emilie   I hope you don't.

Gentleman   Everyday.

Emilie   Yes.

Gentleman   Forever.

Emilie   God yes.

Gentleman   You are . . . You are . . .

Emilie   Speak, soldier-poet.

Gentleman   The surprise of my life. The hope of my heart.

Soubrette *runs on and takes* **Emilie***'s place as they kiss.* **Gentleman** *and* **Soubrette** *exit.*

Emilie *makes many marks under* **LOVE***.*

Emilie   There must be a trigger in women that sways us to forget the bruises of certain activities like childbirth, men, and other dangerous sports. It's either madness or martyrdom or . . . hope.

V *enters.*

Voltaire   I've decided that I'm happy.

Emilie   Glad to hear it.

Voltaire   For you.

Emilie   Oh. Thank you.

Voltaire   You love him?

Emilie   I do. V, he's effortless. Passionate but gentle, and his poetry's not bad at all. And he makes me want to . . .

She jumps in place. **V** *cackles.*

You think I'm a fool.

Voltaire   Gave that up a while ago. But you knew that.

Emilie   I'm glad we're friends, V. It'd be a shame to waste all that history.

Voltaire   My favorite alchemy is the process by which happy hindsight turns tragedy into comedy.

Emilie   Alchemy's not good science. But you knew that.

Voltaire   Knowing better never really worked for me.

Emilie   I recall. You are hard to forget.

Voltaire   That was the general intention.

Don't let this boy distract you. You've got work to do.

Emilie   So do you.

Voltaire   Just take care of yourself. Please.

V *jumps, exits.*

Gentleman, *as Saint-Lambert, returns.*

Emilie   I thought the Duke—?

Gentleman   The Duke can wait. I love you. I said, *adore*. But I meant love. Love is what I meant. I mean. Now I don't know what you think, but I think you think like I think, and I think we're fated for each other and without a doubt completely and utterly in—

*She kisses him hard and true. **The lights go off with a huge crack.***

*A spot comes on. **Emilie** is alone, and remains there waiting for the lights to return.*

*One light comes on. In it **Soubrette** and **Gentleman** are moving together sweetly. This may be sex or dancing. But it's calm. **Emilie** watches.*

Emilie   "Love" is an overused term, but this is like air and water: pure, clear, and known to move mountains. This is it. Happy mind. Happy heart. Thank you god . . . and your best equations.

The lights still aren't on all the way.

But too much of anything, even the best things, can overwhelm.

A light crackles on, and as the scene rebuilds itself some lights are dimmer or don't come on.

*She starts to put a mark under **LOVE** but stops . . . **Emilie** realizes . . .*

Gentleman, *as Saint-Lambert, approaches.* **Soubrette** *looks at him, touches her stomach, she is worried.* **Gentleman** *realizes.*

Emilie and **Soubrette**   The surprise of my life. The hope of my heart.

Soubrette *lets **Gentleman** escort her offstage.*

V *enters, as does a card table.*

Emilie   The scene in which . . .

Emilie *sits and plays. To* **V**.

I'm pregnant.

V *stops.*

Voltaire   Are you sure?

Emilie   It's always a bit of a mystery but all facts point to it.

Voltaire   And the boy knows?

Emilie   He's not a boy, and yes he knows.

Voltaire   And the spouse?

Emilie   These things happen.

Voltaire   "These things happen?"

Emilie   I need you. You can't be angry.

Voltaire   *I'm not angry.*

V *throws his cards on the table.*

Emilie   I'm too old.

Voltaire   Quite possibly.

Emilie   It's not a good time.

Voltaire   I agree.

Emilie   Younger than me have died.

Voltaire (*bursting*)   Yes, they have.

Pause. A supportive tone.

I'm sorry.

Emilie   Help.

Voltaire   I'm sorry.

Emilie   I have to finish the Newton.

Voltaire   You have nothing to worry about.

Emilie   Every moment I should be working.

Voltaire   You'll be fine.

Emilie   The calculations are good.

Voltaire   You are the picture of health.

Emilie   The illustrations need work.

Voltaire   You'll be fine.

Emilie   I'll be fine.

Voltaire   You can't—

Emilie (*scared now*)   I really can.

Voltaire   The world would stop.

Emilie   It wouldn't blink.

Voltaire   The sun would fade.

Emilie   Shine on and on.

Voltaire   This is not how . . . Emilie . . .

Beat. Locked into each other. Breath. They both gain composure. Tonal shift.

You know, I think we should categorize this child under your miscellaneous works. You are so multitalented.

She laughs. She goes to touch his hand but the lights hiss at her. She stops.

Emilie   This child could be . . . like me.

Voltaire   Two of you . . . I wouldn't want to miss that.

But first we take care of you.

Emilie   I'll need some of our equipment from Cirey. For the Newton.

Voltaire   Why do you need equipment if you're translating?

Emilie   Because I'm close, V. I've almost figured out how Force Vive works *with* Newton, and if I can do *that*? That's real.

Voltaire   Isaac be damned.

Emilie   Isaac would be proud. Now will you help me or continue being an ass?

Voltaire   Although I so enjoy being an ass, as you know, I will, of course, help in any way Madame Marquise.

Emilie   V. I won't leave till it's done.

Voltaire (*a compliment*)   Then I hope it confounds you forever. Though that's unlikely.

V *goes to exit, but stops. He doesn't hear this . . .*

Emilie   We speak so well. Tight sentences delivered with confidence. And I wish that I could tell you what I actually mean. I am not this presentable inside. I've got no etiquette. I scream and cry. I don't want words anymore. No use. Just be. Simple be.

V *exits.* **Emilie** *makes a mark under* **LOVE**. **Gentleman**, *as Saint-Lambert, enters.*

And you. New and true love. You are easiest to me, thank god. For us I wish a real chance . . .

Emilie *makes a mark under* **LOVE** *as* **Gentleman** *changes into her husband—or into his memory.*

And you. Husband. Constant enthusiast. I wish you could know how much I honor you. And that I'm sorry for this.

Gentleman *exits.* **Emilie** *makes a mark under* **LOVE**.

I'm sorry. I'm sorry.

Beat. She is alone. No one's coming on.

And here I am. Sorry, running out of time, and no closer to knowing anything new.

giving up.

Which was a grand expectation in this first place.

So *STOP.* Just stop. We don't have to go on anymore. I understand.

Emilie's desk returns, two huge books as well—one is Newton's Principia *and one is hers for writing.*

I said I understand. I don't want to do the rest.

Soubrette *enters carefully. She opens both books to their first pages.*

I know what happens! And I want to stop!

Pause.

WHY NOT?!

Soubrette *turns to her.*

Soubrette   Incomplete.

Emilie   I don't care.

Madam *enters.*

Soubrette   Time and space—

Emilie   Are on my side tonight. So tell them to quit this. It's over. I'm done.

Madam   Incomplete, Emilie.

Emilie   I know the end of this story. Completed, thank you.

Madam   Time and space—

Emilie   *Yes.* Time and space have been very kind, but I don't want any more.

Madam   You don't decide.

Emilie   It's my life! Who else decides!?

Madam   Time.

Soubrette   And Space.

Emilie   I know this story, and I don't care for this last bit, so let me go.

Madam   You can't go.

Soubrette   You have to finish.

Emilie   Then do the rest without me.

Emilie *starts to leave the stage.*

Soubrette   Emilie!

Madam   No!

V, *and* **Gentleman** *run on stopping her.*

Gentleman   *Wait.*

Voltaire   You can't.

Emilie   Can't what?

Gentleman   Exit.

Emilie   Why not? What's out there?

Madam   Nothing.

Soubrette   Real Nothing.

Gentleman   All this is for you, Emilie. Not us.

Voltaire   All you.

Soubrette   And you're not done.

Madam   You're not.

Soubrette   You can't be.

Madam   Because.

Soubrette   You're not complete.

Madam   That question of yours?

Soubrette   Unmet.

Madam   Your story?

Soubrette   Untold.

Gentleman   So finish this. If you don't, all the Nothing wins.

Emilie   But, I don't know what it means.

Gentleman   Because stories aren't equations.

Voltaire   Lives aren't either.

Soubrette   They don't have solutions.

Emilie   Then why am I here? I want answers!

Madam   Answers aren't always solutions.

Emilie   I don't understand.

Gentleman   Maybe you will.

Madam   If you get to the end.

Pause.

Soubrette   Let me.

Madam *gestures to* **Emilie** *to sit, which she does.* **Soubrette***, as Emilie, gets into place.*

I rise at eight and work till three. Café from three to four, and resume work. Stop at ten for a bite to eat alone.

V *walks to her.*

Talk with V till midnight.

V *exits.*

Resume work till 5.

Gentleman *walks with her, reading to her.*

Walk with Jean-François every day. A new poem every morning.

He exits. **V** *walks to her with a book.*

Work until V brings me news and books.

He exits. **Gentleman***, as the Marquis, enters.*

Dinner with my husband. More work.

Gentleman *exits.*

Because above everything. I must risk all for all, and do this work. This work is . . .

Emilie   All.

Soubrette   This work is . . .

Emilie   Mine.

Soubrette   This work is . . .

Emilie   Me.

Soubrette *nods to* **Emilie***, then exits.*

Beat. Eureka . . .

Because *lives aren't equations* . . . they are variables *inside* them.

The governing equations are universal, but a life lived fully can still change the universe.

I can still change the . . .

Emilie *squares to the equation:* $\mathbf{F=mv^2}$.

Force Vive—The Living Force—Life's there—*I'm* in there.

A bed enters.

Wait wait—No—I know what's coming and I know its coming fast but—I have to know what all this means!

Soubrette *crosses the stage very pregnant helped by* **Gentleman**. *She contracts, moans—They exit as.*

Not yet. I'm close. More time. Give me time!

Emilie *fills the walls with Force Vive equations* . . .

My answer's in there. WHERE IS IT?

Soubrette *wails from offstage—* **Madam** *comes running . . . this baby is on its way.*

The scene with the book and the baby.

V *runs across the stage as* **Soubrette**, *offstage, screams and the baby is born.*

Madam *crosses with the swaddled infant as* **Soubrette** *is led onstage to her bed by* **Gentleman**, **V**.

Gentleman *kisses her forehead.*

Emilie   Not yet. No . . .

V *kisses her forehead, hands her a book.* **V** *exits with* **Gentleman**.

I don't understand yet. So slow down—I'm not—I'm *not*—

Soubrette *closes the books.*

Soubrette   Done.

Emilie   *NOT DONE*. There's *more*.

Soubrette   Done.

Emilie   "Done" isn't an answer.

This is not an answer. You said I'd understand. And I don't. And I'm dying. *And— Where's my answer*?!

The Players and **V** *appear. Very quiet at first.*

Madam   We thought you'd like to know . . .

Gentleman   Jean-François is devastated. Never thinks of another like you.

Voltaire   V eulogizes you well. And often. "Half his soul," he says.

Madam   And means.

Gentleman   Husband never marries again. Wouldn't know how or whom.

Madam   The baby girl dies in a year. Laid with you in tomb, poor thing.

Gentleman   There's a revolution you'll be glad you missed.

Madam   But the book survives.

Emilie   It does?

Voltaire   So does that little 2.

Emilie   What about it?

Gentleman   The work, the woman lives hundreds of years on.

Madam   And becomes the work of hundreds after you.

Voltaire   Progeny, Emilie.

Emilie   What kind?

Gentleman   Legacy, Emilie.

Emilie   *What kind?*

Madam   Complete, Emilie.

Emilie   *NoNo, NOT* complete. NOT enough. I'm NOT DONE!

But the **Gentleman**, **Madam** *and* **V** *are gone—*

I died thinking that the first time, and *I'm not doing it again.*

Emilie *fills the walls with Force Vive equations.*

Time and space have obliged tonight—They have obliged ME tonight—It is MY time and MY space—and equations—and Living Force and Force of Living and . . .

She looks at $F=mv^2$.

Force of . . .

Because when you square it . . . you *give it life* . . .

Looks at **Soubrette** . . .

Or life gives you

A day out of dark;

The chance or two

To make your . . .

She marks the **F** *into an* **E** *—it reads* $E=mv^2$. *Smiles.*

And I don't even know what that means . . .

The revelation . . . she turns to us . . .

But *you* do.

And *that's* my answer.

Not *what* we mean, but *that* we mean.

Beat. Full, changed beat.

Emilie *and* **Soubrette**, *the <u>two</u> of them, connect.*

Emilie and **Soubrette**   Done.

A brave beat. She's ready.

Emilie   The scene in which I die.

But not yet.

Emilie *grabs* **Soubrette***'s hand—**The lights crack and wail—**

NOT YET.

The lights do not go out—

The scene I never got. The scene that no one does. The scene when *I* hold my hand—when I *am* all I need—because in this scene? Nothing gives me meaning but me.

A moment between the **Emilies**. *Bittersweet but strong. To* **Soubrette***—only for* **Soubrette***.*

This is it.
The weight of the world. The knowing and the not.
And for all your knowing, you are blessed with more—
Questions. Love and so many questions.
And all the answers may not come—
But the asking makes us last—
And that makes you right *and wrong,* done and *never* done—
And that's the point, Emilie.
That's it.
This is it.
Thank god . . . .
And your best equations.

Emilie *holds* **Soubrette** *tight as* **Soubrette** *dies—**The lights rise into flaring white, then plunge out.**

One light on **Emilie***,* **Soubrette** *is gone. Beat.*

The light is going out again, and so is she . . .

She knows this is her last speech.

She is precise with it, in awe of it, ready . . .

All we have is the moment of having.
And the hope that we knew something real.
All we have is the meaning of having,
All we have is the force and the life
This moment, this meaning, this having—
And this.
And this.
And . . .

Breath. Blackout.

End of Play.

The Revolutionists

The Revolutionists was commissioned and first produced by the Cincinnati Playhouse in the Park (Blake Robison, Artistic Director; Buzz Ward, Managing Director) in February, 2016. It was directed by Eleanor Holdridge, the scenic and costume designs were by Marion Williams, the lighting design was by Mark Barton, the sound design was by Scott Killian, and the stage manager was Andrea L. Shell. The cast was as follows:

Olympe de Gouges	Lise Bruneau
Charlotte Corday	Keira Keeley
Marie-Antoinette	Jessica Lynn Carroll
Marianne Angelle	Kenita R. Miller

Characters

Olympe de Gouges, *38. Badass activist playwright and feminist. Theatre nerd, excitable, passionate, a showman. Widowed and never remarried to ensure her personal freedom.*

Charlotte Corday, *25. Badass country girl and assassin. Very serious, hardened by righteousness, never been kissed. Has a pocket watch she keeps checking. Also plays* **Fraternité** *in a mask.*

Marie-Antoinette, *38. Less badass but fascinating former queen of France. Bubbly, graceful, opinionated, totally unaware, unintentionally rude, and oddly prescient. Never had a real friend. Also plays* **Fraternité** *in a mask.*

Marianne Angelle, *30s. A badass Black woman in Paris. She is from the Caribbean, a free woman, a spy working with her husband, Vincent. Tough, classy, vigilant, the sanest one of them all.*

Setting

Paris, the Reign of Terror (1793).

A safe place, a study, a prison cell, the Tribunal.

Then the scaffold.

Punctuation as Rhythm Primer

(—) Dashes at the end of a sentence are cut-offs by the following line.

(—) Dashes within a sentence are self cut-offs, an acceleration into the next thought.

(. . .) Ellipses at the end of a sentence are trail-offs, unsure of what's next.

Breath. is a small, personal pause.

Pause. is a shared pause of average duration.

Beat. is a longer pause in which a personal change or revelation happens.

Levels of Intensity Indicated by Dialogue Font

Italics are more intense than not.

ALL CAPS ARE VERY INTENSE.

ALL CAPS AND ITALICS ARE THE MOST INTENSE.

Notes on the Play

The play is mostly *a comedy*.

The play is based on real women, real transcripts, and real executions.

But remember it's *a comedy*.

The play runs with a seamlessness that necessitates less-realistic sets. **Fraternité** is an almost commedia presence, a stock character of a bad guy, masked.

In the end, the entire play is in Olympe's mind as she walks up the stairs, onto the scaffold, and to her death.

The Song

Act One

Prologue

In the dark.

A time of unrest in Paris—crisis—danger—threat.

The hum of "Our Song" faintly wafts in.

The sound of a scared breath that we are breathing.

It's our breath—we are trying to steady our breath
Breath
Breath—

Then a sharp white light on, or the engorging shadow of . . . A guillotine, its blade rising to the top.

A gasp.

Which slams into:

Scene One

Olympe *standing at her writing, startled into an idea for a new play . . .*

Olympe   Well *that's* not a way to start a comedy.

With an execution? That's just basic dramatic writing: Don't start with beheadings. Audiences don't want plays about terror and death—no—they want . . . hope. Yes, I have to write about . . . grace and power in the face of crisis. Artistic defiance. Yes. That's good. There we go.

Spitballing now, testing out ideas as they come.

OK, what if I write a play that is the voice of this revolution, but not the hyperbolic, angry-yelling kind. I will write the wise and witty kind that satirizes and inspires and says to the held breath of a rapt audience . . ."something . . . profound."

So yeah. We're gonna have to cut the guillotine.

Marianne *has entered with a bag—luggage.*

She wears a red protest sash that reads: "Revolution for all!"

Marianne   Cut that thing! Serves it right.

Olympe   Oh my god, Marianne!

Marianne   I know this is crazy to just show up like this but hello and surprise!

Hugs!

Olympe   Hello and surprise! Oh my god, for a second I thought you were the national guard.

Marianne   Are they coming for the writers already?

Olympe   Only the important ones. I should be fine. Come in, come in. What are you doing here?

Marianne   Many things including, I hope, staying with you. Is that OK?

Olympe   Of course! Oh my god. Stay as long as you need.

Marianne   Thank you thank you.

Olympe   Don't thank me. I'm so glad to see you. I thought you went back to the Caribbean.

Marianne   Vincent went back, I stayed in Nice.

Olympe   Ooh Nice is nice.

Marianne   For some. For me? A lot less beach and a lot more political reconnaissance.

Olympe   What does that mean?

Marianne   Gathering intelligence to send home. That's why I'm back. Things are heating up and we need an eye in Paris and I'm it.

Olympe   So wait. I've been restarting the same play for a month while you became a damn spy?!

Marianne   I mean . . .

  Olympe   GIRL.

    Marianne   I know.

      Olympe   Look at you!

Marianne   Well, we decided we needed our own intel, really tap into the political machines or we'll never figure how to break them.

Olympe   You are my spy friend! God, you make me so much more interesting.

Marianne   Well don't get comfortable, I'm also here because I need you.

Olympe   Playwrights *love* hearing that. It's so rare.

Marianne   I need you to write for us. Pamphlets, articles, treatises about slavery—

Olympe   Monologues?

Marianne   Abolition human interest stories.

Olympe   But *as* monologues?

Marianne   Just—sure. Help us! You're the best writer I know.

Olympe   How many do you know?

Marianne (*lying*)   *So* many. (*Not lying.*) And you can help people understand what we're fighting for, freedom, justice, humanity, come on.

Olympe   Of course I'll help! But why don't *you* write this?

Marianne   Because I'm a better spy than I am a writer. Please.

Olympe   Yes. I'll write anything you want . . . as soon as I write my play.

Marianne   The play you can't even start? I'm rebelling against slavery and you're battling writer's block.

Olympe   *I'm not blocked.* I'm just . . . mentally . . . hibernating. There's a lot of pressure to write something profound these days. And then I keep thinking if I come up with a good title it'll get me started. Something tantalizing but really vague like . . . "*The Revolutionists.*"

Marianne   You could do better.

Olympe   I know. Nothing's working. There is drama everywhere you look these days, why can't I write any of it?!

Marianne   You can! Pamphlets! For me! Write the truth that needs writing.

Olympe   But that's *your* truth. Which I will totally write, I will, but I also really need something of my own. I need a play that's good and important and annoyingly prescient.

Marianne   Then write the truth of an artist staring down a civil war.

Olympe   And end up with a play about a playwright writing a play? I'd rather watch a guillotine.

Marianne   So would everyone.

Olympe   Would they? Dammit. Back to guillotines.

Marianne   That's not what I meant.

Olympe   Setting: Now. Paris, France, 1793. Guillotines are very big these days. Actually they just came out with small ones too, for kids to kill mice and for wives to make salad.

Marianne   That's so messed up.

Olympe   It is. Everything is. Which is why the people's revolution has risen up with force enough to remove the king from power—

Marianne   and from his own head.

Olympe   Exactly. Danger, unrest. An epic battle for freedom and peace—

Marianne   For white men.

Olympe   Exactly. Which is why *my* play . . . (*A great idea.*) could be about *women* showing the boys how revolutions are done. Yes! Fighting for their rights to life, liberty, and . . . divorce.

Marianne   Divorce and decapitation?

(*Slipping into couplets.*) I hope it's better than it sounds.

Olympe   It's comical yet quite profound

Marianne   Just doesn't sound like comedy—

Olympe   I know, but that's what it could be.

Marianne   You know it's always in the timing,

Olympe   Are you hearing all this rhyming?

Gasp.

Maybe I'm writing a musical!

Marianne   Oh god, no one wants a musical about the French Revolution.

Olympe   Probably right. How about a solemn, bracing political exposé—

Marianne   You're losing me.

Olympe   How about a thrilling, hilarious political exposé that will gather us as one community, to be inspired by great French art and—

Marianne   To boo at whichever new play they want.

Olympe   *They did not boo my play.* The abolition one from last year? No. That sound was the natural cathartic release from years of repressed racism and misogyny.

Marianne   So you're writing fantasy now?

Olympe   The people leapt to their feet.

Marianne   And to the exit.

Olympe   To tell their friends.

Marianne   That it was . . . "interesting."

Olympe   My plays piss off just the right kind of people thank you very much. Excuse me for trying to do something revolutionary during this revolution. This is our time to make a better world for everyone . . . who sees my plays.

Marianne   You're always so close to selflessness.

Olympe   Thank you. See now you've got me thinking. What about a passionate sociopolitical comedy about women's rights and—

Marianne   A feminist comedy? Girl, *don't.*

Olympe   OK, what if my play *starts out* as a comedy, but it'll *end* as a drama. That's fresh, right? We don't even have a word for that but—

Marianne   Like . . . "Life"?

Olympe   Just go with me on this: At first the play is witty and fun, maybe some puppets.

Marianne   *Why do you always add puppets.*

Olympe   Because!

Marianne   You might as well go back to the musical.

Olympe   *OK* I'm trying to do something important here.

Marianne   Which is maybe why it's sucking so bad.

Olympe   *Sometimes conviction sucks.*

Marianne   I'm just saying that nobody wants to be *told* what to feel.

Olympe   I'm not *telling* them what to feel, I'm *forcing* them.

Marianne   That's what pamphlets do! Look. Most people don't have time for the grand dramas, it's the intimate ones that matter. So write your political theatre but remember that for most people it's not about being righteous, it's about being real. So find the heart. Not the . . . art.

Olympe   Why are you better at this than me? I've been trying to come up with a cute couplet like that for days, but I keep dreaming of guillotines and resorting to puppets. I have to write something! This is a revolution! Everyone is making history without me!

Marianne   Listen—

Olympe   I can't listen when I'm whining.

Marianne   You're just blocked. Writers get blocked. It's not a tragedy. Being ripped from your country, stuffed in the belly of a ship, carted across the world, and forced to break your back to make sugar for French pastries is a tragedy. The French are fighting a revolution for *freedom* while running a *slave colony* in the West. That's why I need you writing pamphlets so we can expose the immoral and hypocritical actions that—

Olympe   *Oh my god I can write about you!*

Marianne   —was not the point I was going for.

Olympe   Yes! You're gorgeous, and empowered, and seem to have a very clear character motivation.

Marianne   We're not gonna stay friends if you write a play about me.

Olympe (*narrator voice*)   Marianne Angelle: Activist for freedom from slavery in the Caribbean, lover of cheeses and universal human rights, strong yet sardonically sympathetic.

Marianne   *No*, she said, sardonically. *Pamphlets.*

Olympe   I am! I will! It will be great research for the play. What you're doing is bold and important. You're a goddamn spy for freedom! That's box office gold! Come on. You make me believe that a better world is possible. If people listen to you. And a lot of me.

Marianne   OK they say write what you know, right? But what if you write what you *want*. That's what we're really fighting for isn't it? Women's agency over their own lives.

Olympe   Yes.

Marianne   The abolition of slavery across the planet.

Olympe   *Yes.*

Marianne   Maybe you don't need to dress your ideas in drama. You can write a monologue? Why don't you write a manifesto.

Olympe   Or . . . a declaration?

Marianne   Sure, yeah. Like the Americans.

Olympe   Like the Americans! "We hold these truths and-the-factthat-women-are-people to be self-evident."

Marianne   That sounds pretty revolutionary to me. Also no risk of puppets. Everybody wins.

Pause. **Olympe** *likes this. Then she thinks. Seriously.*

Olympe   Marianne. Do you dream of guillotines? Every night?

Marianne   No. Chains.

KNOCK KNOCK KNOCK on the door.

Olympe *and* **Marianne** *freeze. Oh no. Then . . .*

Knockknockknockknockknock—like a hummingbird knocking, fast and fluttery.

Marianne *gets on one side of the door with a book held as a weapon if needed, through the door . . .*

Olympe   Who's there?

Charlotte   Who's . . . *there*?

Olympe   Well. *You're* the one at the door, who are you?

Charlotte   You're obviously at the door too, and I'm here for a writer.

Marianne   Did she say a writer?

Olympe   I think that's what she said.

Charlotte *bursts in with a book.*

Charlotte   YES IT'S WHAT I SAID, I SAID A WRITER, I NEED A WRITER, WHO IS THE WRITER AND WHAT'S MY LINE? Are you a writer? If not— (*Turning to* **Marianne**.) are *you* a writer? This isn't a complicated question. *Where do they keep the writers, I need a line.*

Olympe   I'm sorry, you need a *line*?

Charlotte   That's what I said, but I don't care what *I'd* say, I wanna know what *you'd* say. Isn't that how this works? I need that to be how this works.

Marianne   And I need you to back the France off. What do you want? Who sent you?

Charlotte   *I* sent me and, I want some dialogue. That's what you do right? You're that real live lady writer guy? You write plays and stuff.

Marianne   And pamphlets about the rights of Caribbean slaves, which means she's very busy and we have no idea who you are or whose side you're on, also you're very loud and immediately unsettling, so why don't we do this another time and/or never.

Charlotte   *I don't have time for another time and/or never.* I have a guy to murder, which will land me on the scaffold, which is why I came to you, which is why, as I yelled upon arrival, I NEED A LINE. My actions will be talked about for centuries and I don't want to sound like a dingbat. I need something that will sink into their memories for all time, something with a lot of "fuck you" in it. So. Playwright. Write.

Olympe   I mean . . . thank you for your enthusiasm but this isn't really my thing—

Charlotte   COME ON. How many feminist playwrights do you think there are in Paris. *One. You.*

Olympe   And trust me that turning down an opportunity to tell someone what to say is *really* hard for me but I'm already juggling a lot now.

Charlotte   Aren't we all: life, revolution, impossible beauty standards. *Help me.*

Olympe   I'm trying to help a lot of people . . . without leaving my office.

Charlotte   Please. It's rare to be in the company of like minds in like corsets, and I know you're a "writery" kind of writer. So. If you write it? I'll say it, I'll shout it, I'll sing it.

  Olympe   Sing it?

   Marianne   NO.

    Charlotte   YES.

Olympe   Can you just gimme some context here. *What* exactly do you need written?

Charlotte   Last words.

Marianne   Last words?

Olympe   Like . . . for a toast? Are you going to a wedding?

Charlotte   No. I'm going to kill Jean-Paul Marat.

By stabbing.

Because he's awful.

Marianne   You're going to kill the journalist Marat?

Charlotte   Yeah. Because he's awful.

Olympe   And by stabbing?!

Charlotte   Yeah. Because he's awful.

Olympe   OK. Well. Now I *have* to write a play about her.

Marianne   *What about my pamphlets?*

Olympe   What about a torrid romance between a gorgeous assassin and a narcoleptic judge!

Marianne   *No.*

Charlotte   What? No. I need *one* line, not a whole (and obviously terrible) play.

Olympe (*making a note*)   No I'm really seeing this. A woman willing to risk it all for vigilante justice. Yes!

Marianne   Should you maybe ask her *why* she's going to kill this guy before you make her a hero?

Olympe   I'm sure it's a good reason, look at that face. Now what if we call the play: "*The Young Assassin.*"

Charlotte *and* **Marianne** *make a "meh" sound.*

Or maybe just, "*Stabbing: The Musical*"! Oh this is gonna be great.

Marianne   Not anymore.

Charlotte   Hold on, is she quoting me? Are you quoting me?

Marianne   Oh, theatre people don't quote, they embellish.

Charlotte   Which would normally just be annoying, but this city is more than a little pissed off at the embellished or have you missed the last few beheadings. They don't like flourish.

Olympe   Theatre isn't flourish. It's fundamental.

Marianne   Here she goes.

Olympe   Story is the heartbeat of humanity and humanity gets really dark when the wrong stories are leading the people.

Charlotte   Well I'm not here to make a *story*, I'm here to make *history*.

Olympe   History *is* a story. Just with . . . an extra . . . "hi."

Marianne   Stop.

Olympe (*using her hand as a puppet*)   Hi, Story!

Marianne   *We said no puppets.*

Olympe   Sorry.

Charlotte   I don't think I was being clear. I'm an assassin. About to assassinate.

Olympe   And we'll get to that, but we have to do some character development first—

Charlotte   I don't understand—

Marianne   It's all part of her creative process.

Charlotte   I did not sign up for this.

Olympe   Because it's a *new* play—

Charlotte   Oh god.

Olympe   Set during the French Revolution!

Charlotte   I don't have time for—

Olympe   Starring lots of furious women!

Charlotte (*being a furious woman*)   *I said I do not have time for such frivolity, I need some last words, and I need to sharpen my knife.*

Charlotte *reveals a long steak knife. Pause.*

Marianne   Yeah. I'd watch a play about her.

Olympe   Right? What if she wears a sparkly mask?

Charlotte   I'm not wearing a mask. I *want* people to know that I did it. Just. How long do I have to sit through this stupid play until we get to the murdering?

Olympe   Well, the exposition, rising action, it'll probably be a while.

Marianne   While we're waiting you could tell us your name?

Charlotte   Right. Hi. Charlotte Corday.

Olympe   Spot on Charlotte Corday, a soon-to-be-killer in revolutionary France.

Charlotte   Well don't say it like *that*. Not in that "You're a killer!" kind of way. Marat is a sick, fundamentalist, political *pundit* who has caused the deaths of thousands of innocent people with no tool as brave as a sword, no, he uses *words*. So really, I'm an editor.

Olympe   I wish I was that young and angry.

Charlotte   Thank you, but you don't seem to get that I am on a deadline. That is not a pun but it could be. And I'm sure this performing art we're in the middle of is lovely but not lovelier than justifiable homicide, and I'm not sure if this *is* the play or if we're still in the prologue, because plays are only for rich people and chandeliers and I'm on a damn mission to maim, so if we're not actively avenging, can we get to the pointy point?

Pause.

Olympe   It's not for rich people.

Charlotte   Theatre?

Marianne   I mean . . .

Olympe   No. It's just . . . I mean the chandeliers came with the space—

Charlotte   So did the starving peasants outside.

Olympe   But I—no—the revolution just opened the theatres to the masses. Playwrights can finally write what they want. Theatre is democracy! Really pretty democracy with great hats and—Am I really writing for rich people?

Marianne   I mean . . .

Charlotte   Yes. The ones who aren't fled or dead. Vigilante mobs always ruin the party. Isn't theatre just another party?

Olympe   No. It's culture.

Charlotte   Isn't culture just another party?

Olympe   Culture is civilization! It's definitive, it lasts, the French are really into it! And I write pamphlets too, and we do a little community outreach and—oh god you're right.

Marianne   Ooh. She never says that.

Olympe   But art is all I know how to do. Truly. I'm useless in the sunshine. (*Getting annoyingly dramatic.*) Only *theatre* gives my soul—

Charlotte   Ohmigod is this going to be a play about a play?

Marianne   *That* is the worst.

Charlotte   That *is* the worst. Art about the rich is one thing, but art about rich people's art is too far.

Marianne   Agreed.

Olympe   Now wait just a minute, the performing arts are a vital part of—

Charlotte   *Art and anything else that fakes its way through this life is useless to real human beings trying to fix the goddamn world.*

Pause. Taken aback by her tone.

Olympe   Well. It might be fiction, but it's not fake.

The beating hearts in front of you are real.

The gathering of people, the time spent is real.

Marianne   Agreed.

Olympe   The story is real when it starts. And this story will capture our hearts.

Charlotte   WHILE THE REIGN OF TERROR TAKES OUR HEADS.

Which I saw them do. To a hundred of my neighbors in one day.

Because Marat told them to.

This revolution is not for the people anymore, it's for the zealots. They are taking over, and they are cruel, and you want to tell me a story? Do you see how insane that seems to a woman who is going to kill a man with her own hands? What the play is about does not matter. What is your life about? *That matters.*

Because sometimes? One man, every once in a while, *really needs to just die.*

Forget the line. I'll do it myself.

Charlotte *starts to go.*

Marianne   Are you in love with someone who doesn't love you back?

Charlotte   NoWhyWouldYouSayThat? No. No.

Marianne   I sense the short temper of the unrequited.

Olympe   Oh *that's* what it is.

Charlotte   I AM NOT THAT. You theatre people—you are so loose.

Olympe (*offended*)   I beg your—(*Not offended.*) That's accurate.

Marianne   So many egos, and tempers, and onstage heavily choreographed embraces.

Olympe   It's bound to spill over.

Charlotte   Yeah. No. I'm gonna go.

Olympe   Don't go now we just started liking you.

Charlotte   The nuns were right. Theatre is the devil's art.

Olympe   Because we get to decide who the real heroes are.

Marianne   The clergy just hate that.

Charlotte   And. Who are the real heroes?

Olympe   We are. If I'm writing it.

Marianne   Stay. Your story's in good hands here.

Pause. **Charlotte** *likes the sound of that. She stays.*

Charlotte   I could stay for a sec.

Olympe   Great. Now. My question is about plot.

Marianne   Me too. You're just gonna walk up to him and stab him? I mean just, stabstab?

Olympe   And because I'm seeing sequel potential, I'm worried about killing off our heroine so quickly.

Marianne   Agreed.

Charlotte   No. I have to do this. I'm the only one with enough guts and cuteness to get away with this, so I will curl my hair, strap a steak knife to my thigh, use my sweet voice to infiltrate his house, stare him down and kill Jean-Paul Marat.

With said steak knife. In his bathtub.

Marianne   His bathtub?

Charlotte   He lives there. Skin condition.

Olympe   Ew.

Charlotte   No, it'll be great. Intimate. Bloody. The water swirling red, the nudity. It'll be so . . . dramatic.

Olympe   Aha!

Charlotte   *Not like that.*

Olympe   Drama wins!

Charlotte   *I said dramatic not theatrical.*

Olympe   All the world's an audience.

Charlotte   All the world's a mob.

Marianne   Sometimes it's hard to tell the difference.

Charlotte   You know what? Never mind, I shouldn't have come.

Olympe   Charlotte, stop.

Charlotte   No, no, the stories you trot out are distractions, and placating the rich, and full of *yelling and bosom and terrible dialogue*!

Marianne (*terribly serious*)   THEN WHY THE HELL ARE YOU HERE.

You know that a good deed needs a good story or else it might vanish like nothing. ever. happened.

You know that or else you wouldn't have shown up. You also know that her words are dangerous, she is putting her life on the line—

Olympe   I am?

  Marianne   To tell a story that is good and good for the world—

    Olympe   My *life* is on the line?

Marianne   She is risking everything for her art. So be nice to the playwright, because she holds fiction like you hold that blade and I know her weapon is sharper.

Charlotte   Than a knife?

Marianne   Than any metal you've got. You tell me which one you want running the world.

Pause. **Olympe** *smiles at* **Marianne**.

Charlotte *looks at both of them . . . changes her mind.*

Charlotte   I mean.

Sorry for the yelling.

Marianne   Uh-huh.

Charlotte   And the aggressive entrance.

Marianne   Uh-huh.

Charlotte   It's just. You two might be the first women I've ever like . . . liked. You're . . . interesting in like a . . . human kinda way.

Marianne   Thank you, young assassin.

Olympe   Such a good title.

Charlotte   Do you mind if I hang here for half an hour until my appointment? You can maybe write my line while I practice my stabbing and scary eyes.

Olympe   Also a good title.

Marianne   Wait. You have an appointment to murder Marat?

Charlotte   Well *he* doesn't know that's what it's for.

So don't let me get in your way. I don't know how this whole "drama" thing works. What do you—like—do all day?

Olympe   Well. I guess I . . . think up interesting people with enormous backstories and lots to lose and force them into action—

Marie *enters, looking lovely and startled.*

Marie   Marie enters! Is she late? Or lost? What were they talking about? Was it her? It's always her. Or is she being her again? It's a confusing time. Hello. Marie . . . (*Whispered like it's a bad word.*) *Antoinette.*

Charlotte   *Holy crap you're Marie-Antoinette?*

Marie   *Isn't it exciting I'mSoFamous.*

  Marianne   Infamous.

    Marie   *Famous.*

    Marianne   Infamous.

Charlotte   Wait. *You're the real Marie-Antoinette?*

Marie   *I am so real!* Sigh. Sometimes I say it instead of doing it. It *used* to be so good to be real. Or did they always hate her? Did she mention her general confusion about this? She has no idea what's coming next, except that one day she woke up in a palace and went to sleep in a prison—not exactly prison—it was one of their lesser bedrooms—*with gunmen outside and no dessert!* The fear in her children's fancy eyes, trying to explain it to the dogs. The pressure, the amount of sudden exposition. It's all too much for Marie!

Marianne   And everyone watching her.

Olympe   Is there anything I can do for you, Majesty?

Marie   I'm not even a "Majesty" anymore, the jerks.

Marianne   You're all Citizens now.

Marie   But who wants a Citizen for a queen? That's ridiculous. (*To* **Olympe**.) I'm here for a rewrite.

Olympe   Oh god.

Marie   Yes girl I need some help. First step: Make me Majesty again!

Charlotte   Marat's the one who wanted to toss the monarchy. It all goes back to him.

Olympe   Exactly. There can be real reform *without* torching centuries of history.

Marie   *Thank* you.

Marianne   But, come on, the royals aren't ready to change.

Marie   No thank you.

Marianne   You aren't. You're dancing while Rome burns. MARIE. First: It's Paris. Second: I had people dance *for* me. Third: We used to like me, the whole country would celebrate my birthday. How did it all turn into this rudeness and . . . murder.

Marianne   There's your title.

Marie   Title? Whose title? I have so many titles.

Olympe   Not that kind of title.

Charlotte   A play title. For a play.

Marie   A *play* play? Which play? I'll play!

Marianne   It's her play. She's writing it.

Olympe   Yes. Olympe de Gouges, Your Majesty. Young playwright, activist, you might have heard of my moving political dramas—

Marie   That's cute, no, I've heard that you're the only lady playwright left in Paris.

Marianne   And you need to rewrite your history because it makes you look bad.

Marie   Most of it *does* make me look bad! You're hilarious.

Marianne   Not on purpose.

Marie   Which is still hilarious! (*To* **Charlotte**.) You're pretty. And young. That must be fun. What are you?

Charlotte   An assassin. It is fun.

Marie   And who is your funny friend?

Marianne   Marianne Angelle. Not funny, not your friend, and we need to talk about colonization in the Caribbean right now.

Marie   Caribbean? Ohmygod I *love* you guys.

Wait. Are you a . . .? Like a real live . . .? LikeASlave?

Marianne   *No.* I'm a free woman. My husband and I came to France to demand full and recognized civil and political equality. We want slavery abolished across the entire French Empire.

Olympe   *I am so for that.*

Charlotte   Yes We Can!

Marie   You know it's the funniest thing, when I walked in here I could have sworn that you were my servant—

Marianne   I AM A FREE WOMAN OF MEANS LIKE YOU AND YOU AND YOU. I AM NO ONE'S SERVANT, I'M JUST STANDING NEARBY.

Charlotte   I like her so much.

Olympe   She knows.

Charlotte (t*o* **Marianne**)   I like you so much.

Marianne   I know.

(*To* **Marie**.) And you, Citizen, should know right now that the men and women of Saint-Domingue, who are dying in the sticky heat of your greed and oppression, the slaves who have suffered under your lash, have started a revolution of their own.

Marie   Two revolutions? At once? Someone should have called ahead.

Marianne   It's the same revolution, the same rights, the same freedoms, just applied to the enslaved instead of your peasants.

Marie   I don't remember any of the other colonies acting this way.

Marianne   We know you need us. You people love our sugar, and coffee, and indigo—

Marie   Indigo! For ribbons!

Marianne   So we have leverage. A country of our own and you get your coffee.

Charlotte   Amazing.   **Olympe**   Damn right.   **Marie**   Your coffee is really good.

Marie   I wish there was something I could do to help. But. I mean I couldn't even start a youth fitness program at the palace, and don't get me started on my rebranding ideas—*which were good*. I mean what *is* a fleur-de-lys? A sad flower? A terrible fork? No one listens to me unless I say something stupid, then it's the talk of the damn town.

Marianne   I feel your pain.

Marie   Thank you.

Charlotte   That was sarcasm.

Marie   I realize that now.

Olympe   WAIT. Wait. I've got it. This is it. This is *it*!

THE QUEEN. CAN BE. IN THE PLAY.

Charlotte   *My* play?   **Marianne**   Oh *hell* no.   **Marie**   I *would* likely
My play?!   What? Uh-uh.   make it more interesting.

Marianne   Olympe, no. You were writing about revolution not royalty.

Olympe   Now wait, you said to write the intimate stories, that's what this would be. A woman at the edge of history, with everything to lose and nowhere to hide—

Marie   Can it be a musical?

Olympe   Under all that vanity she's still just a person.

Marie   Just a *fabulous* person.

Olympe   I mean it's not *her* fault that she's the queen.

Marianne   *Can we please not call her that anymore.* She's not my queen and she shouldn't be yours. She bankrupted your country!

Marie   I mean we reduced a lot.

Marianne   The people have no food, and she had a palace!

Marie   So did the dogs—mini ones—hilarious.

Marianne   She is everything wrong with a class of people so vacant-hearted that they can't see the horror of their own luxury.

Marie   OK I had no choice in becoming royalty, it was thrown at me. And by that I mean a mountain of free stuff and undeserved compliments. What would you do? *You'd take them. They're free.* But just to be very clear, I did *not* say that bit about the cake. That was out of context. I thought I was ordering lunch.

Charlotte   Cake for lunch?

Marie   Uh, *all* lunch comes with cake.

Marianne   *And all cake comes with sugar and all sugar comes from families dying in the drowning heat a world away.* Figurehead or actual head it's *hers* that should roll, not ours.

Marie *is silent.* **Marianne** *didn't mean to go that far.*

Marie (*sincere*)   I know what most people think of me. It's not very nice. And I deserve . . . some of it. And I have a feeling I might die sooner than later, but I would very much like Later to know that I was a real person. Who bled and gave birth in a closed room with two hundred people watching so give me a little credit here. I just . . . I care. I care so much about my people and my country. I just need better press. You can do that for me Madame de Gouges. I was hoping that you would. I would be honored to be in your play. (*To* **Marianne**.) And try to earn your respect. Via meaningful connection . . . and minor revisionism.

Olympe   I know I shouldn't but I kind of like her.

Marianne   She's not worthy, Olympe. She doesn't belong with us. She is not a revolutionist.

Charlotte   Yeah, what would your declaration be? "We hold these *jewels* to be self-evident."

Marie   Well they are.

Charlotte   So shiny.

Marie   Did you say declaration? Like the Americans? They do *great* declarations. I know Thomas Jefferson if you want any advice. He'd like you. (*To* **Marianne**.) Actually he'd like *you*.

Marianne   *I feel like that should make me really mad. You need to go.*

Olympe   Wait—What if she could help us?

Marianne   Help us? Help *us*? No.

Marie   I mean sometimes a revolution needs a woman's touch.

Charlotte   Or you know . . . stabstab.

Marianne   It does need a woman's touch, but that is not a soft thing, Citizen Cake.

Marie (*showing her dominatrix side*)   Oh. I know it's not. Not at night, not in secret, not when you're a tall, red-haired American diplomat in my goddamn country. Then it is a hard hand that knows your every weakness, and is firm and red and shuts you up and makes you sit and you better do what it says or else you're damn right there'll be a revolution.

Pause. The others are surprised and impressed.

Marianne I mean . . .	**Charlotte** She is kinda. awesome	**Olympe** Yeah I really like her.

Marie   Question. Are there snacks? I'm used to a lot of snacking. Treats? Sweets? Anything? Nothing?

Charlotte   I have a mint.

Charlotte *takes out a plastic-wrapped mint. Hands it to* **Marie**.

Marie   A mint! How darling. *Merci, mademoiselle!* Now tell us of our play, Madame de Gouges.

Olympe   Oh. Well I haven't started writing anything just yet but—

Marie   Let the synopsis begin!

Olympe   OK. Um. Well. Think of the power of a play that shows the entwined lives of real women—

Marie *starts to open the mint—the wrapper crackles.* **Olympe** *stops,* **Marie** *stops.*

Women who, even through their differences—

Marie's *mint wrapper crackles.* **Olympe** *stops.*

Marie *stops.* join forces to protest the deep injustice of—.

Marie *crackles the hell out of that wrapper—*

Marianne That is so loud.	**Charlotte** OHMYGOD, STOP.	**Olympe** Can you figure that out, Your Majesty?

Marie   *Sometimes good things make a lot of noise.*

Olympe   See? Musical.

Marianne No.	**Charlotte** No.	**Marie** Yay!

Marie *frees the mint, pops it in her mouth, smiles.*

Olympe   OK look. I don't know what I'm writing just yet, but I know that our voices deserve the stage. We deserve to be our own heroes, everyone's heroes. We're all of us more alike than we are different, and if this revolution is what I think it is? This is our time to be known, and heard, and—

Charlotte (*checking her watch*)   Oh crap I have to go kill a guy.

Olympe   Come on, that speech was getting good.

Marie   You're killing a guy? Which one?

Marianne   Marat in the bathtub with a steak knife.

Marie   Oh kill him! I hate that man! He put my name on a list. *With other people.* Can you imagine? You know my husband, he always said Marat was a bloodlusty wacko. And then he chops my husband's head off. That shows how right he was.

Olympe   OK but—Charlotte. What if you miss? What if he gets you first?

Charlotte   Steak knife pretty much always beats naked-guy-in-a-bath.

Olympe   And he deserves it, but you don't. We don't want to lose you. Don't do this.

Charlotte   Then who will. The entire city is scared of him. Well I'm not.

Marianne   That's right, girl. I got your back.

Olympe   *Marianne.*

Marie   Me too, me too! StabStabStab!

Olympe   Would you stop encouraging her. I'm trying to save her life, because there is no doubt that *she will die for this.*

Charlotte   AND THAT DOES NOT SCARE ME.

Not for this.

I am not afraid to die for this.

Pause.

Olympe   What's that like?

Pause.

Charlotte   Like knowing your lines.

Pause.

Marie   Does she love someone who doesn't love her back?

Charlotte WHY DOES THAT MATTER? God, that has *nothing to do with—*	**Olympe** Yes she does.	**Marianne** That's what I said.

Marie   Is it your tutor? Is his name Jacques? I know these things.

Olympe   Just wait, Charlotte.

Charlotte   No. Jacques knows what he did.

Olympe   I'm talking about Marat. The little assassination you're about to attempt. Have you really thought this through? Have you thought about Madame Guillotine?

Charlotte   Well yeah, who hasn't.

Marie   I hate that bitch.

Marianne   It's the efficiency that most offends me.

Marie   Too quick.

Olympe   Too easy.

Marianne   They say it's egalitarian.

Marie   Bullshit, it's cheap.

Olympe   I mean take some care.

Marianne   We're not cattle.

Charlotte   To them we are.

Olympe   Carting you through the city to your doom.

Marianne   In a wagon.

Marie   No grandeur.

Olympe   Trash at you.

Marianne   They cut your hair.

Charlotte   They cut my hair?

Olympe   Weren't you aware?

Charlotte   No! That's not fair!

Marianne   Maybe it could be a musical.

Olympe (*to* **Charlotte**)   Just think about this. If you die? They could vilify you, call you witch or make him a martyr. Then it's like Marat wins.

Charlotte   Which is why you have to tell my story so they understand it.

And do *not* let them cut my hair.

Olympe   But. We didn't get you your last line. It might take a while. A long while.

Charlotte   Then I'm gonna have to go with: "May God have no pity, you motherfuckers."

Olympe   Lemme work on that.   **Marie**   Hilarious!   **Marianne**   I mean . . .

Marianne   You could always sing. That's what I'd do. A song sticks.

Charlotte   A song? That's not a bad idea.

Olympe   You said no musicals!

Marie   What about the writer's last words? That must be a lot of pressure since that's kind of your thing.

Olymepe   I don't need last words, I am of the theatre, we just go on and on. And on.

Marie   But you must've thought about what you'd say if they—

Olympe   I DON'T KNOW.

I don't know.

Pause.

Marie   Well. I do hope that my last words are sympathetic. I just don't want to sound silly because I AM STILL THE GODDAMN QUEEN OF FRANCE NO MATTER WHAT THOSE FUCKERS SAY.

And I. Will die. Royally.

Do you have another mint?

Charlotte   No.

Marie   *Merde.*

Olympe   Charlotte we can find another way to stop Marat—a protest, a scathing farce—

Charlotte   Thank you, but . . . it's what you said. We're all in a play that someone else is writing.

Olympe   Did I say that?

Charlotte   And I am certain that this is my cue.

Marianne   A word of advice, young assassin, aim high and strike deep.

Olympe   Wait. Charlotte—

Marie   And tie back your hair. I know a little about stabbing.

Marie *gives* **Charlotte** *a red ribbon like it's a secret weapon.*

Olympe   *Charlotte.*

Charlotte   Thank you, ladies. Gotta go make some . . .

Hi, story.

Olympe *smiles—that was her line!—as* **Charlotte** *exits.*

Marianne *grabs paper and pen and she follows* **Charlotte**.

Marianne   OK. I think this might be worth writing home about.

(*To* **Olympe**.)   You, keep writing. (*To* **Marie**.) You, keep quiet.

Marianne *exits after* **Charlotte**.

Marie   Enjoy your exit.

Marie *picks up the book* **Charlotte** *left.*

Marie   Oh, the little murderer left her book. Plutarch. *Parallel Lives.* Hilarious.

Olympe *thinks and thinks . . .* **Marie** *is expectant but still.*

Marie   So . . .

I generally just wait until someone comes to get me . . .

Or I hear trumpets. I usually have to go if I hear trumpets.

She listens. No trumpets.

I'm good.

Olympe (*distracted but polite*)   Uh-huh.

Marie   Or maybe I'm not good at all. Is it hot in here or is that just . . . mortality. Or sudden lack of sugar. And coffee. And husband. Not a great king. But a man. He's at least a man, you know? You shouldn't need to be great to be spared.

Olympe (*distracted but polite*)   Uh-huh.

Marie   When did it all turn so cruel? Did I do this? Be honest, you seem honest. Is all of this because of me?

Olympe   Not . . . exactly.

Marie   But did I make it worse? I did, didn't I. Am I . . . too pretty?

Olympe *is on thin ice . . .*

Olympe   Definitely too pretty.

Marie   I thought so. Maybe if I change my hair, or perhaps less bosom?

Olympe   That would be a public service.

Marie   Ugh. God. It's always the women who have to do the changing, isn't it?

Olympe   What did you say?

Marie   Oh you know. Change this, Change that, ChangeYourEntirePersonalityAndAllegiance.

What about what *we* want? You know? I could tell you a few things I'd like to change and they are *not* my last name.

Now for the play, would you write me with different hair? I'd like to do my part for the cause.

Olympe   I don't think . . . I'm going to write a play anymore.

Marie   Oh. I thought this was scene one?

Olympe   It was. And then it wasn't, then it was, now it's not again.

Marie   That makes sense.

Olympe (*an idea is forming, a good one*)   It does actually. Because we don't write what we know, we write what we want. And you're right, we don't need to change, *they* need to change.

Marie   I'm right?! Gasp! Sometimes I say it instead of doing it.

Olympe   Yes. I can't waste time on a play—Marianne's right—A Declaration! For the Rights of Women! I could just take Thomas Paine's declaration and switch the gender. Oh that's great. See? OK—

Marie   I starting to think this might not be OK.

Olympe   I will not only *write* this Declaration, I will *declare* this Declaration!

Marie   Wait—

Olympe   Theatre and politics coming together!

Marie   You thought they were separate?

Olympe   I will go to the National Assembly myself, and stand up and—

Marie   You're going to the Assembly? In person? On purpose? Girl. Hold up. They're awful, they're overrun by Jacobins, like frothy mean Extremists that killed my husband. They will not like this.

Olympe   What good is a declaration if everyone already agrees?

Marie   Yeah I'm really not seeing this ending well.

Olympe   It never ends well unless you write the ending yourself. If I have the right to die by their hand, I have the right to speak my mind. And I will.

Olympe *starts to write . . . and write . . .*

Marie   I mean . . . Sigh.

Transition . . .

Scene Two

Charlotte . . .

Standing beside a bright white claw-foot tub full of water.

She holds the knife. She wears her red ribbon. She recites her letter.

Charlotte   It is to you, the good people of France, that I must define these actions. I am doing this with the full knowledge that I will be soon in the quiet arms of Madame Guillotine, but . . . JeanPaul Marat, by eight o'clock tonight, shall be dead.

Switch to **Olympe** . . .

Olympe *stands at a podium in a loud, cavernous room full of angry men. She reads with verve:*

Olympe   When will women ask ourselves . . . What has this Revolution given *us*? And if the answer is *nothing*? When will we take it for ourselves?

Charlotte   Until Marat is silenced, you, my friends, will live in danger. So. I will avenge us all.

Olympe   So. I now present this Declaration of the Rights of Woman and the Female Citizen.

Article One: Woman is born free and lives equal to man.

Male objection resounds! **Olympe** *stands there, breathing in the moment.*

Charlotte   As the murderer Marat draws his final breath, there will at last be peace in France.

You're welcome.

Charlotte Corday.

With a swift strike **Charlotte** *"kills" Marat and the water in the tub bloodies.*

She stands there, bloody, breathing in the moment. Switch to **Marianne** . . .

Marianne *reads a letter.*

Marianne   My dear Vincent,

We fight for this better world *together* even if we are a world away.

I fight harder with you in my heart.

More news of the Paris revolution enclosed. Be safe and write soon.

She stands there breathing in the paper and the memory of her husband.

Blackout on **Olympe**.

Blackout on **Charlotte**.

Blackout on **Marianne**. *Switch to* **Marie** . . .

To no one . . . except maybe her ribbons.

Marie   So here's what I don't get. Isn't the definition of *a revolution* "the turning about of an object on a central axis thereby landing its journeyman in the same exact spot whereon they started"? Because that seems like a waste of *everyone's* time.

Which transitions to . . .

Scene Three

Marie *still waiting, playing with some ribbon.*

Marianne *runs in . . .*

They had both hoped to not be alone with each other. They make each other nervous . . .

Marianne   It's happening. It's all happening. *Olympe?*

Marie   Nope. Lady writer left a while ago.

Marianne   So. It's just . . . me and Marie-Antoinette.

Marie   Is it ever *just* Marie-Antoinette. Ribbon?

Marianne   Why don't you keep it.

Marie   Oh, I was going to.

Marianne   Excuse me, I have to go do something useful.—

Marie   *PleaseDon'tLeaveMeI'mScared.*

Marianne *stops.*

Marie   It's so . . . lively out there. Unless you're Marat.

Marianne   Touché, Citizen.

Marie   I made a touché?! I've always wanted to do that. Wait. That means she did it? She killed him? Did you see it? Was it awesome? She is such a badass. Or a crazy person. I mean, the chutzpah of that girl. And such good hair. Tell me everything.

Marianne   I mean . . . OK, she walks right in, front door, I'm watching from the street, it's quiet for a few minutes, and then I hear her yell "FOR FRANCE!," then this scream and splash, and the white curtains spackle red. Commotion in the house, the housekeeper wails, the authorities rush in, then they take a perfectly collected Charlotte Corday to prison in a cart. She was amazing. Perfect form, flawless execution.

Marie   Touché too!

Marianne   Touché too.

They smile. They don't mean to become friends but perhaps they are.

Marie *is oddly profound . . .*

Marie   I fear we shall not know the rightness of our revolutions nor the heroes of our stories for generations to come.

Marianne *registers this profundity with surprised respect. Pause.*

Marianne   Uh. Yeah. Exactly. That was—

Marie   Unexpectedly profound. It happens sometimes.

Marie *might play with her ribbons like a kitten.*

. . . And . . . you're, like, *not* a queen?

Marianne   No. Revolutionary. And a mom.

Marie   A mom, me too! I forget about that sometimes, but I am. How old are your kids?

Marianne   Well Annabelle is ten.

Marie   Awww. Lots of bows?

Marianne   She loves bows. On everything—the cat, the teacups.

Marie   Me too! Teacup bows are the best!

Marianne   And Vincent is eight. He's named after his dad.

Marie   So are mine. Isn't it funny when they start talking alike—father and son? I just think it's so funny. They sneeze the same. They say "spoon" the same. Hilarious. And now sad.

Marianne   The world found it just despicable. No nation, no matter how revolutionary, should kill a king that way.

Marie   Aw, thanks. I mean. He was a lumpy man, but he had good moments. I didn't dislike him. In fact I liked him, when he would just stand there looking serious. He was best when he was just . . . standing.

Marianne   How did you meet?

Marie   On our wedding day. I wasn't supposed to marry him, you know. But all the rest of my sisters had smallpox so it fell to me. Which was fine. I mean the finery was exquisite. Everything else was a bit strained. You know we didn't consummate the damn thing for *three goddamned years*? Can you imagine? *The tension?* And the whole country blames me! And I'm like "nuh uh! I'm totally down! He's the one who—" Turns out? He had to have an operation on his Little Prince before he could— Yeah. So that was anti-hilarious. Then finally little Marie-Thérèse came along, then little Louis-Joseph, then little Louis-Charles, then little Sophie poor dear. Then they killed him. In the square that used to be named after his grandfather. The rest is . . . I talk too much. What about your husband?

Marianne   Oh. We don't have to . . .

Marie   No please tell me. It's so nice to pretend nothing is wrong in the world. Is yours a love story? I love love stories.

Marianne   It is a love story.

Marie   Brava, then. *Allons-y.*

Marianne   Well. Vincent is a catch. He's strong, and tall, with these eyes that just make you tell him every little thing.

Marie   Ooh.

Marianne   And he doesn't walk. Oh no. Vincent *strides*. Long legs and swinging arms, you know.

Marie (*getting a little too excited*)   Uh-huh.

Marianne   And when that man wears a suit? Just give up, just don't even try to look away. But when he takes it *off*?

Marie   TELL ME EVERYTHING.

Marianne   He courted me for months, but the truth is I thought he was too handsome.

Marie   Too handsome is not a thing.

Marianne   Well, you don't want them *that* dashing, it'd make me worry.

Marie   Not me—Dash Dash! OK, Vincent is a dream, he swings his arms, when is le smooch?

Marianne   Well I kept thinking "yes, he's very nice" and "yes he's from a good family." But I just wasn't sure I *really knew* him. Until. He let loose this *laugh*. We were talking about—I don't know—and out comes this rumbly, and loud, and big-old-stupid laugh.

Might we hear this laugh?

And that's when I agreed to marry him.

Marie   That is literally hilarious!

Marianne   They're perfect when they're just a little flawed. You know?

Marie   I do *not* know, but that sounds so fun!

Marianne   I miss him. And our kids, they're with my mom. Revolutions aren't for children.

Marie   Work-life balance, I get it.

Marianne   It's hard. When Vincent went back to Saint-Domingue last month I . . . I knew it was the right thing. But even when we're apart for a day. I miss him.

Marie   What's that like?

Marianne   Like. Sending a letter to your best friend that keeps getting returned.

Marianne's *expression darkens. Something's wrong.* **Marie** *awkwardly pats* **Marianne**'s *hand.*

Marie   I don't usually comfort other people, am I doing it right?

Marianne   You're doing fine.

Marie   Love letters lost . . . that is the saddest thing in the world. You know you could use one of my ships to find him? I think I still have some ships. I used to wear them in my hair, little ones with sails and everything, which does seem a bit excessive in retrospect. Anyway, we'll find out what happened—

Marianne   I think . . . I think he might be dead.

Marie   *What?*

Marianne   I think they might have killed him.

Marie   Oh my god.

Marianne   I don't know if they did but I swear I can tell that something is wrong, is profoundly and terribly . . . gone. And I don't know what to do. What do I do? Do I leave? Do I stay? What do I do?

Marie *hugs her like a best friend. A perfect comfort.*

Marie   I understand this feeling. Don't go.

Marianne *is surprised by the relief she feels telling someone.*

Marianne   We each carry a final letter to the other in case something happens to one of us. So we know.

Marianne *takes out a red-ribboned letter—hers to Vincent.*

Marie   This is his?

Marianne   No. Mine to him. I haven't seen his yet—

Marie   Well there you go. Hope. Because we will not give up on him, we will find him.

And I will help you with everything I have left, Citizen Marianne.

She hands her some ribbons. **Marianne** *actually means this . . .*

Marianne   Thank you, Citizen Majesty.

Marie *is stunned and appreciative.* **Olympe** *enters with—*

Olympe   GoddammitGoddammit*Goddammit*. I'm gonna let you ladies guess how my little solo show at the National Assembly went?

Marie   Um . . . Poorly!

Olympe   Poorly does not properly convey the reviews it received. They booed me. *Hundreds of men booed me as I spoke.*

Marie   Well, what good is a declaration if everyone already agrees.

Olympe   Well they could agree *a little*. How can these men hate a declaration of women's *equality* when that's exactly what *Egalité* is!

Marianne   But *Fraternité* it is not.

Olympe   *Goddammit.* What the hell is this revolution about? Ugh. World changing should be easier.

Marie   I mean, my wig choices have done it on numerable occasions, (*Talking about Vincent.*) but we were just talking and Marianne is worried about—

Marianne (*deliberately not talking about Vincent*)   Marie don't, just—

Marie   What?

Marianne   There's no need to say anything—

Olympe   What's going on?

Marie   Her husband.

Olympe   What about him?

Marie   She's worried that something might have happened to him.

Olympe   Marianne, what's she talking about?

Marianne   I . . . I haven't heard from him in weeks. Something's not right. I don't know anything for sure but—

Olympe   Have you seen his last letter? The last letter he keeps for you?

Marianne   No, but—

Olympe   Then I'm sure he's fine. You'd know if he wasn't.

Marianne   Yes, but it's just strange that he hasn't—

Olympe   Don't worry before there's a problem. There's enough going on already. You should have seen the way those men at the Assembly glared at me. One guy threw a shoe. I mean it's so obvious what I was asking for and they wouldn't even hear me out. Maybe I start killing people like Charlotte. That seems to make them listen.

Marie   It's making people *talk*, not listen.

Olympe   I just can't believe she actually did it.

Marie   I can. That girl. She has some—

Olympe   Conviction.

Marie   Cheekbones.

Marianne   Upper body leverage.

Olympe   I wish I had her certainty.

Marie   You mean cheekbones.

Olympe (*to* **Marianne**)   Ladies, I can't help but think this revolution might not be for us anymore. But I want it to be, I want to have faith in justice.

Marianne   I do.

Olympe   In common sense.

Marie   I do not.

Olympe   *In a good story.* But what are they doing for us at the moment? Not much. Makes me want to abandon everything

Marianne   No. Don't say that. You need to remind yourself what we're fighting for: conviction, sacrifice for the greater good. Come with me to see Charlotte.

Marie   To a prison? Oh no. I'm afraid they'll never let me out.

Marianne   Olympe, come on. She needs us.

Olympe   She needs us to be implicated and die with her? I don't think so.

Marianne   She needs you to tell her story.

Olympe   I will. From here.

Marianne   You're really that scared.

Olympe   I'm not scared.

Marie   You sound a little scared.

Marianne   And you cannot give up now, none of us can. Because it seems like it's going to get worse—

Marie   A lot worse.

Marianne   Before it gets better.

Marie   Not that much better.

Marianne And that's when this country is going to need us the most. Especially the writers. When they give up all is truly lost.

Olympe I mean I'd like to tell her story, I liked her, but it stopped being fun when she actually killed someone. Now it's totally different than I was going to write it. Reality messed up my narrative.

Marie I hate when that happens.

Marianne You don't always get to pick the ending but it doesn't mean it's not a good story. She needs her friends now.

  Olympe Well we really just met her.

    Marianne She needs a dramaturg.

      Olympe Don't we all.

        Marianne She needs the last words you promised her.

Pause. **Olympe** *writes on a slip of paper and gives it to* **Marianne**.

Olympe OK. Give her this. If I'd had more time it would've rhymed.

Marie Is she good on ribbons? 'Cause I have a few extra if, y'know, that might beat back the tide of fate coming hard against us all.

Marianne (*to* **Olympe**) I'm just saying . . . for a dramatist you seem awfully scared of drama.

Marianne *exits.*

Marie Ooh. Would you write me an exit line like that? I've always wanted to be like—"blah blah blah RETORT" and then just leave and the scene is—like—*over*.

Pause. **Olympe** *glares.*

Blackout.

Scene Four

Charlotte *in a prison cell.* **Marianne** *is visiting her.*

Charlotte And after all the shoving and the yelling, they get me to the prison. And I'm exhausted right? And then they had to check my *virginity*, of course. And they were like "She's a virgin!" And I was like "not after you checked, I'm not." And it wasn't the intimate violation of it that bugged me—though I swear to god some guy hit on me *on the way to prison*—It was that they were *sure* there was a man involved. "She wouldn't have avenged her people on her own, she must have been fucked into it." I mean Jesus Christ a girl can't even assassinate someone without judgment. I'm joining Olympe's group.

Marianne What's Olympe's group?

Charlotte I heard that she declared something at the Assembly. Some big women's group? For girls to go scouting or something?

Marianne I don't think that's what she was—

Charlotte Oh yeah, that's what they were saying in my virginity check.

Marianne No, it was a Declaration for all Women. *Egalité* means equality for everyone, that's her point.

Charlotte Exactly what I'm saying! Who checks the boys' virginity when they go to prison for murder, huh? *No one.* That'd be equality, that'd be . . . something . . . good.

Marianne You OK?

Charlotte Me? Fine. Good. I mean . . . I did the deed. StabbityStab, he's dead, what I wanted. So . . . yeah.

Marianne You know, they're calling you the Angel of Assassins.

Charlotte Oooh. Really? That's not bad.

Marianne Yeah, kind of a girl-next-door-meets-Joan-of-Arc vibe.

Charlotte Nice. Wait. They think I'm crazy?

Marianne No.

Charlotte Because Joan of Arc was kinda crazy. I'm not crazy, I'm fed up, I *had* to kill him, it was a civic duty . . . that felt fucking awesome. I mean the *feel* of it? Of righteous vengeance is just . . . floral, like a blooming of power and rightness and— goddammit it's what sex must feel like.

Marianne I mean . . .

Charlotte The way that man looked at me with my knife in his chest. I was this close to him, his breath on my lips, leaning into him, and I said—I actually said this—"You. Die. Now." But that's not crazy that's . . . just very literal.

Marianne I mean . . .

Charlotte Did I tell you some guy's painting my portrait? That's kinda cool. Wait till Jacques sees that. Fucker. And people are reading my letter? The last line might have been a bit much but I didn't have Olympe's help.

Marianne Yes it's circulating in a pamphlet. Widely. But . . .

Charlotte What.

Marianne There's also some . . . celebration . . . of Marat.

Charlotte *Wait what?*

Marianne Now this was bound to happen, but some idiots are trying to turn him into a martyr.

Charlotte   Some? I mean . . . not *many*, not *some*. A faction. A small but vocal faction? Right?

Marianne   . . . right.

Hard pause.

Charlotte   Well. Sometimes history judges slowly. My trial is tomorrow. It'd be nice to see a familiar face. I am preparing my Steely Look of Unwavering Calm, but I may need a high-five before I go onstage.

Marianne   You mean on trial.

Charlotte   Same thing. All the world's an audience.

Marianne   Are you quoting Olympe at me?

Charlotte   Am I? Oh god. Never tell her this.

Marianne   I would never.

They share a smile.

And I'll be at the trial. You're an example for us all to keep fighting, do what we have to, even if it means being very . . . literal.

Charlotte *lets the upset overwhelm her—tears even.*

Charlotte   Would you. Please fight for me too. I don't think I finished the job.

Marianne   I don't know if we'll ever finish it.

Charlotte   But I don't even know if I helped. *Like at all.* What if I just made it worse? Oh god, am I crazy? Did I do the right thing? I mean I know technically murder is wrong most of the time but—oh god this is not—oh god—

Marianne   As a wise and weird woman once said: We may not know the rightness of our revolutions nor the heroes of our stories for generations to come.

But I think you're one of them. And I will carry you into every fray I can find.

The sound of approaching men unlocking steel doors. They're coming for her.

Charlotte   OK tell people—tell them—I don't know. I'm not great with words. Tell Olympe to find the words.

Marianne   She found these.

Marianne *hands her a slip of paper.*

Charlotte   For me? Really? Oh thank you, *thank you.*

Marianne   Don't thank me. Or her. It was literally the least she could do.

Charlotte   No it's not. It's everything. Absolutely everything.

Marianne (*re: her new line*)   Now when you say that . . . Look up, find your light, and say it loud.

Charlotte   OK. Um. I'm really scared.

Marianne   Of course you are. And that's OK.

Charlotte   I'm so scared.

Marianne   I know. But don't let anyone else know it. You're brave, and ready, and not alone. Good work, young assassin.

Charlotte   Thank you. Thank you.

Beat. The ending builds out of **Charlotte***'s preparing for death.*

OK.

OK.

Across town **Olympe** *holds her pen, trying to tame her ideas.*

Across town **Marianne** *holds her final letter to Vincent.*

And **Marie** *listens for trumpets and caresses her ribbons.*

Marianne   OK.   **Charlotte**   OK.   **Olympe**   OK.   **Marie**   OK.

Blackout.

End of Act One.

Act Two

Scene One

Olympe *starts this scene in a rush, writing in her study with furious inspiration . . .*

Olympe   OK, yeah, this is going to start moving really fast now. Marat's death has made things very bad, very quickly. The revolution has turned violent, anything done or said against the Republic is now treason and treason is punished by death. There are mobs in the streets, Marat's a martyr, Charlotte's on trial, and I've finally found something to write about—!

Marie *reads over her shoulder.*

Marie   Marie! OhMyGod, is that *me* Marie? The *Queen* Marie? The Me Queen?!

Olympe   Yes, can you not yell *all* of your revelations as you have them.

Marie   Gasp! Sigh! Retort! Oh that seems like *such* the right move.

Olympe   Well the declaration was a bust and you're really interesting.

Marie   Right?

Olympe   Back to plays. Fiction I can fix. Reality is way too hard to write. At least drama has some structure. We're headed somewhere clear. And I have to admit that this play might be good. Like actually good.

Marie   And it's really about me? That's hilarious!

Olympe   Actually, it's a very serious epic historical political drama with a few songs that will be a vindication for generations! Because it will last five hours.

Marie   *Ugh.* But the title. Something cute, something that says "She's Innocent!" Perhaps, "*The Lovely Queen*" or maybe, "*Braveheart.*"

Olympe   NO. It has to be sweeping and profound. Something like . . . "*France Preserved*"!

Marie   Sounds delicious.

Olympe (*a better title*)   OK maybe . . . "France *Saved.*"

Marie   Oh that's nice. I'm thinking "Ooh, is France an ingénue tied to a train track? And what are trains?"

Olympe (*the extended title*)   "*France Saved; or, A Tyrant Dethroned.*" There we go, that's it.

Marie   De-WhatNow? De*throned*? Who's dethroned?

Olympe   I want a country that owns itself and I don't think we can do that with a monarchy so this play—

Marie *Silence.* No queen? That is not—no—wait. Do I die in the end?

Olympe Well I haven't written the end.

Marie You said "we're headed somewhere clear, drama has structure." Well where the hell are we headed and why is it not a beach?

Olympe Look—

Marie No *you* look. I'm the main character of this thing, right? So let's make me stay queen and not die, OK? *Let's do that.*

Olympe Sometimes the story tells itself.

Marie THEN YOU BETTER TELL THIS DAMN STORY TO BEHAVE.

I have precious little time to force history to like me. *Now tell me what you're writing.*

Olympe I don't have time to go back, I'm halfway through the story.

Marie *Aren't we all. Tell me.*

Pause.

Olympe Setting: The queen's private chamber in the palace on the eve of the fall of the monarchy.

Marie That's a bad day to set a romantic comedy.

Olympe It's not a romantic comedy.

Marie *whines,* **Olympe** *pushes through it.*

You're desperate. You're plotting any way to uphold the crumbling royal institution while the revolutionary forces are at your door.

Marie (*like she's talking to a scary movie*) Get away from the door Marie!

Olympe Then a woman comes to you, to convince you to let go of the old ways and embrace the new, to compromise. Her name is Olympe.

Marie Hold the throne. You're writing about yourself now?

Olympe It's a character.

Marie Named after you.

Olympe Well yes but—

Marie Isn't that confusing? I'm confused. I hate when theatre confuses me.

Olympe I call it "Meta Theatre." The point is to be a little confusing.

Marie I hate it. I already hate it.

Olympe You don't hate it.

Marie The play is trash!

Olympe *The play could save us both.*

Pause.

Marie   *Comment? (French: "How?")*

Olympe   By showing *you* learning a goddamn lesson for starters.

By showing people that revolutions needn't be so bloody. That they can be kind and creative. I'm telling you, Your Majesty, This play. Will be. Important.

Marie   If it's not a romantic comedy nobody will come.

Olympe   I'll add a butler.

Marie   Hilarious!

Olympe   Now, the first act ends with Olympe convincing the queen to work *with* the revolutionaries to create a Constitutional Monarchy that truly embraces Liberté, Egalité—

Marie   Sororité.

Olympe   *Yes.* The country is saved by its women. (*Beat.*)

Marie   That I like. Keep writing. And if you want . . . the production may borrow my wigs.

Olympe   I'll make sure to thank you in the program.

Marie *suddenly hugs* **Olympe** *like a child hugging a mother.*

Olympe *is shocked, then hugs her back.*

Marie   It's finality that scares me most.

Olympe   That's the hardest part. Writing the ending.

Marie   *Oui. C'est vrai.* That was my fear as a child. Never seeing people again. Or dogs. How are you supposed to understand when you're so young? Never? What is "never"?

Never is now, Young Marie. Never might be now.

Olympe   I don't know, Your Majesty. Never might not come to you. You're a very compelling woman. I'm the one that should worry. My attempt at immortality is on paper, scripts in actors' pockets. It's not as glamorous as it looks.

Marie   Oh, don't worry, it doesn't look very glamorous. But I like your stories. I'll remember them. And I'll tell my grandchildren and they'll tell their grandchildren, and their grandchildren will invent new ways to watch never-ending plays on ever-tinier stages. May I nap on you?

Marie *fills her lap with the growing pile of ribbons that are now a pillow for* **Marie**.

Olympe   A play that doesn't end. If I'm writing what I really want? That'd be it.

Marie   Then tell me that story, and let's not have an ending, shall we? A cliffhanger will do. Something that makes you want to come back for more and more and . . .

Olympe *inhales to begin her a story but—* **Marianne** *runs in.*

Marianne   They lied—there was no trial—Charlotte's headed to the scaffold. Right now.

Oh god.

Blackout.

Scene Two

Lights on.

The guillotine.

Marianne *joins* **Olympe**.

Olympe   Oh god. OhGodOhGod, I can't watch this.

Marianne   You have to. If you don't capture it, they will. Write it down, Olympe.

Olympe   I can't, I do fiction, this is way too real.

Marianne   *That's why you need to write it.*

Olympe   I need to stay alive, and that's becoming harder and harder because of her. She's made them scared and they're taking it out on half of the human race. *Our half.* We have to get out of here now.

Marianne   I'm not leaving her, and neither are you.

Olympe   She doesn't need us now! All the sane people are leaving. Only the heartless wackos are left.

Marianne   And if you don't put the heart back in this revolution, *who will?* If you don't write this down, *who will?* *They* will. And that's how they win. And you don't want them to win. So stay right where you are, buck up, and witness this. That's what she deserves. What we all deserve. You said we're the heroes if you're writing it. So write.

Olympe *really wants to go—makes herself stay.*

Olympe   OK. Yes. OK. Scene: Charlotte Corday mounts the scaffold.

Charlotte *mounts the scaffold. The crowd is rowdy. She wears a white bonnet and dress.*

Olympe   The red thing creaking as she stands tall against the grain. The crowd is rowdy this morning. They heave fat words at her, they bark. But she is not marred. The hem of her white dress flips in the wind like a ring of small fish at her feet.

I'm loving this narration, perhaps I should write novels.

Marianne   Focus please.

Marianne *and* **Olympe** *wave to* **Charlotte**.

Charlotte *delights when she sees them and waves back. Then goes back to her Steely Look of Unwavering Calm.*

Olympe   The young girl, a fair and beautiful creature in white, looks out towards the horizon, with posture braver and taller than any man gathered below the scaffold to watch her . . . die . . . Oh god. I can't. I can't. I'm sorry—

Marianne   Olympe, don't—

But **Olympe** *runs off—she can't take it.*

Charlotte *doesn't notice . . . but* **Marianne** *starts narrating to cover.*

Marianne   Uh. So. The executioner yells: "Does the condemned have any last words?"

Charlotte   Uh. Yes. I do . . .

Marianne   And. With confidence, and clarity, and a voice like a church bell ringing across the city—

Charlotte   I KILLED ONE MAN, TO SAVE ONE HUNDRED THOUSAND.

VIVE LA REPUBLIC! VIVE LA FRANCE!

TELL MY FATHER I'M SORRY I DIDN'T GIVE HIM GRANDCHILDREN.

A sound of the guillotine, cheers, and a blackout cut her off . . .

Immediately a bright-white spot on **Charlotte**.

A moment alone with **Charlotte** . . . *breathing . . . a moment suspended in this purgatory.*

So so softly she sings . . . or her voice plays around her . . .

(Sung so softly, simply.)

> Who are we, without the riot?
> What is a song, without a band?
> What plays on, during the quiet?
> Is the beat of the beat, and beat of the heart, and the heart in our hand.

Blackout on **Charlotte**. *Which gives way to . . .*

Olympe *in the corner of the city—breathing—scared.*

That was too much to handle.

She's losing it. A gunshot or clamor in the distance startles her and sends her running off again.

Scene Three

Olympe's *study.* **Marie** *holds a letter—wrapped in blue ribbon—she's stunned by it, scared of the letter, can't look away.*

A sound of trumpets in the distance. **Marie** *whips to the sound. Uh-oh.*

Marie   Trumpets.

Marianne *runs in; she heard the trumpets too.*

Marianne   I heard them, they're coming for you, we have to—

Marianne *sees the letter* **Marie** *holds.*

Marianne   What is that?

Marie   It just arrived, and I—I think it's—

Marianne   No—

Marie   I'm so sorry—

Marianne   Oh god.

Marie I'm so sorry, my friend, . I'm so sorry. I'm so so sorry	**Marianne** Oh god, oh god, oh god. Oh god, oh god, oh god.

Marianne *grasps the letter and falls on her knees. Vincent is dead. She knows this now.*

Marie *immediately cradles her, holds her, a true and great friend in this moment of terrible truths becoming known.*

Marianne   We worked so hard. And fought so hard. But right now. In this moment. I really don't know what I'd say if you asked me if I'd rather have the cause or have him here. In this moment? I might just toss all the revolutions for one more . . . anything. Stride.

   Marie   Stand.

      Marianne   Laugh.

         Marie   Spoon. Yes. But.

There is more to do, much more. Who will give your daughter her present if not her fearless, unbreakable mother?

Marie *reveals a beautiful little teacup with a big satin bow and a note.*

Marianne (*reading the note*)   "Teacup bows are the best. Love, Marie"

Marie   They really are.

Marianne   Thank you.

Marie   You're very welcome. And it will never be truly all right after losing him, but I'm going to say that it will because it's really nice to hear it sometimes. So. "It'll be all right. It'll be all right."

Marianne (*taking out her last letter to Vincent*)   I never . . . I never . . . sent my last letter. He never read it. He'll never—

Marie   Read it now. To me. I'll hear it for him. What did you want to say?

Marianne *gets out the red-ribboned letter, reads from it—*

Marianne   I love you.

Marianne *folds a page and drops it.*

I love you.

Marianne *folds another page and drops it.*

I love you.

A heavy KNOCK KNOCK KNOCK on the door.

Marie   Here we go.

Marianne   *No, not yet, don't leave, not yet.*

Marie   I wish "yet" would listen.

But if we're honest we all knew this was coming.

What should I . . . Should I take a book? Or my play?

I'll give him your letter. And don't be sad for us. When you laugh? We will too.

Marie *smiles to* **Marianne**, *gathers all her ribbons . . .*

The door creaks open—

Marianne   It'll be all right.

Marie   I think so.

And **Marie** *exits.*

Marianne *is alone for a moment. She feels alone.*

Then **Olympe** *runs on.*

Olympe   Are they gone? Did they take her? Did they take anything of mine? Did they take the—

Marianne   I cannot talk to you right now.

Olympe   But she's gone though right? She's gone? She's—? *Oh god, where's my play? The new play? Did she take it?* Nonono, not that play. Not *that* play.

Marianne   How could you leave her, leave us all?

Olympe   *I will be with you in one minute but I think that MarieAntoinette took my goddamn play.* Which means *they* have it now, which means . . . suddenly I wish I'd written a romantic comedy.

Marianne   *No one cares about your stupid play.*

Fiction doesn't matter if you're only using it to hide from reality—our reality—this reality, the one where your friends need you and are dying alone and you're trying to get your lines right.

Olympe   My . . . No. I'm trying to save our lives.

Marianne   There's nothing to save if you don't stand for anything.

Olympe   No, there's nothing to save if they kill us because they find my script in Marie-Antoinette's pocket. Now. (*A decision.*) Burn the pages. All my scripts, all the pamphlets. Anything left. We burn them, drown them, eat them, just get rid of them.

Marianne   No.

Olympe   Yes. We have to. And we leave tonight.

Marianne   No. No more of this running and dodging.

Olympe   If I don't, if they find any trace of my writing about any of us, they come for me, so start burning shit.

Marianne   And if you destroy them you destroy Charlotte and Marie and me. You destroy me. Because no one writes me down.

But I thought you were. Sisterhood of heroes. Bullshit.

Olympe   Hey.

Marianne   NO. (*Talking about Vincent now.*) If you burn this story then everything we've fought for, everything that's happened, *every single person that has thrown their life into this will be as blank and mute as the paper you can't seem to fill.*

Olympe   You seem upset. I get that, but I'm just saying what we know is true: This fight isn't winnable any more. It's unstoppable this violence and—

Marianne   Isn't winnable?

  Olympe   It's not.

   Marianne   It is.

    Olympe   It's not.

Marianne (*furious*)   *My husband died for this and you tell me that "this isn't winnable"?*

Olympe   Wait—what?

Marianne (*furious sarcasm*)   *It's just a game and he lost? NO.*

No—

Olympe (*she gets it*)   Marianne, wait—

Marianne   *It can be won, and it will be won, because people like him died for something real, unlike you and your goddamn stories that you abandon just when it's your time to stand for something.*

Olympe   I didn't—I'm sorry—

Marianne   They killed him like he was theirs to throw away as they pleased, but he was mine. *He was mine first.*

Olympe   Oh Marianne I'm—

Marianne   THIS IS NOT YOUR LINE.

Olympe   I'm sorry, I'm saying I'm sorry.

Marianne *is fucking furious.*

Marianne   You're always saying, saying, saying, and you never listen.

Because this is all about you. Because you cannot feel anything unless it's staged.

Well I'm gonna blow your mind here and tell you that this might not be *your* story in the end. Yes—Holy shit, the lady who has the time to sit down and write her little skits *might not be the hero of the French Fucking Revolution.*

Olympe *You came to me,* you all came to *me,* and asked for *my* help—

Marianne *And you are failing us because you're not writing what's real.* The real world, the world you say you want to change, is too much to bear and you run. You run. You are allowed the privilege of telling stories, of naming yourself but here you tremble, afraid of your own power. Maybe that's why your writing *doesn't mean anything.*

Olympe   Doesn't mean anything?—I went to the National Assembly myself and—

Marianne   Told them what you thought they could handle. It didn't work. Now you're cowering in the shadows, abandoning your friends. Where is my pamphlet, my declaration, huh? You wrote half a play for *Marie-Antoinette because she's easy to stage. Where are my words, Olympe?* Or am I one of those breathless puppets to which you so often resort.

Olympe   You can't berate me and call me false and then beg me to help you.

Marianne   I'm not begging for anything from you. I don't need you.

Olympe   Finally! I've been waiting for you to declare *your damn self* and stop waiting for me.

Marianne   And I'm waiting for you to realize that you can't write the world if you're not in it! You can't change it if you can't see it! And you can't be a hero if you're too scared to show up. Or is this all just another drama you'll never finish?

This chills **Olympe***.*

Olympe   At least I'm trying to create something. You're *just watching.*

Marianne *Witnessing isn't just watching.*

Olympe *And fear isn't weakness.* Fear is how you know you're paying attention.

Marianne   Maybe real revolution doesn't have time for either fiction or fear.

Olympe *Because you don't think art matters.* You never did—*you never did.*

Marianne   Oh please—I have *always* stood by you.

Throwing every bit of anger at **Marianne** *with this—*

Olympe   You have *always* judged what I do, and doubted it, and mocked it and truly, in your honest heart, thought that *words don't work*. You would rather have twenty Charlottes in this fight than *one* sane artist because theatre seems to piss you off, but *death doesn't bother you.*

Marianne *smacks the papers out of* **Olympe***'s hands violently, like she's slapping a face.*

Both **Marianne** *and* **Olympe** *are shocked that she did. Beat. Beat.*

Marianne   If your story is so easy to burn you won't need my help.

Marianne *leaves.*

Olympe *is alone . . . really alone now. Freaking out.*

Gathers her papers—will she burn them? No. She can't. What does she do now?

Trying to conjure up a new character . . .

Olympe   Perhaps a . . . new friend enters?

Nothing.

Or an old one?

Across town trumpets announce . . .

Scene Four

Marie, *standing behind a rail, the ribbons fallen at her feet, defending herself at the Revolutionary Tribunal.*

Marie   Marie enters.

This is not her usual crowd.

Marianne *enters,* **Olympe** *isn't here.*

Charlotte, *as Fraternité, in a mask presides.*

Marianne   The Trial of Marie-Antoinette. This is big. The world is watching. Even so the prosecutor knows that this is not a trial but a roast as he says:

Charlotte/Frat   "Prisoner 280, STATE YOUR DEFENSE."

Marie   Well. I didn't do . . . it?

Charlotte/Frat   "The Tribunal accuses the former and immoral Austrian queen of crimes against humanity, morality, and the Republic. These crimes include: Being queen—"

Marie   Oh, I *did* do that.

Charlotte/Frat   "Calling the former king a coward—"

Marie   Definitely did that.

Charlotte/Frat   "Conspiring with the enemies of France to promote war and destroy the populace—"

Marie   I did not do that—

Charlotte/Frat   "Orchestrating orgies at the palace—"

Marie   No one told me about *that*.

Charlotte/Frat   "She sent French treasury money to her true homeland of Austria, designed the massacre of Swiss Guards, and—"

Marie   Well this is *not* hilarious.

Charlotte/Frat   "And we're not done yet, folks. This woman is also accused of incestuous relations with her own son."

Marie   NOW YOU LISTEN HERE. YOU MAY PUSH ME BUT DO NOT PUSH MY CHILDREN, NEVER MY CHILDREN, YOU DO NOT. SLANDER. CHILDREN. That accusation is a disgusting lie that *you* dreamt up, not me, which says a lot more about *the dreamer than it does the accused* you sick, pardon my American, DICKS.

Marianne   And the women in the room were taken with her passion, for how many of them had been accused of being bad mothers by strangers.

Marie   You think you're making things better with this charade? But you're not, you're setting us all up for a—All I'm gonna say is watch out for ambitious little emperors whose names rhyme with *Shapoleon*.

Marianne   The prosecutor knew he risked losing the crowd so he got right to the point:

Charlotte/Frat   "The Tribunal has reached a decision."

Marie   YOU CAME IN HERE WITH A DECISION.

Charlotte/Frat   "Prisoner 280, Marie-Antoinette, otherwise known as the Former Queen of France and Navarre, otherwise known as the Bitch, Madame Deficit, the Widow Capet, and the Soon-To-Be-No-More.

You are condemned and sentenced to die by the guillotine. *Now.*"

Marie (*summoning up her deepest, most regal power for this laserlike take-down of her enemy*)   Then you, sirs, bear not the marks of men, but the instincts of animals. And with your mouth of hate and hands of hair, you rip not your enemies in half but your country, *your country is gored on your watch*—so you, Followers of Animal Order, will remove the squint from your eyes so that you may fully see with whom you are dealing. Do you see? Do you see this woman, this mother, this citizen queen, do you See. Me. Now?

You do. And now we are linked. And now, like a simple song played on and on, you will never. forget. me. Proceed.

A quick shift to a guillotine.

Marie's *wig is suddenly gone, her hair is short and messy.*

Olympe *finally shows up . . . terrified to be there, to witness.*

Olympe   They cut her hair.

Marianne *hears this, sees that* **Olympe** *is there.*

Olympe   She aged a decade in a moment. To her, she *was still* France. And today, France was losing its head in a dirty gown. But she doesn't betray herself. She doesn't weep. She acts every bit the royalty.

Marianne   Then the wind drops

Olympe   The world hums to a hush.

Marianne   And the world begins to never forget.

Marie *looks to* **Marianne** *and* **Olympe** *who nod and smile supportively.*

Marie (*quick and quiet*)   Marie enters. Is she late? Or lost? What were they talking about? Was it her? It's always her. Or is she being her again? It's a confusing time. Hello. Marie.

Charlotte/Frat   Does the condemned have any last words . . .

Marie   Yes.

I . . .

She accidentally steps on Frat's foot.

(*To him.*) I'm so sorry, I didn't mean to—

A sound of the guillotine,

Marie *reveals and drops one red ribbon. Cheers and a blackout cut her off.*

Immediately a bright white spot on **Marie** *suspended in whatever purgatory this is. She sings, so softly, so simply . . .*

> Who are we, without our power?
> What's a truth, none understand?
> Fame's a force, building era from hour,
> and the beat of the beat, and the beat of the heart, and heart in our hand.

Marie *breathes, mourns, breathes, then looks right out at us before . . .*

Blackout on **Marie**.

Scene Five

Olympe *in her study.*

After seeing **Marie**'s *execution she's disgusted, horrified, scared as hell.*

Papers everywhere, scripts, pamphlets.

She hates hates HATES them all.

Olympe *throws the papers, scatters them, hurls them.*

Olympe   WHY DON'T YOU WORK?!

Air and ink and make believe and nothing is working and nothing is helping and nothing that I'm doing is real. *An entire life of nothing that's real.*

Marianne *enters . . .*

Marianne   That's not completely true.

Olympe *swings around to see her friend—a rush of feeling.*

Olympe   *Marianne,* you're here, oh my god, I'm so sorry. You're right. What am I doing with all this? What's the point, what's real? I don't even know anymore.

Marianne   You showed up for Marie. *That's* the point, that's real.

Olympe   I know I let you down. I'm not brave like you, I'm just . . . loquacious. A fact that's probably going to get me killed.

Marianne   You're not at the end yet. You're stronger than you think, and your words do matter. They are braver than you are. Let them loose and they'll outlast you. That's what I think. And . . . I'm sorry too.

Does **Olympe** *hug her here? Need her, grip her hand, something.*

Marianne   And you'll be happy to know that you were right.

Olympe   Oh. About what?

Marianne   I am better at this than you. I wrote my own pamphlet, which was so good it became a declaration.

Clears her throat. The declaration from memory:

"We, the free and proud women and men of Saint-Domingue, deny the unjust power of France and her agents of torture and greed. The sun of this island shines on an independent nation of liberty, not property."

Olympe   Not. Bad. Citizen.

Marianne   Oh ya know. Writing what I want.

Olympe   What we want . . .

Marianne   You know what I really want? I want people to live their lives and make babies and eat too much and do experimental theatre.

Olympe   Now there's a France I can believe in.

Marianne   And let's be kind, shall we. In honor of Vincent, and Charlotte, and crazy ass Marie-Antoinette, let us *laugh too loudly and too often,* and call out the hypocrites of our age until they are the butt of the joke. That's what we give our children. A good laugh.

Olympe   My son. All grown up with a son of his own. What will he think of me?

Marianne   He'll think his mom doesn't take any shit from anyone, says what she believes, and is willing to die for it.

Olympe   But—yes—but I don't particularly *want* to die for this. I would rather live for it.

Marianne   Uh. Yeah. I think the real win is changing the world and living to enjoy it.

Olympe   Right? This stuff is scary as hell.

Marianne   This is the "Reign of *Terror*" not the "Reign of Agree to Disagree."

Olympe   *OK*, I was trying to be brave because you were, but goddammit I want to outlive these fuckers.

Marianne   Me too!

Olympe   Let's just skip to the part when we're all over this bullshit and we can tell our grandchildren how we beat these idiots.

Marianne   Beat them black and goddamn blue.

Olympe   With our drama!

Marianne   And our sashes!

Olympe   And our fists goddammit I want to punch those assholes in their eye sockets!

(*To those assholes.*) You want a revolution? COME AT ME.

Marianne   COME AT ME TOO.

Olympe   OK, come at her first and then me.

They share a much-needed smile.

Marianne   OK. One of us has to survive this. Whoever does will have a lot of work to do. And three really chatty ghosts making sure they do it.

Olympe   I think it'll be you.

Marianne   I think it'll be you.

Marianne *hands* **Olympe** *a pen.*

Marianne   Either way. *We're* the heroes. If you're writing the story.

Olympe   I should probably hurry up then.

Olympe *smiles. Grabs the pen to write . . .*

KNOCK KNOCK KNOCK at her door. **Marianne** *holds her hand and she:*

Olympe   The Trial of . . . Me.

> *BANG BANG BANG of a gavel.*
> *As a swift surge into . . .*

> "The Trial of Olympe de Gouges"

Scene Six

A podium swings in front of **Olympe**. **Charlotte** *and* **Marie**, *as* **Fraternités** *in masks, enter.* **Olympe** *is surrounded, arguing for her life on all sides.*

Charlotte/Frat   BY THE AUTHORITY OF THE COMMITTEE FOR PUBLIC SAFETY, YOU ARE HEREBY TRIED WITH TREASON FOR CONSISTENT AND AGGRESSIVE THEATRICAL ACTIONS.

Olympe   OK. So. The thing about that is . . .

Will she deny it or not? Not. She takes a stand.

Yes. Yes. If being a traitor is loving my country enough to shame it for being less than its best self, then I am one, yes I am, and god knows I don't do anything less than aggressive theatre.

One of the Frats reveals **Olympe***'s play—a threat to her.*

Charlotte/Frat   Your play is a treasonous tract,

Charlotte/Frat and **Marie/Frat**   a shameful drama, poorly penned—

Olympe   First draft, Jesus.

Charlotte/Frat   maliciously and purposefully composed to attack the sovereignty of the people.

Olympe   I would never attack the sovereignty—

Marie/Frat   Your play depicts the former queen, does it not?

Olympe   Well yes but not in a fine light.

Charlotte/Frat   You portray that woman as a sympathetic figure for all to see.

Olympe   Nonono, the whole point is that the queen learns a lesson. A lesson about the true north of the Republic.

Marie/Frat   And she learns this lesson in your play?

Olympe   Yes.

Marie/Frat   So she's capable of learning?

Olympe   Yes.

Charlotte/Frat   Which makes her a sympathetic figure.

Olympe   *It just makes her human. I'm* the sympathetic figure in the play. And *I'm* the one that convinces her that democracy is better than royalty. That character is Olympe de Gouges SO AS NOT TO BE CONFUSED WITH ANYONE ELSE BUT ME. This play proves I'm a patriot. And anyway, I haven't even gotten to the end of it.

Marie/Frat   What happens at the end?

Olympe (*making this up—deliberate* Les Mis *references*)   Uh . . . we'll probably . . . hear the people sing? And the sound of distant drums?

Marie/Frat   It's a musical?

Olympe   For the whole family. You'll laugh, you'll cry, there's a barricade.

Charlotte/Frat   By unanimous decision, this Tribunal states that Olympe de Gouges, the female playwright—

Olympe   Just *playwright.*

Charlotte/Frat   —is guilty and shall be punished by death—

Olympe   You can't kill me for this, I work in the theatre, it's a nonprofit.

Charlotte/Frat and **Marie/Frat**   We kill a lot of people, Miss de Gouges.

Olympe   No. You *can't* kill me. I'm pregnant.

Pause.

Charlotte/Frat and **Marie/Frat**   The Tribunal does not think you're pregnant.

Olympe   But I am. Definitely pregnant.

Charlotte/Frat and **Marie/Frat**   We're pretty sure that you're not.

Olympe   Gimme a few weeks.

Charlotte/Frat   The condemned shall be killed tomorrow morning and justice will hereby be served.

Olympe   THIS IS NOT JUSTICE. You say you fight for freedom and equality but that means art and ideas which is my life's work. A work *in progress* you might note.

I mean you can't kill the writers, that's Democracy 101.

I AM NOT THE PROBLEM, *YOU* ARE THE PROBLEM.

Charlotte/Frat and **Marie/Frat**   The Tribunal does not think we're the problem.

Olympe   *Goddammit—come on—no—NO—YOU GUYS? YOU GUYS ARE FUCKING UP THE REVOLUTION.*

Swift transition as the world around her empties, vanishes, leaving—

Scene Seven

Olympe.

Alone.

Olympe   Not like this. No. No, it's not ending like this. *I'm not ending like this.*

Trying to tear out the stage curtains, the floorboards, her costume. How does she stop this play?!

THIS IS NOT. *THE END.*

She stops, realizes.

You don't write what you know, you write what you *want*. OK. (*Trying to narrate her way out of this.*) Olympe de Gouges. Thirty-eight, very well liked and respected in her field and all the politicians and revolutionaries and theatre critics think she's great, and she will live a long time, and eat as many macarons as she can carry, and she will make it out of this, and she is just walking home from rehearsal, and enjoying Paris in the fall and —

Charlotte *appears.*

Charlotte   You know that's not as good a story.

Olympe   I don't care if it is.

Charlotte   Yeah you do. I know you do.

Olympe   No, THIS IS MY LIFE, NOT A PLAY. A PLAY YOU CAN WALK OUT OF.

Marie *appears, only ever repeats her last words.*

Marie   I'm so sorry, I didn't mean to—

Olympe   Marie—help—*ribbons*.

Marie   I'm so sorry, I didn't mean to—

Olympe   What is she saying?

Charlotte   Her last words. I think that's all she remembers—

Marie   I'm so sorry, I didn't mean to—

Charlotte   Do you have your last words worked out yet?

Olympe   NO NO I DON'T.

Charlotte   You should think about it, writer.

Olympe   *I am not this kind of writer!*

Marianne *enters.*

Marianne   What kind of writer are you?

Olympe   The *really scared kind.*

Charlotte   Scared that you didn't matter?

Marianne (*re: Marie*)   Or that she's going to be more famous than all of us.

Marie   I'm so sorry, I didn't mean to—

Olympe   No No *NO*. I'm scared of . . . of ending.

Marianne   Then don't. Turn the end into a beginning.

Charlotte (*a bad idea*)   A play that doesn't end? Oh god.

Olympe (*a great idea*)   A play that doesn't end? Oh god!

Marianne   You're writing what you want, right? So defy them with your story. They can't touch the play in your mind.

Olympe   The play in my mind?

Marianne   Yeah. Play that one.

Olympe   But. I need *real help here*, not fiction.

Marianne   It might be fiction, but it's not fake.

The beating hearts in front of you are real.

The gathering of people is real.

The time we spend together, this time, is real. The story is real when it starts.

The lights rise slowly on the real audience.

Olympe   Has it? Started? But it can't write itself.

Marianne   Oh girl. It already is.

Olympe *starts to see the audience around her.*

Marianne   Your story isn't yours now.

Marie   I'm so sorry, I didn't mean to—

Olympe   But . . . whose is it?

Charlotte (*pointing to the audience*)   I think . . . theirs.

Olympe *sees the audience. Is amazed. Have they been there the whole time?*

Olympe   But . . . who are . . . who . . .?

Marianne   I don't know. But they showed up and seem to be listening.

Olympe   Are they armed?

Charlotte   I think they're just . . . interested.

Marianne   Which is what you wanted, isn't it? An audience.

Charlotte   A message.

Marianne   A story of our own.

Marie *giggles softly.*

Olympe   Yes. (*Absolutely overwhelmed by this.*) What a thing.

What does she say to a live audience? Tearfully but proud. To us . . .

Thank you. For your time. For listening. Thank you.

It's an honor to . . . stand before you and—

As she stands before us . . .

The world around her changes . . . To the scaffold. We become the mob.

Exactly as we heard in the prologue . . . Anticipation. Wood creaking.

*And the sound of a scared breath—***Olympe***'s breath—Except it's everywhere, it's our breath, it's history's breath.*

Breath—Breath—

To stand before you and—

Charlotte *and* **Marie** *start singing "Our Song."*

Olympe   This whole time . . . I've been standing . . . before you and—

A sharp white light on, or the engorging shadow of . . . A guillotine, its blade rising to the top.

That's not a way to start a comedy.

Marianne   I don't know about you, but when good stories end I always want to go right back to the beginning.

Olympe *hears this, understands, grips* **Marianne***'s hand. She concentrates, conjuring up the ending to her story exactly as she would have it go.*

Olympe   The death of Olympe de Gouges.

Marianne *narrates for her . . .*

Marianne   A bright fall day, four p.m., light lingering on the trees and slanting low on the Place de la Révolution. Olympe de Gouges walks up the wooden steps onto the sturdy stage. Yes, she thinks, a stage.

Olympe   A stage . . .

Marianne   She thinks of Marie-Antoinette, who was on this very spot only weeks ago.

Olympe   Marie.

Marianne   She thinks of Charlotte Corday—

Olympe   Charlotte . . .

Marianne   and the wildness of her hands and heart, also here not long ago.

Olympe   All of us.

Charlotte   She also thinks of a woman she passed in the streets a few weeks ago who held her head high and wore a red sash that said "Revolution For All." To Olympe she looked like the symbol of freedom.

Olympe   *La Marianne.*

Marianne (*sung*)

Who are we, without a story?
Lost at sea, in search of land . . .

Charlotte   That woman hummed a soft song that slipped into Olympe's ear that day.

Marianne (*sung*)

We survive the roughness of glory

Charlotte   A song sticks.

Marianne (*sung*)

By passing the beat of the beat of the heart.
From hand to hand.

Marie *and/or* **Charlotte** *continues humming the song.*

Olympe   A simple song played on and on.

Charlotte   And on and on.

Marianne   Now Olympe never actually met these women, but

On the scaffold in that moment—

Olympe   Her moment.

Marianne   She writes what she wants: her own story.

Olympe   *Her own story.*

Marianne   And her story is one of . . . sisters.

Charlotte   Sisters know what you mean when you don't have the words.

Marianne   So she tells herself a story as she looks out on the masses of people.

Olympe   Yes. She finds herself with an . . . audience. And a monologue. This she can handle.

So she quiets that fiction in her mind.

Charlotte *and* **Marie** *stop humming "Our Song" . . .*

Olympe   And she summons up her truest self.

And the time is now.

And the stage is set.

Marianne   "Does the condemned have any last words."

Olympe   And she knows that a story is more alive than a fact. A story is what lives.

Olympe de Gouges stands before them.

And she is good.

And she is not alone.

And with her last moments, she calls out like a queen, like a righteous girl, like a mother of nations, she calls out: "Children of France. Avenge my death."

Marianne   Which wasn't exactly what she meant. She really meant:

Olympe   "Please do my plays after I'm gone."

Marianne   Or:

Olympe   "Don't settle for the story that they're giving you."

Marianne   or maybe she just meant:

Olympe   "May God Have No Pity, You Motherfuckers."

Charlotte   That's my girl.

Marianne   But the crowd understood her.

Olympe   And a downpour of applause rained on Olympe like the curtain call she'd always wanted.

Marianne   Which surprised the executioner so much that he held the blade longer than he'd ever done before. And that pause cracked him right down the center. And in that crack grew a rustle, that turned into a rumble, that turned into a . . .

Marie *giggles.*

Charlotte   The executioner *laughed*. Not at her, at himself. He caught a glimpse of his own hypocrisy. Which was horribly, terribly funny.

Olympe   And the vindication of Olympe de Gouges started, as it should, with a joke.

Charlotte   And a song was sung that Olympe could only hear—

Olympe   That Olympe could hear only—

Marianne *sings to* **Olympe** . . .

Marianne (*sung*)

   Who are we, without a story?

Olympe   As the blade fell.

Olympe *takes a slow, proud, grand bow thanking her audience for listening. At the nadir of the bow—The sound of the guillotine.*

But **Olympe** *stands tall again to tell us* . . .

Olympe   And a story . . . begins.

Blackout.

End of Play.

Ada and the Engine

Characters

Character list

The play may be performed with 6 actors or 4 actors; doubling is indicated below.

Ada Byron Lovelace, *(18–36) Curious, funny, brilliant, aware of her brilliance, stories, aware of her story. Never met her famous father. Tries to be a "good girl" but just cannot help her curiosity and love of all things impossible. A woman of our time stuck in hers.*

Lady Anabella Byron, *(35–55) Ada's mother, harsh strict, jealous? Yes. But realistic. She has had a hard life largely due to Ada's father. Projects his sins on her.*

Charles Babbage, *(40–60) Ada's soul mate, friend, mentor. Lauded genius of London. A holder of famous salons, an inventor, a mathematical scholar, a dreamer who just cannot seem to make his dreams into the metal they require to be real. Almost perfect for Ada. Almost.*

Lord Lovelace, *(25–45) A gentleman who becomes Ada's husband. He'd rather that he was more rich and more lordly but he'll manage with his lot. A proud man. A wanting man. A serious man. Is not madly in love with Ada but she'll do just fine.* (Can be doubled with Byron.)

Mary Sommerville, *(40–60) Charles' friend and colleague and Ada's mentor. There are no women as successful and respected in science and math as her. Pragmatic, sharply friendly, someone who will tell you when you're wrong.* (Can be doubled with Lady Anabella Byron.)

Byron, *(36) A charming man, darkly funny, unpredictable, emotional, brooding but self-aware. A poet.*

Setting

England, 1835–52.

The Victorian era. The houses of intellectual elites.

Music

To hear The Kilbane's song at the play's end, go to tinyurl.com/AdasVision

Aesthetic contradiction is fun. Since the play ends with a pop rock operatic blossoming of music, the rest of the play can wrestle with an anachronistic modern sound too. The ending musical moments may be choreographically as balletic or simplistic as you like. The song is critical, however, as Ada's biggest idea was her vision of a computer writing music.

> "The engine might compose elaborate and scientific pieces of music of any degree of complexity or extent."
>
> —Ada Byron Lovelace, 1842

Transitions and Letters

Transitions should be active, fluid, and fun. When letters are delivered let them be in buttressed by music, choreography, or physical storytelling. Let us see the life in these letters, most of which were actually written by the historical figures themselves.

For the Audience

She Walks in Beauty

She walks in beauty, like the night
Of cloudless climes and starry skies;
And all that's best of dark and bright
Meet in her aspect and her eyes:
Thus mellow'd to that tender light
Which heaven to gaudy day denies.

One shade the more, one ray the less,
Had half impaired the nameless grace
Which waves in every raven tress,
Or softly lightens o'er her face;
Where thoughts serenely sweet express
How pure, how dear their dwelling-place.

And on that cheek, and o'er that brow,
So soft, so calm, yet eloquent,
The smiles that win, the tints that glow,
But tell of days in goodness spent,
A mind at peace with all below,
A heart whose love is innocent!

—Lord Byron, 1813

The Rainbow

Bow down in hope, in thanks, all ye who mourn;—
Where'in that peerless arche of radiant hues
Surpassing early tints,—the storm subdues!
Of nature's strife and tears 'tis heaven-born,
To soothe the sad, the sinning, and the forlorn;—
A lovely loving token to infuse;
The hope, the faith, that pow'r divine endures
With latent good, the woes by which we're torn.—

'Tis like a sweet repentance of the skies;
To beckon all those by sense of sin opprest,—
And prove what loveliness may spring from sighs!

A pledge:—that deep implanted in the breast
A hidden light may burn that never dies,
But bursts thro' clouds in purest hues exprest!

—Ada Byron Lovelace, 1850

"But words are things, and a small drop of ink,
Falling like dew, upon a thought, produces
That which makes thousands, perhaps millions, think."

—Lord Byron

Act One

Scene One

Augusta Ada Byron *stands in a lushly appointed room of her and her mother's house in London. She is 18, perpetually curious, slightly odd, and in an hour will be attending one of her first society events. She looks beautiful in a formal gown and jewels but doesn't look exactly comfortable in satin.*

But this is **Ada.** *And while other girls would be primping, she works on her mathematics. But* how *she works on maths is . . . musical. She hums as she works.*

Then she sneaks a slim book of poems out from a hiding place.

She reads a poem that she knows by heart, but she still likes to see it on the page. Perhaps she touches it like a friend . . . like it's family.

The words become a simple song . . .

She softly taps the rhythm of the poem, its heartbeat, against her chest.

Ada
    She walks in beauty like the night
    Of cloudless climes and starry skies;
    And all that's best of dark and bright
    Meet in her aspect and her—

Lady Anabella Byron *enters. She is Ada's mother, cold, perfect, bitter.*

Anabella   Ada.

Ada *hides the book behind a maths text.*

Ada   Yes—What?—Ready—I'm ready—Are you ready? To go? Because I am. Ready. What?

Anabella   You are talking. Too much. It makes the rest of us uncomfortable.

Ada   Sorry. Is it the dress? I hate this dress. Or *dresses.* As a concept they are irrationally cumbersome and weighty in their diaphanous . . . ness.

Anabella   What did I just say?

Ada   Words. Too many. Sorry.

Anabella   *Ada.*

Ada   Yes.

Anabella   What are you reading?

Ada   Nothing. Maths. The new tutor suggested I work on a geometric progression but I'd rather focus on the factorization of primes—

Anabella   What. Are you reading.

She is caught. Hands her mother the book of poems. **Anabella** *recognizes it immediately, hates it . . . And starts to calmly rip out each page as she talks.* **Ada** *winces at every page.*

Daughter. We have so much against us already.

Ada   I'm so sorry, Mother.

Anabella   I don't think you are. I think you enjoy this rebellion. I think it lights you up, I think it fuels you.

Ada   I didn't mean to—I just found it—I didn't know it was his—

Anabella   This deception and defiance is at your core.

Ada   No, Mother please—

Anabella   Do you know *how* I come to know this?

Ada   Mother, please—

Anabella   Because *he* is rooted in you. You cannot help that you are his daughter—

Ada   No I cannot. Which is why I likewise cannot help my curiosity about him.

Anabella   *Know that he left you. Like any harlot he was done with.*

Ada   *Mother.*

Anabella   Darling if that shocks you, I'd drop the curiosity where you stand. Your father poisoned every pond he passed. He left wreckage and desperation and depravity with his every step. And I defied him. *I* did. For you. Now I know that you think you're very modern, but darling . . . what I had to do for you. *That* was unheard of. Women do not leave their husbands, even when their husbands are philandering, ne'er-do-well erotic obsessives.

Ada   You said he left us.

Anabella   He did. To wander the world from bed to bed. And yet, if I had not acted in the way I did to protect you from him fully and completely, you would have been taken from me and forced into your father's life. I fought for you in the courts, in the press. And what did he do?

He died sick and alone, mocked and sunk in the thought that no one loved him enough to save him from himself. Does that sound heroic? The genius Romantic? And yet the world gives him power through obsession.

Ada   He doesn't have any power, he's dead.

Anabella   That *is* power. Dead a decade and still haunts us with rumors vile and sticky. He is a constant downpour.

Ada   He's gone. Why shield me from him any longer?

Anabella   Not from him. From his nature in you.

Ada   I know what they say about him.

Anabella   Good. It's all true. The darker the truer.

Ada   They say that he was great. Flawed and—yes—dark, but a great genius of our age.

Anabella   Do not idealize him.

Ada   That's what we do with genius, and I hope there is some of that genius in me. I would better like to be dark and genius, than sunny and useless.

Anabella   You underestimate the vileness of his damage. Do not think his darkness was part of his genius. It cut his genius short, and it will do the same to you if you do not brace against it.

Ada *hears this.*

Ada   It's words, Mother. Just words. It's not an attack, it's only a poem.

Anabella   A poem you thought was about you, I'm sure. They all think his poems are about *them*.

That's exactly what **Ada** *thought . . .*

Don't be an idiot, darling. It's about some shivering bit of flesh from before you were born. I'm sure he abandoned her as soon as the lines were penned. Like you. Paste your name in a few lines, call it love, and never be seen again. That was his general *modus operandi.*

Ada   What lines? My name in his lines?

Will **Anabella** *tell her the truth?*

She finishes ripping the volume . . . but reserves one page.

Anabella   Canto Three. All for show of course. To lighten his image after he sailed away from you never to return. Who would abandon a child they loved? Who would fill a young girl's life with rumor and scandal she cannot ever escape?

Ada *takes the page from* **Anabella** *and reads the passage.*

Once you're married and you can't mess up your life any further, I'll answer any question you have about him, but not before. It's hard enough to find a man of worth to marry a strange girl, but more so when you have your very public lineage.

Ada (*a fleeting edge of defiance*)   You married him, not I.

Anabella (*vicious*)   And when I see his instincts in yours I cringe, I weep, I long for the power to rip him from your fiber.

Pointed pause.

But tonight? Tonight we will give them nothing to whisper except compliments for your grace, your beauty, your deference. Tonight we prove our poise. Don't we?

Ada   Is this your debut or mine?

Anabella *slaps her face.*

Anabella   None of that cheek, my dear. That simply won't do.

Ada   Yes ma'am. I am sorry.

Anabella   Good. Posture.

Ada   Yes.

Ada *straightens herself.*

Anabella   Spin.

Ada *spins for her mother to see her outfit. Small talk . . .*

Your tutor tells me that you have almost completed the second book in the calculus series.

Ada   Yes. He is competent but not very interesting.

Anabella   Then let's try not to elope with this one shall we.

Ada   That was just once.

Anabella   For you, the difference between zero and one is your entire world.

Now. We shall have no discussion of tutors nor maths for the rest of the evening.

Ada   I'm not allowed to discuss maths at the party?

Anabella   Absolutely not.

Ada   But Mr. Babbage is the Lucasian Chair *of Mathematics.*

Anabella   I know who he is.

Ada   And Mrs. Sommerville. She has written tomes—

Anabella   And you are not there to discuss her tomes, you are there to find a husband.

Ada   Then why have me tutored in maths since I could talk and *not let me talk about it.*

Anabella   Because maths is the opposite of passion. It was necessary to direct your focus to keep you uncorrupted.

Ada   And despite your studies, he "corrupted" you.

Anabella   I will strike you again if you speak to me in that manner for one moment more.

Ada   And perhaps this time I will strike back.

A standoff between them.

Anabella   There he is. Right there. Under your skin. What must that feel like. Sickness? Itch? That's why they look at you, Ada, why they whisper. They wait to see you fall as he did. Fall into beds, into debt, into a depravity the complete description of which I have spared you thus far. And you will do well to swallow back any hint of his . . . steam or else you will be lost to it and die as he did, alone and unloved. That is your future if you do not present yourself the lady, find a husband with titles, and diminish. your. temper.

Beat. **Ada** *is . . . emboldened with hate for her . . . or just scared.*

I think we're ready now.

Anabella *leaves. As we swiftly transition . . .*

Ada *reads from that scrap of paper. Her father's words . . .*

Ada   Is thy face like thy mother's, my fair child!
  ADA! sole daughter of my house and heart?
  When last I saw thy young blue eyes they smiled,
  And then we parted,—not as now we part,
  But with a hope.—
  Awaking with a start—

Which lands us . . .

Scene Two

Babbage*'s House, 1 Dorset Street, London. A festive salon is bustling with London's elite. The audience are the gathered saloniste—the sound of mingling, drinking greets . . .* **Charles Babbage***, a striking man who leads with intellect and articulation. He is the gravity of the party, all drift to him. He gestures to a device offstage [unless you can build a working model]: the model of the Difference Engine.*

Charles   Friends! Why don't we gather please. Right here, this way, thank you. Welcome and again, many thanks for your attendance tonight. For those so compelled, I offer you a glimpse at the muchdiscussed if-you-stand-next-to-me Difference Engine. It's only a small model of what will soon be a machine of cogs and wheels the size of a carriage. Now this machine does not dance nor chirp like some mechanical curiosities of our age, some of which you can see in the parlor. This machine calculates. But *what* it calculates and the *speed and accuracy* with which it calculates can save men thousands of hours and errors. The flawless mathematical tables it can produce by the simple turn of a crank will revolutionize navigation, industry, finance. All made better, faster, more perfect. I can bore you with the technical details, but for those ready to get back to dancing, know this . . . When it is manifest, and soon it will be thanks to your government's generous funding, the world will know a new way of knowing.

Now someone should hand me my rum so I stop ruining a perfectly good party.

Ada *runs up through the "crowd."*

Ada   Mr. Babbage. Hello. Your machine. May I ask what order of polynomial it can manage?

Charles   Certainly, my dear. This model can process to the third.

Ada (*disappointed*)   The third? Oh.

Charles   Well. This is just a model. A fragment. The final engine can evaluate to the seventh.

Ada   A seventh order? Well that's more impressive isn't it.

Charles   I certainly think so. And if you care to know, the final engine would have thirty-one-digit accuracy.

Ada (*like "what a great song!"*)   Thirty-one? What a prime. I do so love primes, don't you? Lonely odd little things.

Charles   A description usually reserved for inventors like myself.

Ada   Oh you are no lonely inventor, Mr. Babbage. You are a titan of intellect. A genius. Are you not . . . *that* Mr. Babbage?

Charles   My pride would like to say yes but my propriety must decline that very kind praise. Did you mention your name, my dear?

Ada   No.

Which arithmetic processes does the engine employ for calculation. Does it multiply?

Charles   Oh no. A machine that could multiply is a far-fetched thing. The complexity would overwhelm any engine. No, the Difference Engine employs a quite useful pattern for calculating the value of a polynomial using *only addition*. The method—

Ada   The Method of Finite Differences. That's brilliant. You can use repeated addition to calculate the whole series. Well done, sir. I have heard many times of your great mind and I finally see its description was accurate.

Charles   That is too kind of you, miss.

Ada   It's not kind, it's true. You know some people mistake charm for brilliance. I don't.

Charles   That's a welcome quality in a lady. It should keep you out of trouble.

Ada   It hasn't yet. I think we should be friends.

Charles   Then I think we should meet. Officially. Charles Babbage.

Ada   Of course I know you. And your work. And now your house, thank you again for the party.

Charles   And your name, my dear?

Ada (*tries not to mentioned the "**Byron**" part*)   Oh. Well. I'm Ada . . . Byron.

Charles   Ada whom?

Ada   Byron.

Charles   Byron?

Ada   Not that Byron.

Charles   *Lord* Byron?

Ada   *No.*

(*Caught.*)   Yes.

Excuse me.

She starts to go, stopped by his—

Charles   You're Mary Sommerville's friend. The young mathematician?

Ada   That I am.

Charles   She speaks very highly of you. She doesn't do that about many people.

Ada   Not many people deserve her praise.

Charles   Indeed. A pleasure to make your acquaintance, Miss Byron.

Ada   I'm am confident that my pleasure is greater. (*Switching from flattery to business a bit too quickly.*) It seems to me that the hardship of producing useful mathematical tables is accounting for human error in the *transcription* of them. I find mountains of errors constantly, and I imagine it's not the *computation* that is incorrect but the *copying.*

Charles   The copying, yes, exactly my thought. Which led me to a simple solution for eliminating such error.

Ada   Corporal punishment.

Charles   No. A printer.

Ada (*like it's a foreign word*)   A printer?

Charles   Automatic and attached. All the values are recorded directly after calculation—pressed into clay—by the machine itself. No man's hands touch them which means—

Ada   Error-free calculating. Mr. Babbage. You know you might've just become, in this very moment, the single most interesting person I've ever met.

Charles   How old are you, Miss Byron?

Ada   Eighteen.

Charles   Then you've got time yet to find better.

Ada   Or perhaps I'll just have to get to know you . . . better.

"Is she flirting?" he thinks. "Am I flirting?" she thinks.

May I write to you? I tend to be presumptuous but you see I'm terribly good at maths and terribly bored with everything else and I sense your depth of wisdom and if you would accept my correspondence I would be most excited—Of course I understand if you are busy, which of course you are. And I am a girl of little use to you, of course I am.

Charles   No, my dear, no. I will admit that I do not often say this to many eighteen-year-old . . . socialites, but I very much look forward to our conversation. Many of them.

Ada   Yes, many. Please many.

Another pause.

Also I play piano. I'm quite good.

Charles   Is that right?

Ada   Yes. Music and mathematics share a language I find. Though I also find a kind of delicious magic in music. Its ability to transport one to a most free and full place of feeling with just a few bars. I will not deny that I live for the times when I am either at my desk in study or at the keys in song. All else fades away. Freedom can look quite caged from the outside, but it's really in the mind, don't you think?

That's it. He likes her very much.

Anabella (*off*)   Ada, my dear?

Ada   Oh god.

Charles   Is someone calling you?

Ada   My mother. I'm off-script. Dance with me.

Charles   Dance with—? I don't think that's very—

Ada *pulls* **Babbage** *into a waltz. With no music.*

As **Anabella** *enters . . .*

Anabella   Ada, darling—

Ada   Here, Mother. Dancing. Just dancing.

Anabella *sees her daughter dancing with the host. Silently.*

Anabella   I do believe you're missing a key element of the waltz.

Charles   Indeed we are. You must be—

Ada   The music is in our minds, Mother. An experiment in timing.

Babbage *stops dancing.*

Charles   You must be Lady Byron. Good evening.

Anabella   Good evening to you, sir and I apologize for the experiment my daughter inflicts upon you, our generous host.

Charles   Not at all, Lady Byron. I am in your debt for the company. Your daughter is a compliment to your tutelage and taste, madame.

Anabella   That is very kind praise. And I am terribly sorry to leave you but—(*To* **Ada**.) Lord Lovelace has requested a dance, Ada.

Ada   Oh. Who?

Anabella   *Lord* William Lovelace, and you have accepted his request—

Ada   Have I?

Anabella   and Mr. Babbage has an entire house of guests to attend to.

Charles   There is truly no trouble.

Ada   The trouble is that I'm supposed to be finding a husband.

Charles   A worthy pursuit.

Anabella   And were Mr. Babbage only slightly younger I would think you were making progress at that aim.

Ada *is titanically embarrassed by this.*

Ada   *Mother.* (*To* **Babbage**.) That's not at all what I was—(*To* **Anabella**.) *Mother.*

Charles   Well. Lady Byron, age cannot be helped, can it?

Ada   I do so look forward to corresponding, Mr. Babbage.

Charles   As do I, Miss Byron. Enjoy the party.

Babbage *exits.*

Anabella   *Ada.*

Ada   I did not talk about maths.

Anabella *turns to go—*

Babbage *reenters.*

Charles   I have a book analyzing Riemann and the distribution of prime numbers that, after our discussion, I'm certain you would enjoy, Miss Byron. I'll send it over tomorrow. Good evening, ladies.

Babbage *exits again.*

Ada   It was only primes.

Annabella *glares and whisks* **Ada** *out of the room . . .*

And into a dance with Lord **Lovelace**—*30 and handsome, serious, surprisingly good dancer. There is some spark between them,* **Ada** *has fun.*

Babbage *watches them dance from the side—aware of their youth.*

Anabella *watches them dance too, congratulating herself. She finds* **Charles** . . .

Anabella   If I may sir . . . My daughter's is a life besmirched by gossips and a wilder side to her character that does not heed. She needs a great man like you to . . . speak on her behalf to young men of titles and property. She will fall to a graceless fate if she does not marry well.

Charles   She looks graceful to me.

Anabella   Yes. I think she does look happy with that one. Don't you?

Charles sees that she does.

But **Ada** *steals a glance at* **Charles**. *It sends a bit of a shock in him.*

During the dance **Ada** *and* **Babbage** *correspond . . .*

Charles   Miss Ada Byron, I do hope you won't delay in attending another of my salons. I am sending you designs for the Difference Engine for your perusal until our conversation continues. May it be soon.

Ada   Mr. Charles Babbage, I must thank you for your letter, your invitation, and the unexpected kindness in sending the account of your Machine. I look forward to pestering you with questions and . . . another dance. Perhaps this time with music.

Charles   Miss Byron, will you join Mrs. Sommerville to dine with me next week?

Ada   Mr. Babbage, I am desperate to visit you and it might not wait till the next week. I am afraid that when an idea comes in my way I have no regard for time, space, or ordinary obstacles. Yours—

Lovelace   Dear Miss Byron.

Ada *and* **Lovelace** *stop dancing at this.*

I would very much like to call upon you this week at your convenience. I have thought fondly of our dance. Yours—

Charles   Yours—

Ada   Yours,

The dancing and letters lead **Lovelace** *and* **Ada** *off as* **Charles** *hurries a note to* **Mary Sommerville***.*

Charles   My Dear Mrs. Sommerville,

It was with great interest that I read your newest *Dissertation to the Mechanism of the Heavens*. I do hope we will discuss this in full at our dinner tomorrow. (*Hopefully.*) Am I to expect Miss Byron as well? (*Hopefully not . . .*) And her mother? Either way, I'll have much to discuss after today's meeting with the prime minister about the Engine.

Yours—

Which slams immediately into **Babbage** *being furious—*

Scene Three

Babbage *and* **Mary Sommerville** *having cocktails at* **Babbage***'s.* **Mary** *is brilliant, takes no shit, one of* **Babbage***'s closest friends and* **Ada***'s mentor.*

Charles   I swear to god, these crooked, idiotic ministers—these bastards—these—

Sommerville   Charles—

Charles   These vampires of industry, that's what they are. They are leeching the soul and the sense out of this country.

Sommerville   *Charles, really.* You're yelping like a wounded animal.

Charles   They took my funding, Mary. And if the government thinks they'll get this engine without it they do not realize the enemy they've made in me.

Sommerville   The government has given you more money than the Navy and all they have seen is an abacus with a crank you show off at your parties. You have to give them something.

Charles   I did. A model. It proves that the concept works. Now I need that funding to finish the real engine but they're saying because I haven't finished it they won't give me the funding.

Ada   It's a loop of logic.

Charles   It's a loop of blasted logic.

Sommerville   It's bureaucracy, Charles. You were the one that got in bed with the government. Sink into spite or fly, it's your choice.

Charles   Nothing is my choice. Not anymore.

Sommerville   There's always a choice. Start over, start again, do something else. All choices.

Ada   He can't abandon the engine. It will change the world.

Sommerville   If the world is ready for change. It's usually not.

Charles   The fact that the Engine won't be built because of some ludicrous political luddite who can't *see* the future and thus digs in his heels to prevent it from arriving, is why I much prefer automatons to people.

Sommerville   If we wanted melodrama, we would've gone to the opera. Settle yourself.

Charles   It must be built.

Ada   It will. It must.

Charles   If the government won't fund it I will do it myself.

Ada   Or with me. Take my money. Please.

Sommerville   Good lord. Your mother wouldn't hear of such a thing.

Ada   I have a dowry.

Sommerville   Which is for your husband.

Ada   But I don't have one, nor do I rather see the point. They seem at best to be boring and at worse to be cruel or tragic or . . . syphilitic. I shall be a bride of *science*. Babbage has lent me his designs for this Engine and I marvel at them. And not at their ingenuity, at the fact that we're waiting so long to bring it into being. I want to help that happen. Let me.

Charles   Thank you, my dear. I can't let you do that.

Ada   Then let me write something for the papers. I have a noticeable name, why not use it for something besides fodder for gossips.

Charles   I would never ask that of you, but thank you so very much. We'll find a way.

Sommerville   That we will.

Ada   I know we will. If anyone can outwit this, you can.

She touches his hand. **Mary** *sees this, intervenes, taking his hand instead.*

Sommerville   We won't give up then. We might just need to give it time. But we won't give up.

Now I'm certain Ada's mother will be wondering where I've stolen her off to. We must retreat for the evening, I fear.

Charles   Of course you must.

Sommerville   Thank you for a fine time and the chance to scold you.

Ada   Yes thank you eversomuch. Each of our evenings together replaces the last as my favorite.

Charles   Thank you both for your company and patience amidst my increasingly regular fits of rage at the incompetent.

Ada   Once you've seen the future it's born. We've seen it in the Engine. And thus it will be. I'm sure of it. Good night. (**Ada** *bows gorgeously, winks at him, before prancing off.* **Mary** *goes to* **Babbage**—*very serious.*)

Sommerville   It won't work.

Charles   The Difference Engine already works in theory, and if they'd give me the money—

Sommerville   Not the engine, the *girl*. You're a brilliant man, you can't play the fool if you tried.

Charles   Of what exactly am I being accused?

Sommerville   She's too young for you. She's too . . . storied. You'll make a mockery of yourself.

Charles   I will do no such thing as I have no intentions in that direction whatsoever.

Sommerville   Good. She's not going to be your wife.

Charles   Have I ever said as much? I have *not*.

Sommerville   No you have never *said* as much. But you write her, you invite her to private dinners, you . . . manage her mother. That's quite beyond the pale for a friend very much her senior.

Charles   A friend indeed. And only that. She's an . . . effervescence for . . . the mind.

Sommerville   Oh dear.

Charles   Leave me be, she helps me think.

Sommerville   Your mind has needed neither help nor fizz before.

Charles   You introduced her to me. You mentor the child. You speak so well of her.

Sommerville   I do. As I do of you. And for both your sakes pursue her not.

Charles   You know me well enough to know better.

Sommerville   I do Charles. I know you. You cannot resist your next best idea.

Charles   I will kindly request that we only speak of mathematics for the foreseeable future, Mrs. Sommerville.

Sommerville   Alright then. (*Meaning: "Don't fall for her."*) Don't carry the one, Charles. Good night.

Mary *leaves him.* **Babbage** *alone.*

He reaches for whatever wine was left and downs it.

As we hear **Ada***'s letter to* **Babbage** *. . .*

Babbage *starts to sketch on his drafting table—he is on to something. A new idea. A better idea . . .*

Ada   Dear Mr. Babbage, I will not delay thanking you for Lardner's Trigonometry. I have had quantities of formulae to work out and have destroyed a great deal of paper in this pursuit. What can I do to help you and your marvelous machine? I do hope to see you soon. Yours truly—

While **Ada** *reads* **Babbage***'s letter she prepares the room for her intended, trying to become wifely . . .*

Charles   At our last dinner you spoke of "the future." The idea of foresight has lodged itself in my temple from that evening on and I find myself in a state of intense thought. A new idea forms in me. It feels as though I stand in a valley thick with fog. I can't see where I am much less where I'm going. But the fog is lifting. A path is revealed. One step at a time I go forward into the future. I thought you would understand. Yours—

Ada   Yours,

Charles   Babbage.

Which smacks into . . .

Scene Four

Lord Lovelace *and* **Ada** *in her parlor.*

This is a third or fourth date. "Date" isn't the right word. All parents and finances and reputations have conspired to bring them together for this match.

Ada   I had a thought.

Lovelace   What kind of thought?

Ada   Well. What if you call me "bird." As a nickname. That's rather lovely isn't it?

Lovelace   What kind of bird?

Ada   No just "bird." "Birdie." "Hello, bird!" Something.

Lovelace (*trying it out*)   Hello. Bird.

Ada   And what shall I call you? Lord Eagle? Master Hawk?

Lovelace   Hawks eat birds.

Ada   Ah yes. That would make a poor metaphor for matrimony. One hopes.

Lovelace   Oh. My sisters wish to offer you their dressmaker for the wedding. They will make all arrangements. Silks and things.

Ada   How kind of them. Though I do have a fine dressmaker here.

Lovelace   Theirs is better.

And I've made arrangements for a honeymoon in Ockham. Then on to Somerset. Perhaps a stop at Ashley. I thought we'd retain a London residence—

Ada   Oh we must, we absolutely must keep a home in London. Mr. Babbage's salons and Mrs. Sommerville will have us for dinners and lectures.

Lovelace   I thought we'd be in London for the birth.

Ada   Oh. Whose?

Lovelace   Whomever you deliver first. I rather like the name Anne for a girl, George for a boy. Children are God's gift and a man's peace of mind.

Ada   And lectures, I suppose, are neither.

Lovelace   I have no opinion on lectures.

Ada   A lecture might help you find one.

A serious turn.

Lovelace   Miss Byron. Will you be a good wife to me? I'll thank you to be honest as I know well your . . . lineage.

Ada   Perhaps a balanced equation is best. I will be as good to you as you are to me.

Lovelace   It seems I must be frank. We are both aware of your need for a husband of my standing, but I need . . . a good wife. I am not smitten by your fame nor your father, and I will not take kindly to a life of excessive . . . attention. I will do everything I can to make you happy but I will expect . . . domesticity, integrity, fidelity. I'd like to know your mind before we proceed.

Ada   My mind? Well that you cannot have. All else, however, as is a wife's duty, I will give to a loving husband. It seems then that it is *your* mind you need to reckon with before we proceed.

Lovelace   Yes. Well. Very good then.

And I hope you know that—that I will be devoted to you. And care for you . . . deeply. And—

Babbage *enters, hurriedly.*

Charles   Miss Byron. Hello. I'm so sorry to rush in.

Ada   Charles I didn't expect you until the evening.

Lovelace   Or at all. Good day.

Charles   So sorry, didn't see you there. Forgive the intrusion. I took an early train. I had to. You see I think . . . I think I have a thought.

Ada   Oh my. Shall we walk?

Lovelace   Now?

Charles   That would be most helpful. If I do not interrupt.

Lovelace   You rather do actually—

Ada   Oh we were just chatting. You don't mind do you darling? When Charles has a thought it's best to take a turn in the garden and extract it for him.

Lovelace   I don't see why it's so urgent—

Ada   Birds fly, that's what they do. Off we go?

Charles   Good day, sir. And many thanks for letting me borrow Miss Byron.

Lovelace   Soon to be Lady Lovelace. Very soon in fact. Huzzah.

Charles   Oh. Isn't that . . . very good. I'll be in the garden.

Babbage *exits suddenly.*

Ada   I was going to tell him. Let me tell him.

Ada *glares at* **Lovelace** *and turns to go too—*

Lord Lovelace *catches* **Ada**'s *arm before she can leave.*

Lovelace   I hope you don't expect Mr. Babbage to have free rein to come and go in my house?

Ada   No. But *this* house is mine.

Lovelace   You know exactly what I mean. It's rather uncouth, don't you think, to carry on like this. I don't understand your relation to him.

Ada   Mathematical.

Lovelace   Miss Byron.

Ada   Well I don't understand it either, but there it is. The nation's genius waiting in the garden *for me*, so I'll take my leave of you all by my little self.

Lovelace   I fear you do not take me seriously in my objection.

Ada   To what do you object? He's my friend. Am I not allowed to keep a few of them after we marry?

Lovelace   Not with your reputation.

That shuts her up.

Ada   That's . . . not fair. Not at all.

Lovelace   Forgive me.

Ada   I do not. No I don't I think I do forgive you. A gentleman would never—

Lovelace   That was sharper than I intended.

Ada   *A gentleman would never say such a thing.*

Lovelace   I'm sorry. My dear, I'm sorry.

Ada   No. No I'm glad you said it actually. You've wanted to throw that at me since we've met. If you think me damaged because of some stupid flirtation as a girl—or is it my father's shadow that makes you flinch. If there is darkness in me and it worries you so *then look away*. I'm not forcing you to marry me.

Lovelace   I want to marry you. I will marry you.

Ada   He's a friend. He's just a friend.

Lovelace   Then. We shall speak of it no more. My dear . . . bird.

Lovelace *offers her a tender kiss on the cheek—* **Ada** *accepts it. And quickly turns away.*

A swift transition as **Ada** *catches up to* **Babbage** *in the garden . . .*

Charles   I was in such a state about the Difference Engine. But the truth is . . . *that* design was never right. And I pecked at it and turned it over and over and then . . . A new design. A better design. So much better than the former.

Ada   But *how* is it better?

Charles   It would be able to perform *any* operation set for it. Not just finite differences, not just polynomials, anything.

Ada   What kind of anything?

Charles   Analysis. An *Analytical* Engine.

Ada   Analysis . . .

Charles   The most elaborate equations, the most complex functions, it could do them in minutes. The Difference Engine was designed to solve *one* kind of equation only. The Analytical Engine would solve anything you put to it.

Ada   But you said a machine that could *multiply* was a fantasy, much less—

Charles   I was wrong.

Pause.

Ada   I don't think I've ever heard you say that.

Charles   I've never needed to.

But the Analytical Engine, as I imagine it, could multiply, divide, find roots, manage polynomials of *any* order. It could process a logarithm in the middle of dividing a hundred-digit number by a thirty-digit number. It could multiply two fifty-digits in one minute.

Ada   Mr. Babbage, this is—

Charles   I know.

Ada   Charles, it's—

Charles   I know. The idea of a computing machine with this kind of power and flexibility? It's impossible. Until . . . Foresight. Pre-vision, *planning*. If you could *plan* the actions in advance, if you could *store* results until needed. Have you ever seen a Jacquard loom?

Ada   On holiday with Mother a few years ago. The most gorgeous patterns made by machine.

Charles   Punched cards.

He takes out a punch card from his pocket—a piece of cardboard with holes punched in regular patterns. She takes it.

Ada   Yes, that's how they tell the loom what patterns to weave. A hook passes through to raise a thread. No hole, no thread. Rather ingenious really.

Charles   For the engine. Punched cards.

Ada   Punch . . . Oh. *Oh.* For the operations?

Charles   For the operations.

Ada   For the engine?

Charles   For the engine.

Ada   Punched cards would let you . . . instruct it.

Charles   To do anything. Instead of weaving threads—

Ada   It would weave numbers. It would be programmable.

Charles   And *re*-programmable.

Ada   Change the cards, change the operation.

Charles   Any computation, any *combination* of computations, any time you like. It would be completely—

Ada   Universal. Charles, it would be *universal*.

Charles   If I can figure out how to make it work . . . yes it would.

Ada   Yes it would. My god. I feel like I'm witnessing the beginning of something . . . absolutely grand.

Another moment between them.

This is a very different feeling than the one **Ada** *has for* **Lovelace**.

Charles   Do I understand that you're engaged?

Ada   Oh. Yes. I am.

Charles   That's cause for celebration then. Isn't it.

Another moment between them.

Nothing can happen between them, though they both play out the consequences in their minds simultaneously.

Ada   One question.

Charles   Yes, of course?

Ada   Why didn't you ask me to marry you?

Pause. She said it. He can't believe she said it.

Charles   I don't know. I mean I *do*. I mean I . . .

Ada   You don't need to tell me. But there was a reason?

Charles   I'm sure there was one.

Ada   The difference between zero and one is the whole world. I find.

Charles (*wanting to tell her how he feels but . . .*)   Whatever you think I am in your mind is more perfect than I could ever be. The theory of a thing is rather faultless.

Ada   The theory of a thing isn't real.

Charles   Some things *can* only exist in the theoretical.

Ada   Some things should be tested before they're locked up in theory. How do you know a thing won't work exactly as you'd hoped it would? Until you make it. And see.

They are still locked in their moment until . . .

Charles   I should—I should—

Ada   Don't. Charles, I didn't mean—

Charles   I should go rest before dinner.

Ada   Please don't. You don't have to go.

Charles   No. But I . . . I should.

Charles *backs away. It's over. As he goes to leave—*

Ada   You're going to make this new Engine. And neither of us can quantify its import when you do. And for two mathematicians that is certainly saying something. Good day.

Babbage *turns—So does* **Ada**, *hiding everything spilling over inside her.*

Babbage *is swept away as* **Ada** *runs into . . .*

Scene Five

Anabella. *She walks in just in time to see* **Ada** *sink into a chair, deflated from disappointment.*

Shockingly . . . instead of scolding her daughter, or straightening her posture . . . **Anabella** *understands everything in a glance. She sits next to* **Ada**, *holds her.* **Ada** *bursts into tears.*

Anabella   Darling. It's always harder for us than them. The freedom I know you want is not handed to women, even lucky ones. We must earn it, we hoard it and use it to save ourselves when the time comes. That's what I did. I used every bit of it I had to break away from your father. Now you must store it up and save it so you can save yourself if you ever need to.

Ada   That's what I'm trying to do. Love saves you. Doesn't it?

Anabella   *No.* Especially if you're in love with the wrong man. Please trust me that *this* is not a mistake of mine I will let you repeat.

In another corner of the house **Lovelace** *runs into* **Babbage**.

Lovelace   Mr. Babbage.

Charles   Oh. Yes. Mr.—*Lord* Lovelace. So Sorry. Good day, sir.

Lovelace   It was, yes.

Charles   Excuse me?

Lovelace   You are a man of good standing, Mr. Babbage, highly regarded in circles I respect, so I trust that I may speak openly. My intended is a sensitive woman, prone to fits of the fantastic and the . . . demonstrative. Her unfortunate inheritance. Too much stimulation and I fear for her well-being.

Charles   You have nothing to fear from me, sir. I want only the very best of this world for her.

Lovelace   Then leave her be.

Charles   Sir.

Lovelace   Either you will. Or I will. I don't think her constitution or reputation is strong enough for the both of us. And I have neither the time nor mind to . . . compete. I'll thank you to excuse yourself tomorrow morning, and perhaps contain your friendship to the epistolary. For the near future. Until she gets settled in the ways of a wife. You understand. Good day.

Lovelace *exits, leaving* **Babbage** *to steam a bit.*

Back to **Ada** *and* **Anabella**.

Anabella   I know you think me harsh. I am. I will not let you suffer as I have. Now you must play along, marry well, and earn the freedom you so want.

Ada   Why don't the men have to earn it?

Anabella   Because they take what they like. For women, freedom comes with legitimacy. Marry well and then you're free. From your past, from me. Lovelace will be good to you. And we'll find him a tutor so he can carry on a conversation with you.

Ada *laughs a touch at this.*

He's rather good-looking.

Ada   That's true.

Anabella   Focus on that.

Babbage *alone—perhaps he looks across the space to* **Ada**.

And don't believe the poets. Love is either something learned or something lost. Make your choice while you have one.

Ada sits up. Breathes. Feels better.

Babbage *sits down. Breathes. Feels worse.*

Transition to . . .

Scene Six

Another series of letters pass back and forth . . . **Ada***'s come as she preps for marriage.*

Ada   My Dear Lord Lovelace,

I don't think there can be any earthly pleasure equal to that of reposing perfect trust and confidence in another, especially when that other is to be one's husband. I am most devotedly yours,

Lovelace   With this you have made me the happiest of the living, my sweetest, rarest bird. In all love and, quite soon, dearest matrimony. Yours,

Babbage*'s letters come as he drafts, sketches, and tinkers with cogs and wheels in his study.*

Charles   Lady Lovelace,

Though it has been months since we've spoken I thought of you when I came across the enclosed book on a recent trip to France.

Congratulations on your nuptials. Sincerely,

Another as she marries **Lord Lovelace** . . .

Ada   Mr. Babbage. Alas, it has been far too long since I have written. Though I read mathematics every day, trigonometry, biquadratic equations. Though *motherhood* might diminish the time I have at my command.

Still tinkering, still in his study . . .

Charles   What a mother you will be. And no less a mathematician because of it.

She is exhausted suddenly, sitting to read . . .

Ada   You may have heard of the tedious illness which has occupied me since our second child arrived.

Charles   My dear, are you not well? Please expedite a response.

Ada   Worry not, dear friend. I am wonderfully improved, though still far from being strong.

I must confess a great happiness that you are still bearing me in mind—

Charles   I am grateful to hear that your health improves. I have been invited to give a lecture in Italy this summer about the Analytical Engine at Turin.

Ada   Don't think me fairy-brained if I presume to attend the conference with you? I would be as light as air and just as quiet.

Charles   I've insisted that someone transcribe it. I shall see it reaches you immediately.

Ada   Thank you for the transcript. Though I'm not sure how an Englishman's lecture delivered in Italy ended up in French. I've translated it myself and am devouring it fully. Won't you come for Christmas, dear friend? Surely the machine allows you a holiday.

Please come. Yours—

Charles   Yours—

Ada   Charles!

He looks up. Walks into a hug from **Ada**.

Lord Lovelace *greets* **Babbage** *with a rather warm handshake, and* **Anabella** *bows coldly like always.*

This transitions quickly into . . .

Scene Seven

Christmas at **Ada***'s house.* **Lord Lovelace** *and* **Anabella** *in one corner,* **Babbage** *and* **Ada** *in another.*

Ada   I have never been more delighted than translating your lecture. I really did feel like myself again.

Charles   I'm so glad, my dear.

Ada   Not half as glad as I. You have made me so *happy* to be working again.

Charles   Are you not happy?

Ada   Oh no, I was. Or should be. Or *am*. I am. Children and husband and . . . all the things one is suppose to accomplish by a certain age. Don't listen to me babbling. How are you? I've missed you. So very much. Our time together . . . it always fills me up whenever I fear lacking purpose.

Charles   You have more purpose now than ever, Lady Lovelace.

Ada   Isn't that a funny thing. A lady.

Charles   And a mother.

Ada   Which is less funny. Quite overwhelming. My mind is always split. Did I ask how you're fairing?

Charles   You did. I'm fine. My mind is rather split as well. No matter what I put myself to I cannot stop thinking through this Engine.

Ada   Of course you can't! Nor should you! The Analytical Engine is . . . well it's exactly what Menabrea wrote, it's *gigantic*. A towering idea. And the separation of duties is truly brilliant. Keeping the results in the Store, while the machine processes in the Mill—it allows for a multitude of operations at once.

Charles   The separation is why it works at all. Any result kept in the Store may be reintegrated at any time into the Mill. And on and on.

Ada   And on and on. It's just magnificent. Your engine not only has muscle but memory. It can be taught.

Charles   It's the punch cards—that's the key element.

Ada   And with them, the Engine can hold the past, the present, and the future, all at once, all together in it's beating metal heart. What a thing. What an impossible thing that is suddenly so obvious.

Charles   You've always had your father's way with words.

Anabella *heard that too. He's on her bad side, just like that.*

I could have used your guidance with my lecture in Turin. Some linguistic flourish wouldn't have been missed.

Ada   Oh stop, I'm sure you were perfectly composed and obviously captivating. Menebrea wrote down everything you said. And it needs to be published.

Charles   It will.

Ada   It will? Oh that's wonderful. When will it?

Charles   If you allow them the use of *your* translation, it will be published within the year.

Ada   Publish . . . *my* translation? Mine?

Charles   Yes. It's rather perfect and I trust its author's expertise on that matter. The *Journal* will publish if you approve.

Ada   *Of course I do! Charles! Thank you! Oh my goodness, thank you!*

She hugs him, **Anabella** *disapproves from across the room,* **Lovelace** *stands and walks to them.*

Charles   No my dear, I must thank you. Though I wonder why you didn't write an *original* paper on the subject with which you are so intimately acquainted.

Ada   An original paper? Wouldn't that be extraordinary.

Lovelace   It appears all the excitement is in this corner.

Ada   Oh darling! Do come here. You know the lecture I was translating, the one about Babbage's engine. It's going to be published!

Lovelace   *Your* translation?

Ada   Yes! Published! I'm going to be published!

Charles   Your wife's work is clear and strong and in every way an excellent specimen.

Ada   I'm an excellent specimen! Isn't that lovely! Could there be a prouder husband?

Lovelace   There most certainly could not.

Ada   Then he approves of his wife, the authoress?

Lovelace   Of course I do. I certainly do.

Charles   Your heritage would indicate such a fate most likely.

Ada   But mine shall be the poetry of science. Less rhyming, more calculus.

Charles   Speaking of which. I was wondering if, along with the translation, you might perhaps add some further explanation of the machine, some notes to give greater context and—

Ada   Oh yes I must. There is a noticeable lack of philosophic explanation that I could readily remedy. Perhaps a table, a diagram of some sort, some way to show exactly how the engine would think, step by step.

Lovelace   Does it *think*? Can it *think*?

Ada Of course.	**Charles** Not exactly.
I mean not exactly *think*, but *process* thought—	Well yes it *thinks*, in that it *processes*—
Exactly.	Precisely.

Lovelace   Precisely . . . what?

Ada   I'm so sorry darling, we're boring *and* confusing and you can only be one of those in polite society.

Charles   Apologies, Lord Lovelace.

Lovelace   No no. It's a certain kind of pleasure to see my bird so . . . animated again.

Ada   Nothing animates like mathematics. I cannot wait to get started on this. Thank you. *Both.*

Charles Of course, my dear.	**Lovelace** Of course.

Odd, brief pause.

Lovelace (*changing the subject*)   What does it look like?

Ada   What does what look like?

Lovelace   The—what is it—Algebraical—

Ada   *Analytical.*

Lovelace   *Analytical* Engine? Yes. What does it actually . . . *look* like?

Charles   Well. It's not built as of yet, but when it is.

Ada   And it will.

Charles It will be a rather large—a *very* large, steel and brass and steam-powered . . . um . . .

Ada *Loom.*

Lovelace A loom?

Charles Yes.

Ada But the size of a ballroom.

Lovelace A loom as big as a ballroom?

Charles Bigger. It could go on forever really, the more gears one adds, the more work it can do.

Ada And I suppose there's nothing stopping you from adding more—

Charles And more—

Ada And more processing power. Columns of steel and steam—

Lovelace What's in the columns then?

Charles The numbers. On gears.

Ada Falling into line as the engine thinks and thinks.

Lovelace So it's a *thinking* loom?

Ada With the heart of a train. Loud like a train too. Clanging and smacking, always beating and pushing, metal into metal.

Charles Gears locking into gears.

Ada Cogs in columns, then dropping (*She claps.*) from one column into another— (*She claps.*)

Charles The noise.

Ada The noise would be titanic, wouldn't it?

Charles But rhythmic.

Ada Yes.

Charles For if it has the heart of a train it has the nerves of a clock.

Ada Ticking and clicking, but not so regular as time passing.

Charles No. As the information passes through the machine towards its solution, entire sections of the Mill—

Ada That's where the "thinking" is done.

Charles Yes, those sections would shudder and convulse—

Lovelace Convulse?

Ada   With waves of switches flipping and spinning down its back like tumbling water but not water, *information*, decimals, symbols

flowing and gliding and dancing—

Lovelace   Now it's dancing?

Charles   Information switching partners—

Ada   changing hands—

Charles   converging and iterating—

Ada   Pirouetting and processing until—

Charles   It stops.

Ada   It stops.

Pause.

Lovelace   What happens when it stops?

Charles   Well it's either finished its job or it's broken.

Babbage *and* **Ada** *laugh,* **Lovelace** *tries to. Realizes he's out of his element.* **Anabella** *walks over.*

Anabella   Ada darling, I believe it's time to bid your children good night.

Ada   My goodness the day has flown by. Excuse me, gentlemen. When I return I shall force Mr. Babbage to describe the Engine's operations transfer in full.

Lovelace   Over dinner?

Ada   It's for the paper.

Ada *steps away giddy—until her mother pulls* **Ada** *aside—*

Anabella   It's getting a bit explicit, darling. The giddiness. Your husband is in the room and you're fawning over another man.

Ada   I'm not fawning, Mother, please.

Anabella   Babbage's letters have been constant, as *I'm sure* has been his affection. I only caution you—

Ada   *Mother, we're working together. I'll have no more of this in his presence nor in my house.*

Anabella   You'd think he would have left you alone now that you're married.

Ada   Wasn't that supposed to be our arrangement?

Ada *walks away from her mother, who exits too.*

Lord Lovelace *and* **Babbage** *chat.*

Lovelace   Your letters gave her great joy. And now this. I haven't seen her this lifted in ages. I thank you for it.

Charles   You are most welcome. I hope you don't mind the correspondence.

Lovelace   I did not and do not. And I . . . I really must apologize to you, sir. For our last encounter. You have been a great friend to her and a steadfast supporter and I hope you can forgive my . . . overemphatic slight. She is lucky to have you as a friend. As am I.

Charles   Well. That's very kind.

Lovelace   You see the births were not altogether easy on her, her health has always been poor, but your correspondence strengthened her throughout her trials.

Charles   And I am grateful for that strength as it is I who take strength from her. She has a kind of . . . electricity to her.

Lovelace   *She* certainly thinks so.

Charles   It is hard to deny. She truly is . . .

Lovelace   Yes she is. Though I always feel I need your aptitude for mathematics to fully deserve her.

Charles   Oh no . . . No.

Pause. Though they both know it's true.

Lovelace   Love is a changeable thing is it not?

The more life we share, the more I care for her. We were in . . . agreement before. But now I do think we are in love . . . of a kind. My understanding was that it went the other way around, but I suppose I don't care which way it goes as long as she is happy.

Charles   She seems happy to me.

Lovelace   Does she? Good. I hope it strengthens evermore until, as they say, death do us part.

Charles   I will tell you, love does not stop at death. Once you share a life, especially children, the soul . . . *compounds* itself. My wife is always near to me even now.

Lovelace   Excuse my ignorance. I did not know you were once married.

Charles   Yes. Georgiana. She was so young when she died, she wouldn't recognize me now. That's an odd thought isn't it?

Lovelace   Good women. Make for better men. Something like that.

These men are both talking about **Ada** *and know it. Pause.*

Would you tell me what a logarithm is?

Pause.

Charles   You might ask your wife.

Ada *enters—*

Ada   The boys are destroying your very kind gift, Charles, but then again that seems to be what boys do with everything—

Lovelace   Darling?

Ada   Yes, dear?

Lovelace *has walked right up to his wife and kisses her, sweeps her into his arms and kisses her.*

Ada *did not see that coming. Neither did* **Babbage***. Neither did Lovelace really.*

When he lets her up, she takes a breath.

Babbage *doesn't know what to say—so he raises his glass to them both as . . .*

The next scene sweeps in.

Scene Eight

Letters pouring out of **Ada** *to* **Babbage***.*

Ada   My Dear Babbage, I am working very hard for you, like the Devil in fact, which perhaps I am. I have made some very important extensions and improvements to the processing.

*Another letter—***Lord Lovelace** *joins her, helping.*

You will admire the table and diagram extremely. Lord L is at this moment kindly inking it over for me. He is quite enchanted with the beauty and symmetry of it.

Lovelace   Birdie. Is this to your liking or—

Ada   NoNoNo. He's got to be able to read it, darling. Please summon up your best handwriting.

Lovelace   This is my best.

Ada   Then summon up someone else's.

Another letter as **Lovelace** *exits with his papers.*

It must be a very pleasant thing to have Fairy in one's service—I, poor Fairy, can only get mortals to wait on me.

Another letter.

I have made Lord L laugh by referring to this paper as my child. I think he is an uncommonly fine baby.

Another letter.

You know I do not believe that my father was such a poet as I shall be an Analyst.

Another letter.

Enclosed is our revised and corrected translation and notes in its entirety.

Your Fairy forever,

Ada

And suddenly they are met.

In **Babbage**'*s office. Evening.* **Babbage** *reviews her work.*

Charles   *Sketch of the Analytical Engine Invented by Charles Babbage.*

Ada   *With Notes by the Translator . . .*

Charles *holds up a thick stack of papers.*

Charles   Good lord. Your notes are twice the length of the translation.

Ada   *Thrice.*

Babbage *reads.*

Ada *waits for him. She fidgets, anxious.*

Points out and reads aloud to make sure he's seeing it.

This bit's rather good I think: "The Engine is not merely adapted for *tabulating* the results of one particular function, but for *developing and tabulating* any function whatever."

Charles   Uh-hmm.

Ada   "A new, a vast, and a powerful language is developed for the future use of analysis—"

Charles   Yes I can—

Ada   "With commands input via punch cards, there is no limit either to the magnitude or the quantity of numbers used—"

Charles   I am reading it.

Ada   And the diagrams I think turned out quite well. Producing the Bernoulli numbers proves that the engine can do anything mathematical. Most professors cannot manage Bernoulli but *it* can—I proved it can.

The program I laid out—(*Pointing out the diagram.*) is flawless. Because I found one of your flaws by the way. Carry the one, Charles.

Now I set down every command given through the punch cards and every corresponding step the engines would take in a calculation of this complexity.

Silence. **Babbage** *engrossed,* **Ada** *anxious.*

And I know you don't particularly agree but, as a small gift to myself, I might have snuck in the bit about the Engine one day writing songs.

Charles   "Supposing that the fundamental relations of pitched sounds were input, the engine might compose elaborate and scientific pieces of music."

Ada   Yes. I rather love that thought. A singing machine.

Pause as **Babbage** *says nothing. Lost in the pages.*

I might combust if you don't say something. I've worked so hard, and I think it's quite brilliant, and as far as I know this work is unheard of—

He looks up.

Charles   It's perfect. Pray do not alter it. Not one word. All this was impossible for you to know by intuition. Yet you know it as thoroughly as I. Greater than I. You see its . . . future.

Ada   I do.

Charles   And the music.

Ada   Well. If the engine can process numerical commands it could theoretically process any symbol. Notes instead of numbers is what I see.

Charles   Yes. Notes, numbers, it makes perfect sense.

Ada   Does it?

Charles   Over and over again, you surprise me. You shock.

Ada   Don't I sound . . . alarming.

She is so relieved and happy that he liked her work.

He is so impressed and amazed.

If he were a different kind of man, he would have swept her off her feet and kissed her.

She would rather that he was that kind of man. They are both imagining that which they cannot seem to make themselves do, but want to do very very much.

Babbage *comes closer to her,* **Ada** *babbles instead of addressing him.*

There are only a few more corrections for the printers. They rather insist on capitalizing all my subscripts which quite alters the meaning of B_{2n-1}. (*Read as:* "B sub 2, n minus 1.")

He is calm even with the electricity coursing between them.

Charles   I hope you know . . . how grateful I am for you. And how much I . . . I hope you know.

Ada   I do. As must you. Know.

They should be making out right now . . . but they aren't. They can't.

Actually they could . . . but they won't. Stuck in the middle of want and won't.

Ada *tries to break the gravity of the moment.*

Then . . . we should both be . . . quite satisfied with ourselves. Our work. The paper. Which truly is the best of both of us. We have finally made manifest so many conversations. Our collective dream it seems is . . . real. We are, in this respect . . . complete.

Charles   Complete.

Ada   Yes.

Charles   Partners really.

Ada   Partners?

Charles   In this respect.

Ada   Oh. Yes.

Charles   Yes.

Their breath is the only thing moving in the room. Breath. Breath.

Ada   I'm so sorry.

Ada *turns to go—but* **Charles** *reaches out and catches her hand quickly and surely. He's not letting her go this time.*

She spins back to face him. Then steps forward towards him. Perhaps he touches her cheek or arm. If he does she lets herself enjoy this for an instant before going back to thinking, "I should leave right now even though I don't want to."

This is the closest they can get to each other in this world. The most intimacy they can manage. All tension and electricity between them has this one single, silent channel. Eyes on eyes, hand on hand, breath so very close to breath. Perhaps he opens his mouth to speak the impossible when—

Blackout.

End of Act One.

Act Two

Scene One

Exactly where we left them.

The energy, the want, the impossibility flowing between them like Faraday's electricity. Hand in hand.

Ada (*a small voice*) I do . . . I have . . . I have to go.

  Charles You *have* to?

    Ada I have to go.

      Charles Ada. Just—

        Ada I must. A train. Catching a train.

          Charles Ada—

            Ada I can't—

              Charles Please.

                Ada I'm sorry. I'm so sorry. I can't. I must go. I really must.

She releases her hand. Apologizing without words.

He nods—perhaps clears his throat. Busies himself in the room somehow. Trying to accept that they won't be talking about their relationship or . . . **Babbage** *moves back to business, partly to change the subject, partly to recover from some embarrassment.*

Charles Of course. And I won't keep you longer than to broach one more issue before you go, if I may.

Ada Charles.

Charles NoNo. I just have a small preface that I wish to see attached to the paper. A short note really. A small introduction to the piece, then your translation, then your marvelous notes.

Ada What sort of preface?

Charles Just—context. Contextualize the engine, its development, its varied history.

Ada Has it had a varied history?

Charles You'll understand when you see it. I do have the draft here somewhere. Where is the damned thing? I'll find it. Here it is. Good.

He gives it to her to read.

It will, I think, add a touch of weight to your paper and some frankly *necessary* blame for the great delay in seeing this work come to its proper fruition.

Ada   Forgive me, you mean to preface the paper with *this* letter? To be published in the journal as well.

Charles   Well yes. The scientific community will, I think, be interested in the sightless ministers of this crooked government who defunded the Difference Engine to the great loss of this country.

Ada   Charles.

Charles   The Difference Engine would have been made if not for the prime minister's complete lack of—

Ada   *Don't do this. This is lunacy.*

Charles   Lunacy. I beg your pardon.

Ada (*reading from his note*)   "The viability of the Difference Engine was without question, even as its first breath was squeezed out by this government's miserly—" Charles, really. You cannot be serious in this. To print this is to shame the government with common libel.

Charles   It is not libel, you know it's not, it's a short statement of only true facts and justifiable opinion.

Ada   Is it signed?

Charles   What.

Ada   Is this short statement signed. by you?

Charles   Well the paper is yours, yours and Menebrea's, not mine.

Ada   So you would have me put *my name* behind this?

Charles   I am not asking you to claim it as yours.

Ada   By not claiming it as *yours*, yes you are. This good work, *my* good work, that took months of my time and you would tarnish it with such foolish name-calling that everyone will know comes from you no matter whose name you put behind it.

Charles   *They didn't fund it because they're sightless and cheap and they need to be pilloried and mocked for it, not reelected.* These ministers are doing damage to the intellectual vibrancy of this nation and they cannot survive if they mock me, they will never mock me again.

Ada   Then stop making it easy for them.

Charles   If this information seems to come from me they won't listen.

Ada   And if it seems to come from me it's a lie.

Charles   You can't refuse me on this.

Ada   Excuse me.

Charles   You cannot.

Ada   Oh I very well can *and will.*

Charles   You will print it, yes you will, it will be printed as I laid it out.

Ada   I will never let it hit the page.

Charles   This I did not expect. That you would end up like the rest of them, burning the bridge as I cross it.

Ada   I'm saving you heaps of embarrassment. The publishers will never consent to printing it either.

Charles   Then you will retract the paper from such idiot purveyors.

Ada   I will *retract this paper? From print?* Who are you? Who would have me efface months' worth of work and time and, if I do say, *leaps of mental acuity* in translating not just the French but your knotted complexity into the vernacular of reality. You would tell your friend to simply retract it?

Charles   If she were a real friend, she'd do it without question.

Pause. Ada is steaming.

Ada   I am. Your very best friend. And thus I cannot and will not support you in acting in a manner not only wrong but suicidal.

Charles   You defy me then?

Ada   Is it not *you* who defy *me? My good sense?*

Charles   Oh yes, *sense* is your family's most rumored feature.

Ada   Do not condescend to me when you are using my name to sell your lies and you know it. I am a prize for you. I am your protégé. And I am every bit the genius you are.

Charles   So you keep telling everyone.

She almost laughs at this. Then she's serious and leaves.

Ada   I see we have turned a corner that I fear will lead us off a cliff. I will see myself out, Mr. Babbage.

Charles   Yes you wouldn't want to "miss your train."

Like a flicked switched she changes her mind to stay and fight.

Ada   Do not punish me for protecting us.

Charles   From what?

Ada   *Each other.*

Charles   I don't need your protection, my dear. Not from myself and not from a socialite.

Ada   Oh my *mind* you'll employ when it serves you, unless the woman attached to it *objects* to a ludicrous thing, then? Then you dismiss her as turncoat fool. Well if you think I would be so easy manipulated you know me not.

Charles   And yet you've done everything I've asked so far.

Ada   Then it's a good thing you're too scared to ask for the thing you actually want.

She means herself of course. Slam.

Charles   It's my engine, Ada.

Ada   It's my program, Charles. My work.

Charles   *Your work is my work, this work, this idea, everything in this is mine first. It doesn't exist without me and neither do you.*

Beat. Shock.

Ada   Like your engines? Do they *exist*? I have yet to see them. The designs of which you boast exuberantly would beg the question . . . where are the machines themselves? Why does not the great man, with the great ideas, produce any *great thing*? Why? Because you're scared.

Charles   Of you?

Ada   Of yourself, you coward.

Charles   *Coward?*

Ada   Perhaps you hate these ministers because you fear they're right. You can't be trusted to produce anything but promises. Oh. *And models.*

Charles   I could say so much worse of you.

Ada   OH yes, the girl with sin in her blood, who talks and dreams and leans in so much closer than other girls do. Is a Romantic worse than a coward?

Charles   I am not a coward.

Ada   *You are scared of your best ideas!* This engine could be made. It should be made. And if it's not made? It will be because of your cowardice and the fact that you turn on your friends.

Charles   My friends turn on me, they always do.

Ada   You're an ass, Charles. *You* are the thing in your own way. You stop yourself. A mountain of your best ideas weigh nothing if they are not made, and because of some counterproductive form of perfectionism *they die in your mind.*

Charles   I won't bring something into being if it's not perfect. If it's not perfect why do it?

Ada   That's a clean way for a coward to sound like a hero.

Charles   *I am not a coward.*

Ada   You're scared of everything except what's in your head. And that is where your best ideas are buried, unmade and unmet.

Charles   You've lost your mind and your decorum and you're not making any sense.

Ada (*talking about them*)   *And You. Make. Nothing.* You dream, you promise, and nothing comes of it, and it's all for naught, and you could remake the world but you're terrified of seeing your dreams in the daylight.

Ada *goes to leave finally but falters—a wave of pain in her stomach comes over her so strongly that she freezes to weather it.*

Charles   What. Ada?

With a firm hand she stops him.

Ada (*holding her rage down to a low flame, but it is a hot one*)   *Do not. Touch me.*

Here is the truth of things. We need each other.

Charles   My dear—

Ada   I am speaking. You are brilliant but unpleasant. I am brilliant but unrecognized. I see only one solution to both save you from yourself, and me from mediocrity: We must continue to work together. Partners is what you said, and I agree.

Charles   I did not mean ours as a business arrangement.

Ada   What if it was?

Pause.

All I want is for the engine to be built, that's what I've always wanted. If I could craft it such that you would do nothing but engineer it into existence, would you let me manage everything else? Let me do that work, while you yours. Partners.

Charles   You call me a coward and then you propose to work for me?

Ada   Well you would really work for me.

Charles   *Are you mad.*

Ada   That's not what I meant. I meant that I could manage the money, the relationships, the business—and if any of your machines are to be made there must be a *business to it.*

Charles   And you would *manage* me? Keep me in check, make sure I played nice.

Ada   *Exactly.*

Charles   *Exactly not. No. Never.*

Ada   A bit of *management* could take you from zero to one. The entire universe is in their difference.

Charles   *If you think small enough.* This is impossible.

Ada   A thinking machine was impossible until *we* told them how it could be done.

Charles   It doesn't think, it takes orders. (*Talking about her.*) Therein lies its value.

My dear you are out of your depth here. Not least by speaking to me like I am an overactive child you need to keep busy lest they ruin the wallpaper. Secondly, I would never, in a millennia, trust you to manage my money when I have consoled you on your gambling losses more than once.

Ada   *The algorithm was correct, the HORSES were wrong.* And I was trying to raise money for you.

Charles   Well stop it. You're embarrassing yourself and me by association. What I need instead of your questionable financial and entrepreneurial guidance is time. Time is what I want. I need peace of mind to talk to the damn thing, and time to listen.

Ada   We don't have time.

Charles   *We* don't have anything, you and I. *We* don't.

Ada   No we don't. Neither friendship, nor sense, nor time, nor the years that we want *to realize this dream, we don't have it, we have nothing, nothing, nothing left and no time TO MAKE ANYTHING REAL.*

Her outburst drains her into breathlessness. **Ada** *leans on something.* **Charles** *is now concerned for her. What's she really talking about?*

Then in a flash **Ada** *cramps so hard that it stops her in full, bends her over—she manages it quietly, but he sees her pain. He steps to her, she waves him off again. It passes.*

Charles   My dear you must tell right now what's wrong.

Ada   Oh. A bit of everything at the moment.

Charles   Ada. What is this?

Ada   Something like . . . the beginning of the end. The doctors—I think they're placing bets on whether I survive the winter.

Charles   The winter? What on earth are talking about?

Ada   It's what I've been battling for years. And it seems it's winning. I'm told there's little for it but prayer and laudanum.

Charles   No.

Ada   Neither of which make me think straight.

Charles   No that's not right.

Ada   You know my father died at thirty-six.

Charles   Ada, no.

Ada   I'll be thirty-five next month.

Babbage *drops every rule of his time and grabs her into a hug—an embrace that is shock and desperation and dependence and love and sadness.*

She holds him back. Releases into him. Grips him, embraces him, needs him.

We see how scared she really is.

After a moment he whispers something to her—we can't hear it—but she nods, thanks him with this. Perhaps he told her that he loves her. She is so imbued by whatever he said that she is speechless, exhausted, vulnerable.

They sit together. Closer than they ever have been.

Ada   I'm still mad at you.

Charles   Good. I'm still mad at you.

Ada   Good. Because I won't accept your pity.

Charles   Well, pity's for strangers. What I have for you is a plan. I have doctors, I have friends at the medical school. And I have a commandable, programmable calculating machine that might or might not write an opera. And it must be built.

She likes the sound of that . . . even though she thinks she won't see it built.

Babbage *sees this too.*

We also must plan to visit the Great Exhibition next month. A world's fair of technology and industry. Inventors for miles. You'll love it.

Ada   I've heard they're covering Hyde Park in glass.

Charles   Yes, the Crystal Palace. A fine design. I could've done it better. Still. Steel and glass and a hundred thousand people inside. And we will go. And see the future together.

She really does love that idea.

Ada   Please don't leave. I fear it will get bad. Byrons don't seem to die easily.

Charles   You are not your father.

Ada   I think of him so much now. It feels like memory, but I never knew him. And yet I . . . I do know him . . . somehow. I know that he died alone. Which is my greatest and growing fear.

Charles   You are not alone.

Ada   When it gets bad and I am not myself, please don't leave me, please.

Charles   I won't, my dear.

Ada   Please, Charles.

Charles   How could I leave. You're far too interesting. And you're the only one who understands me.

Ada   *And* puts up with you. Did you know that you said you wanted time to "talk to the Engine"? Did you know you said that?

Charles   Said what?

Ada   You said "I want time to talk to the damn thing." You meant the Engine.

Charles   No, I didn't, I didn't say that.

Ada   Yes you did, I heard it clear as day. You're a bit poetic after all, talking to inanimate objects.

Charles (*teasing now*)   Hush you.

Ada   Hush *you*, titanically rude malcontent.

Charles   I'm a malcontent if you're a—

Ada   What am I? Tell me.

Charles   A . . . harpy, of some sort, I don't know.

She laughs just a little at him. He laughs at himself.

Ada   I'm a bird.

Charles   Not a fairy?

Ada   I suppose both have wings. I made wings once as a girl. Almost dove off the roof if the nanny hadn't grabbed me. Though I like to think I would've flown. Or perhaps I am just a flightless bird.

Charles   An emu.

Ada   Did you say emu?

Charles   Flightless bird. You said.

Ada   You're calling me an emu?

Charles   I'm not, you're calling you an emu.

Ada   That's the worst thing anyone has ever said to me.

Charles   I didn't say it, you did.

Ada   No gentleman should call a lady an emu.

Does **Charles** *do an "emu" gesture, whatever that is? If he does, she laughs at it.*

A moment.

Charles   What can I give you, Lady Lovelace?

Pause.

Ada   All the impossible things. And hurry.

He looks at her . . . she looks into the great grand future in her mind.

Scene Two

A letter from **Babbage** *takes over—though perhaps they do not move an inch from the previous moment. They sit together, he holds her, they both look out . . .*

Charles   My Dear Ada,

Lovelace *appears, unsettled, upset. He is in the near future while* **Babbage** *and* **Ada** *are holding fast to the present.*

Lovelace   Dearest Lady Byron,

Charles   I find it quite in vain to wait until I have leisure so I have resolved that I will leave all other things undone and set out for you—

Lovelace   Your daughter's health slips in rapid decline. Her pain brings her fits of either howling or whimpers. The laudanum is the only tool I have to calm her.

Charles   I take with me papers enough to enable me to forget this world and all its troubles and if possible its multitudinous charlatans—everything in short but the Enchantress of Numbers.

Lovelace   She is not as she once was. I know not how to help her.

A letter from **Ada**.

Ada   Dear Babbage, I write to entreat that you will act as my executor in the event of my sudden decease. No mutual knowledge of any two human beings in this life can give such stable ground for faith and confidence as ours.

Lovelace   As her mother I ask you to consider joining us in residence to ease her end.

Ada   Most affectionately,

Charles   Farewell my dear and much admired Interpretess.

Lovelace   With haste,

Charles   Evermost truly yours—

And now **Anabella** *directs a letter at* **Babbage**.

Anabella   Mr. Babbage.

Ada *is grabbed by her mother from* **Charles**.

Anabella   My daughter is not well and not improving. I am left to manage her affairs as she is no longer capable.

Lovelace *helps* **Ada** *across the room and administers her laudanum.*

From a brown bottle he drops many drops of the liquid into a glass of water. She drinks it, breathing through her pain. After she downs the drink she relaxes—sleepy—high.

Anabella   I ask you to leave her in peace. Let me be clear. You are not welcome here any longer.

The letter ceases as **Babbage** *confronts* **Anabella** *at the door to* **Ada**'s *room.*

Charles   Lady Byron, you've known me almost twenty years now, you know my deep concern for your family, you cannot push me out.

Anabella   Your concern has always been, even when deeply inappropriate, for my daughter, who is no longer accepting visitors.

Charles   I am not a visitor. I'm the executor of her will.

Anabella   I don't care what honorifics she threw at you while in one of her stupors. You are not family and not welcome.

Charles   I insist on seeing her.

Anabella   You may insist, Mr. Babbage, but you will not enter.

Charles   I know you are writing letters in her name. I know her hand and this is not it.

Anabella   She cannot do it herself.

Charles   *And she would not want you speaking for her.*

Lovelace *joins* **Lady Byron**.

Anabella   Mr. Babbage.

Lovelace   Mr. Babbage. Your concern is noted. Thank you. And please leave.

Charles   Sir. I was explaining to Lady Byron that I—

Lovelace (*explosively*)   *Please leave, sir. She is no longer your concern, nor your puppet, nor the woman you, nor any of us, knew her to be. There is nothing for you here. Good day.*

Babbage *doesn't know what to do but leave . . .*

A breath.

Ada *and her mother and husband.* **Ada** *is high and delirious on the couch.*

Anabella   Coming around almost every day now. No propriety at all.

Lovelace   I don't really care about propriety at the moment. I just want peace. I want her well.

Anabella   She's not going to be well. Not ever again. We must hold fast to etiquette.

Lovelace   Etiquette does not help her pain. She's drowning in it.

Anabella   Well. She doesn't talk to the deacon, she doesn't pray, she refused the mesmerist I sent, she doesn't even get off the couch—

Lovelace   She *can't stand.*

Anabella   You push that drink down her throat all day—

Lovelace   It's the only way she sleeps, it's the only thing that helps her pain.

Anabella   *Suffering is the price we pay for sin.*

It is not elegant, but it is sometimes necessary. Only God can forgive and relieve us.

Ada (*oblivious*)   Excuse me.

Lovelace   Good thing He gave us opiates.

Ada (*going for more laudanum*)   Excuse me.

Lovelace   And no more of your deacon round this house, I'm sick of it. Evangelists and mesmerists do not help her.

Anabella   Then she cannot be helped.

Ada   Excuse me.

Lovelace (*to* **Ada**) Yes. I'm sorry. Yes, dear.

Ada   We shall be late for the Exhibition if we do not collect ourselves at once. All of our friends will be there. At the Crystal Palace.

Lovelace   She's been talking of the Great Exhibition all week. She thinks it's last year.

Ada   Charles will meet us at the grand fountain.

Lovelace   Ada. The Exhibition is over.

Anabella   And there shall be no more mention of Mr. Babbage.

Ada   But we're going to see the displays of industry and technology. The Crystal Palace is all light and glass, have you seen it? A world of windows and Charles is taking me today.

Lovelace   Please stop this, Ada.

Ada   He's going to miss me if I'm not there. And the children. No one should miss their father.

Anabella   Their father?

Lovelace   It's the laudanum. She's delirious, she doesn't know what she's saying.

Anabella   What do you mean their father?

Lovelace   I do not want to hear her ramblings, I just want her to sleep.

Anabella   The soul cannot rest unconfessed.

Lovelace   She's not confessing, she's drunk. (*Turning to* **Ada** . . . *prompting her.*)

Ada   Do you know Charles? A great man. He builds engines and I tell them what to do. Do you know our Engine can sing? Birds and machines.

Lovelace   Ada, please—

Anabella   And you confess your love for that man then?

Lovelace   *I will not have you fuel this fantasy in her.*

Ada   When we met we danced with no music. But I imagined the music. I hear it still. Do you hear it? It's in the in-between of things. That's where love is. And every other impossible thing. You know you've made it there when you can hear the song. (*To* **Lovelace**, *like he's someone new and unknown. He is instantly devastated.*) Can you hear it, sir?

Lovelace *puts all his life into one look at her face. Then turns on her.*

Anabella   God will purify her now.

Lovelace   I don't care what he does with her.

You're the lady of this house now.

Charles (*offstage—banging on the front door*)   Lord Lovelace. Lady Byron, please—

Anabella   God help us. It's him again.

Lovelace   You know she asked me to be buried next to her father in Hucknall. Her father. Not near you, nor I, nor her children but the man she only knew in . . . myth. She'd rather that than the life we gave her. That says something about her doesn't it. Or us.

More knocking from outside.

Let him in.

Anabella   I will not.

Lovelace   Just let him in.

Anabella   Not when she's just cleansed her soul of him.

Lovelace   She needed and hated you in equal parts. You know this, don't you?

Anabella   *Excuse me.*

Ada   Are you a nice man, sir?

Lovelace   What?

Ada   I think I know you and I think I know that you are good.

Lovelace   Very few people are in the end.

Ada   Oh. Is this the end? I have a book I'd like to take with me.

Ada *reveals the pieced-back-together book of her father's poems from the very first scene. She's kept it all these years.*

Anabella *doesn't know what to say.*

Charles *knocks on the interior door—he's right outside.*

Lovelace (*to* **Charles**)   COME IN. (*To* **Anabella**.) Someone should be here who cares.

Charles *enters as* **Lovelace** *exits.*

Charles   Sir, if I may please say that—

Lovelace   You may not.

Lovelace *goes for good. Exits with a slam.*

Anabella   Mr. Babbage, for god's sake.

Charles   Lady Byron. I will see this woman and there is no respectable reason why you should stop me.

Ada   Darling, I was going to meet you at the Crystal Palace.

Anabella   You should have stopped yourself, Mr. Babbage. From the beginning you should have been a gentleman and a—

Charles   I was never any other kind of man to her.

Ada   The whole place is glass. The whole thing's a prism.

Anabella   You should have let her go.

Ada   Rainbows and light.

Anabella   She was never going to leave you, the grand man of science, the father she never had. You should have done the honorable thing and left. her. alone. Now look at her. Abandoned and ruined. Laudanum's on the table. I'll be outside.

Ada   Goodbye madam.

Anabella *leaves.*

(*To* **Charles**.) I don't much care for her really.

Charles   Ada, my dear. What can I do? I came every day, she wouldn't let me in.

Ada   We were going to the Crystal Palace today. Because the whole thing's a prism. And our boys will see the future.

Charles   What's this now?

Ada   But I can't play the piano anymore. My fingers are stuck. And the music is coming. Can you hear it?

Charles   Music?

Ada   Yes. You see there is music in everything. Because there is mathematics in everything. Hidden all around us like a prism hides a rainbow. Until it lets the colors free. I wrote a poem about a rainbow. It's rather good I think. My father's a poet. I'm meeting him at the Crystal Palace.

She gets up trying to find the paper—the pain, even on drugs, overwhelms her.

She clutches him. Breathes through it, whimpers. He holds her.

Charles   I'm here. I'm right here. Why don't we rest—*He helps her lie back down.*

Ada   Before we go to the Crystal Palace.

Will he play this fantasy with her? Yes.

Charles   Yes. Before we go we'll rest.

Ada   And . . . what will we do there?

Charles   We will . . . walk.

Ada   Under the glass?

Charles   Yes. And by the fountain.

Ada   I do so love the fountain.

Charles   So we'll sit by the fountain.

Ada   And wait for the boys. They'll want their father to show them all the feats of wonder.

Charles   Yes. The boys will meet us there. And our girls, of course. Three boys and six girls.

Ada   That many?

Charles   Oh yes. Our house was overflowing.

Ada   Was it? It was. Yes it was.

Charles   It was.

Ada   The children. You must find them and show them what we've made. The engine and the music and the children must be shown the future.

Charles   The future.

Ada   Yes. It will be lovely I think.

She is fading—tired—

I think I'll rest. And then we'll go. To the future.

Charles   Perhaps I'll sit here with you. If that's all right?

Ada   Of course my darling, that'd be lovely.

She kisses his cheek like a wife would.

Charles   Would you like a poem? A poem might be just the thing to help you rest.

Ada   Did you know that poems have heartbeats? My father taught me that. There's a bit of maths to them too. One *Two*, One *Two*.

Babbage *picks up her father's book. From now on* **Charles** *cannot hear* **Ada**.

Like the beginning of the play she taps her chest like a heartbeat along with the iambic cadence of the poem that **Charles** *now reads to her.*

Over the next pages **Ada** *gradually turns back into herself . . . though* **Charles** *doesn't notice.*

Charles   She walks in beauty, like the night

Ada   (*a numeric heartbeat*)

Of cloudless climes and starry skies;

One *Two*, One *Two*, One *Two*, One *Two* . . .

And all that's best of dark and bright

One *Two*, One *Two*, One *Two*, One—

Meet in her aspect and her eyes: Thus
mellow'd to that tender light Which
heaven to gaudy day denies.

Ada *is not delirious now, she is fully herself again. She has a thought,* **Charles** *cannot not hear or see her.*

Ada   Oh dear god. What if . . . what if . . .

Charles   One shade the more, one ray the less,

Ada   What if the number *system* is what's stopping us.

Charles   Had half impaired the nameless grace

Ada   What if we changed the decimals to—

Charles   Which waves in every raven tress,

Ada   Yes. We could increase the memory if there's only—oh that could work.

Charles   Or softly lightens o'er her face;

Ada   With only *two* symbols it could recycle more commands, more results, it could process faster—

Charles   Where thoughts serenely sweet express

Ada   Two numbers, not ten.

Charles   How pure, how dear their dwelling-place.

Ada   On, off; hole, covered; one, two—

Charles And on that cheek, and o'er that brow,	**Ada**
So soft, so calm, yet eloquent,	No. Of course it's not.
The smiles that win, the tints that glow,	Obviously.
But tell of days in goodness spent,	It's not one and *two* . . .

Ada   It's one and *zero* . . .

Charles   A mind at peace with all below,

Ada   Zero and one . . .

Charles   A heart whose love is—

Ada (*standing with more energy, more herself every minute*)   Over and over in every combination, for every command in the world. That's it, that's the . . .

But **Charles** *doesn't see her standing. He sees her still lying down . . . not moving . . .*

She also sees that she has stopped the heartbeat she was tapping on her chest.

She knows what this means.

The future.

Charles *stands sharply—looks "at* **Ada***" lying on the couch, even though she stands next to him. To* **Charles Ada** *is gone. He catches his breath. Gone. Then he sits next to her. Can't move.*

Ada *realizes she's gone too.*

She can only look at her soul mate from afar now, even though she's so close.

Now what the hell does she do.

As the world around them changes, fades away. It suffuses with . . .

Light. Prism-inflected rainbows flicker about her. This place is in between the others . . .

The Crystal Palace . . .

Charles *takes no note of it . . . never leaving "*Ada*'s" side. He is in the world she just left . . .*

Ada   Is this . . . the future?

Into this in-between walks . . . a man.

Byron   I'm not exactly sure. Feels more like nostalgia to me. Or poetry?

Ada   Excuse me.

Byron   They're very similar. Lots of pining, nothing to be done. Rather lovely though.

Ada   Did you say Poetry?

Byron   Yes I can't seem to escape it.

No matter what I do, everything ends up verse. Hello.

Ada   Hello. You're a poet?

Byron   Precisely. Or regrettably if you're my wife.

Ada   I'm sorry. I . . .

Byron   What?

Ada   Oh dear. Are you . . . Mr. Byron?

Byron   No. I am *Lord* Byron, a title I, in the traditional English manner, did very little to deserve. And you are?

She is stunned.

Forgive me, do I offend you? Have we met? Or fought? Or . . .?

Ada   No. I . . . no, we haven't met. Exactly. Once, I'm told, but not . . . I'm so sorry I'm at a loss for our . . . exact . . . function.

Byron   I'm sorry, a function?

Ada   A relationship involving one or more variables. It's a metaphor.

Byron   I'm usually quite good with those but you put me at a loss, my dear.

She thinks . . . then recites . . .

Ada "Is thy face like thy mother's, my fair child!	**Byron**
ADA! sole daughter of my house and heart?	Ada.
When last I saw thy young blue eyes they smiled,	Ada.
And then we parted,—"	

Byron   Dear god, child. Ada?

Ada   Correct.

Byron   Oh my dear.

Ada   Also correct. I suppose. Hello.

Byron   Hello.

Pause.

I have . . . thought of you. Often. Very often.

Ada   Likewise. Well. Three nights in five. Or four in seven. The percentage is certainly in your favor but I'm afraid it's not one hundred.

Byron   So she turned you into a mathematician? To spite me? She did, didn't she?

Ada   I'm afraid so. Even geography was too potent a subject.

Byron   What did geography ever do to her?

Ada   Gave you more places to run to. She turned me into a scientist.

Byron   And what in god's name is that?

Ada   An explorer of the fundamental principles of the universe. Like I'm told a poet is of the heart.

That pleases him to hear.

Byron   You speak very well. I'll take credit for that. Did you read my poem?

Ada   Yes. I've read them all.

Byron   I wrote about you.

Ada   I realized that. Once Mother told me who you were.

Byron   Which took how long?

Ada   Eighteen years.

Byron   That woman.

Ada   She was not a fan.

Byron   I married the one person I couldn't charm.

Ada   Why did you do that?

Byron   Why *did* I do that?

Ada   She's not very nice.

Byron   Well, neither was I. We all have our magnetisms and our mistakes.

Ada   Sometimes that seems to be all we have.

Byron   It certainly tends to be all we remember.

Ada   Memory taunts me. What could have been but wasn't.

Byron   That's not memory then. That's regret.

Ada   I have never found them separate.

Byron   You have a shadow to you, my dear.

Ada (*starting to turn on him, mad, resentful—*)   Yes, well, perhaps you should take credit for that too.

Byron   Excuse me?

Ada   Actually you'll need to excuse me. I am about to repeat what I know about you and to most people it will seem like a torrent of insult, but I wish to hear from you what is true.

Byron   You needn't say any more.

Ada   You know of which you're accused? Adultery and abandonment—leaving your women and daughters across Europe to fend for themselves while you prance off to the next bed.

Byron   I have never pranced in my life.

Ada   And that's not even the worst of it. Not the even the worst—

Byron   I know what you're going to say, you don't have to—

Ada   Is it true?

Byron   Oh for god's sake—

Ada   *Incest.*

Byron   *She was a HALF sister—No one was hurt.*

Ada (*fighting him, blaming him, calling him out*)   *I was hurt—I was.* Everyone thinking my father disgusting and disgraceful and that all of that was in me waiting to bleed out. I spent my life glared at or gawked at or gossiped about. I couldn't live my life because of yours.

Byron   *And why was that?*

Ada   *Because I was your daughter and not your son.*

Byron *hears and understands her. He takes a new approach.*

Byron   The human condition is spent along the tight wire between want and ought, what we crave and what's expected. I would not live a life of expectation certainly if it was not my own making. *Nor should you.* To live for passion, to live at *all*, that was a choice I made and I could not have made any other. Your mother knew that my wandering was inevitable. She knew it and she waited for it and she lived drunk off of her dramatic suffering in spite of it.

But I was always wandering back to you. I just never quite made it.

Ada   Why not.

Byron   Because I've always been the most comfortable . . . amiss.

Ada   "Amiss" is your excuse? For blackening my life, for leaving me never knowing if I was—

Byron   I'm sorry.

  Ada   I never knew—

    Byron   I'm sorry.

Ada   *I never knew if I was real to you.* Do you know what that's like? Not knowing if you're real or a dash of fiction in your father's mind? *It's unhealthy.*

Byron   *Might it also have made you unusually comfortable with the power of imagination to set the world on fire.*

Pause.

Ada (*pissed*)   I'm not sure if you are defying my expectations or perfectly adhering to them.

Byron   I will excavate a compliment in that.

And attempt to convey my . . . apologies. Oh god I don't know—What is the etiquette of this? For leaving you, my dear, I am sorry. But I think we both must acknowledge that I would have likely made your life much darker in the end. I tend to do that.

Ada   I just . . . wanted some of your . . . greatness. In my life, in *me*. And I might be the only woman in England that doesn't care what you did. You were a great mind, a great man.

Byron   Yes. Just not a good one.

Pause.

She breaks—weeps—she lets it all out—her pain, her regret— he goes to her instinctively. Holds her like a . . . father. She accepts this embrace immediately—she needs it so much— but he is shocked by it—by his paternalism, his caring.

Ada   I've been in such true pain for so long . . . and I suddenly realized I wasn't.

This is very important to him suddenly. He focuses just on her.

Byron   I never imagine you hardened, or sad, or lonely. In my mind you're still a child with no worry.

Ada   You missed the middle bit then.

Byron   I meant that I tried to imagine you happy, I wished for that for you.

Ada   Wishes are rather useless things I find. There is no metal to them.

Byron (*Luddite in full*)   A metal wish? Doesn't that sound like a nightmare.

Ada   Does it?

Byron   *Yes.* Yes it does. Dear god I hope you're not one of those modernists.

Ada   Of course I am. Who's *not* a modernist that doesn't hope to see the future? Machines *are* that future.

Byron   Like hell they are. You cannot make things better than people.

Ada   But people can make things to better the world.

Byron   Machines cannot better us, if they've got no heart. Machines cannot love.

Ada   Good for them.

Byron   You would really want that? To be heartless and cold?

Ada   Painless and unburdened, yes I rather think I would've preferred that.

Byron   And this from the daughter of a Romantic.

Ada   From a daughter who trusted numbers more than people. Numbers do not lie, nor leave, nor die.

Impressed pause. **Byron** *looks at her, really looks. Drops the charming poet bit . . . honest and true.*

Byron   I like you very much. Most people can't say that of their children.

An honest flood. He is not charming her with this, he is confessing.

Had I known you. The words I would have spilt. For you. A million verses vanished when I left your side, and I see it now, and it is agony to imagine them.

This means so much to her. But she can't help the tease.

Ada   I will excavate a compliment in that.

Byron   There is truly no higher one that I have. Truly.

Ada *is so struck by this she confesses as well . . .*

Ada   You know I . . . I don't exactly know why but I . . . asked to end up next to you.

In case you wonder whom that strange girl is beside you. It's me.

He hugs her again. Really starting to feel the pride and pull of a parent.

Byron   I know it's you. I know you and you are not alone, my beautiful, brilliant, impossible girl. And you are free. And you are free. And now you are free.

He starts to release her—but she holds him fast, not letting him go, needing him more. This is what he can do for her. She has a thought . . .

Ada   Here I always thought true freedom was impossible.

Byron   Not everything that seems impossible stays impossible.

The idea lands on her, strikes her, she is held in awe.

Ada   Oh my god.

What if he built it? He actually built it.

   Byron   Built what?

     Ada   Or someone did.

       Byron   Built *what*?

Ada (*so proud of* **Charles**)   The Engine. It could . . . if he made it, it could . . . hold the past, present, and future. Together. Like it seems to be doing right now.

Byron   I'm sorry, did you say an *engine*? Like a train or—?

Ada   Like a mind.

Byron (*deeply skeptical*)   An engine with a mind?

Ada   No. The Engine *is* the mind.

Byron   Which is all the more impossible.

Ada (*agreeing*)   Isn't it?

Talking about them, together, talking right now.

Isn't *this*? Impossible things don't stay impossible. Once you can imagine it then they start to exist. What if *it* exists—now it exists, which is why *we* exist, which is why we're here at all!

Byron   Which would make all a figment of someone's imagination?

Ada   Yes. And computation.

Ada *looks around the room.*

She must experiment to know for sure.

So she does . . . offering the space a tentative . . .

One.

The space chimes one note. Confirmation. My god she's right. As soon as it confirms her thesis she is thinking at light speed, from this point until the song starts the lines are fast, urgent, pick up cues, go go go—

(*To him.*) Do you hear that? *Can you hear it?*

Byron   Yes, but—

Ada (*to the machine*)   Zero!

The note silences. Another confirmation for **Ada***!*

Byron   What is that, what are you doing?

Ada (*to him*)   I don't know but— (*To the machine.*) One!

Another note! Yes!

(*Back to him*—) I think I might be programming it to make music.

Byron   Programming what?

  Ada   The Engine!

    Byron   The Engine makes—?

Ada   Yes! Music! (*To the machine.*) Zero!

The note silences. She is loving this!

Byron   But where is it coming from?

Ada (*to the machine*)   One!

Another note!

The same place *we're* coming from— (*To the machine.*) Zero!

No note.

(*Back to him.*) the in-between of things, the impossible future that isn't impossible!

Byron   And you're programming the impossible?

Ada   Well. Someone has to teach it to sing. (*To the machine.*) One.

Then . . .

The Engine suddenly starts up around them—music and machinery.

They are inside the memory of the Analytical Engine. They are part of the machine, which clanks and clamors with metal on metal sounds wrapping them in.

They marvel at this.

They exist together in this space, this sound, this impossibility. Their song starts. His is poetry, hers is binary . . .

They dance as they sing and the Analytical Engine whirs and clanks around them.

Ada (*sung—rubato*)   and all the gears are spinning round they spiral up, they tumble down it fills the room this dream of mine the numbers falling into line

Piano arpeggio 1x alone.

Ada   she walks
in beauty
like the
night

of
cloudless
climes and
starry

ski—i—i—i—ies . . .

and all the gears
are spinning round

    Byron she walks
    in beauty
they spiral up,   like

they tumble dow—   the night
ow—own . . .

    of
    cloudless
    climes and
    starry

it fills the room
this dream of mine   ski—i—i—i—ies . . .

    she walks
    in beauty
    like   **Babbage** *sings*
        of
the numbers   the night   *their machine.*
falling into li—i—   *He can see Ada*

i—ine . . .   of cloudless   *again in this*
    climes   *dream . . .*
    and
one zero, zero, one.   starry   **Charles**
    ski—i—i—i—ies . . .   and all the gears
        are spinning round
        they spiral up,
one, one one zero,   they tumble down
zero, one.   it fills the room

one, one   she walks   this dream of mine
one zero, zero, one.   in beauty   the numbers

    like the   falling into line

	night	and all the gears
one, one	of cloudless	are spinning round
one zero, zero, one.	climes	they spiral up,
	and	they tumble down
	starry	it fills the room
	ski—i—i—i—ies . . .	this dream of mine
		the numbers
one, one one zero,		falling into line
zero, one.		and all the gears
one, one		are spinning round
one zero, zero, one.	she walks	they spiral up,
	in beauty	they tumble down
	like	
	the night	it fills the room
		this dream of mine
		the numbers
	of cloudless	falling into line
	climes	
	and	and all the gears
	starry	are spinning round
		they spiral up,
	ski—i—i—i—ies . . .	they tumble down
		it fills the room
		this dream of mine
		the numbers
		falling into line

Byron *touches* **Ada** *goodbye for now. As she turns her attention to* **Babbage***:*

one,	
one,	
zero.	one,
	one,
one,	zero,
one,	one,
zero	one,
	one,
one,	zero
one,	one,
zero	one,
one,	one—
one,	she walks
zero—	in beauty

                         like the
                         night
                         of
                         cloudless
                         climes and
                         starry
                         skies . . .

Babbage *says goodbye too—doesn't want to, must leave her.*

Ada   all the stars and all the clocks and all the lines and where they cross

and all the clouds
and all the trees
and all the spaces
in between

and all the birds
and all the bells
and all the stories
they can tell

and all the steam
and all the steel
and all the secrets
they conceal

all the stars and all
the clocks and all
the lines and where
they cross

and all the clouds
and all the trees
and all the spaces
in between

and all the birds
and all the bells
and all the stories
they can tell

and all the steam
and all the steel
and all the secrets
they reveal

and now the world
is fading white
numbers spinning

into light

and now the world is
fading white numbers
spinning into . . .

Ada *is alone . . . her ones and zeros now echoing around her, outside of her. She is not singing but sound is all around her. The song and the numbers funnel down into a spotlight on her.*

The spotlight and song gradually fade as a strange blue light and a strange new sound takes over . . .

It's the blue light of modern computer screens—laptops, iPhones, iPads—all giving off their ghostly light on her.

All playing her song.

Blackout.

End of Play.

Silent Sky

Silent Sky was commissioned by and premiered at South Coast Repertory (Marc Masterson, Artistic Director; Paula Tomei, Managing Director), in Costa Mesa, California, with support from the Elizabeth George Foundation, as part of the 2011 Pacific Playwrights Festival. It was directed by Anne Justine D'Zmura; the scenic design was by John Iacovelli; the costume design was by David Kay Mickelsen; the lighting design was by York Kennedy; the original music was by Lewis Flinn; the projection design was by John Crawford; the dramaturg was John Glore; and the production manager was Joshua Marchesi. The cast was as follows:

Henrietta Leavitt	Monette Magrath
Margaret Leavitt	Erin Cottrell
Peter Shaw	Nick Toren
Annie Cannon	Colette Kilroy
Williamina Fleming	Amelia White

Characters

Henrietta Leavitt (LEH-vit), *30s, brilliant, meticulous, excited—almost always wearing a period hearing-aid.*

Margaret Leavitt, *30s, homebody, creative, sweet, sister.*

Peter Shaw, *30s, the head astronomer's apprentice . . . and the man.*

Annie Cannon, *40s, the leader, terse and sure, grows into a firebrand.*

Williamina Fleming, *50s, smart as a whip and fun, Scottish.*

Settings

1900–20.

Star field.

The Harvard Observatory second-floor offices.

Leavitt home, Wisconsin.

Ocean liner on the Atlantic.

Henrietta's home, Cambridge, MA.

Notes

Sets: Simple, representational, flexible—e.g. a period desk, not a whole room. Swift transitions are key.

Stars: The star field from the Northern Hemisphere should be almost ever-present; even if the stage lights disappear, the stars shine and cradle the set.

Photographic Plates: These should be black and white windowpane-sized glass of the star field. They are negatives of the true night sky—stars are black and sky is white.

Music: Margaret's piano composition and playing should be live (seemingly), then augmented by a fully encompassing sound as the stars take over.

Magellanic: MAJ-eh-LAN-ic
Cepheid: SEH-fid
Andromedae: An-DRAH-muh-DIE

"In our troubled days it is good to have something outside our planet, something fine and distant for comfort."

—Annie Jump Cannon

Act One

Scene One

The late evening sky outside **Henrietta** *and* **Margaret**'*s father's rural Wisconsin church—about 1900 . . .*

A ruddy sun sets on **Henrietta**—*a fiercely smart woman, curious, energetic, spilling over her own traditionalism. Dressed primly and warmly, she points to the sky above her.*

Henrietta   Heaven's up there, they say. "Pearly clouds, pearly gates," they say. They don't know much about astronomy, I say. (*The sun is gone and the sky darkens into night.*) The science of light on high. Of all that is far-off and lonely and stuck in the deepest dark of space. Dark but for billions and billions of . . . (*The first star to peek out. A single note accompanies it.*) Exceptions. (*As the sister stars emerge. Another note.*) And I insist on the exceptional. (*As the night sky suddenly brightens into stark day—***Margaret** *sneaks up on* **Henrietta** *and pinches her.*) Ow—What are you doing?

Margaret   You know church is about to start. You know this and you're avoiding it and you've been caught.

Henrietta   I haven't been caught, I've been attacked.

Margaret   With love.

Henrietta   With pinches. What kind of world is this.

Margaret   You're not wearing your hearing-aid, you're fair game. Church. Now.

Henrietta   I can't right now.

Margaret   Oh yes you can, We're Waiting I'm freezing Come In.

Henrietta   Margie, I'm sorry but I cannot sit still right now.

Margaret   The only thing you have to do in church is sit still. Now tell me what's going on or come inside.

Henrietta   I've been trying to tell you all week but you're busy and you're barking and—

Margaret (*bark-like*)   *I don't bark.* I'm running the house, and Daddy's running the church, and *you*—What are you doing? Staying up all night? In the cold? Like a moth?

Henrietta   What is wrong with you this morning, Miss Jumpy.

Margaret   I'm not jumpy—

Henrietta   I'm not a moth—

Margaret   Why are we still outside?!

Henrietta   *Because.* They have a job for me at Harvard. At the Observatory. Actual astronomy.

Margaret   Since when were you even looking for a job.

Henrietta   Since they offered. Margie, this is an extraordinary thing. They need mathematicians and they asked me specifically—

Margaret   Harvard asked *you*?

Henrietta   Yes and please don't hold back your tone of shock.

Margaret   This is shocking—I am shocked.

Henrietta   And I'm . . . leaving. I'm taking the job and I'm leaving. (*Holding out a letter. Beat.*)

Margaret   You've always been leaving.

Henrietta   Next week.

Margaret   Next . . .? Oh Henri. Now wait. We need to discuss this as a family.

Henrietta   Margie, this could be my best life and it's right in front of me.

Margaret   And I'm still freezing. (*Turns to go.*)

Henrietta   Margie, talk to me—

Margaret   Fine—yes—I know that we were never going to be grow-old-next-to-each-other kind of sisters, and the way you drive me crazy makes that for the best—but—Henrietta this is extreme.

Henrietta   Exactly. Come with me. (*Small pause.*)

Margaret   Oh, Henri, please.

Henrietta   Both of us. Come on.

Margaret   What are you talking about? That's absurd.

Henrietta   Only a little! You're the only person who understands me, and you're always up for an adventure, and I *do* want to get old and scrappy with you.

Margaret   I did not say scrappy.

Henrietta   You should come with me and fire up your heart!

Margaret   What are you talking about?

Henrietta   The edge of the wide world!

Margaret   It's Boston.

Henrietta   A blaze of learning!

Margaret   A *blaze*?

Henrietta   A blaze! And Radcliffe is nearby and they have a music school.

Margaret   Henri. Slow down.

Henrietta   You don't have to stay here. You can be happy, you can loose yourself—

Margaret   *Loose* my—? No. Stop. Do not start wearing bloomers.

Henrietta   Margie.

Margaret   *Wait.* There are women these days, and they wear pants, and it's ridiculous. Now I have to play the hymns for the service that started ten minutes ago, and thank you, sister, my fingers are numb.

Henrietta   *I need you to convince Daddy to give me my dowry.*

(*This stops* **Margie** *cold.*) I'm serious. Very. Please talk to him.

Margaret   *Why do I get all the yelling jobs?*

Henrietta   You're so good at it.

Margaret   This is your future, Henrietta. You know for certain that you'll never marry, you'll never fall in love—people do that. Uncoordinated, unplanned emotion—Just the word "spinster," Henrietta, please.

Henrietta   I need to start my life . . . with Daddy's money.

Margaret   Next the bloomers. Whiskey with suffragettes.

Henrietta   I'm not a cowboy.

Margaret   You know what I'm talking about.

Henrietta   I'm talking about astronomy. You keep talking about terrible pants.

Margaret   *It starts with pants.* It's a changing world. And some things should be sacred. And I'm not saying you shouldn't go—but I worry. It's far away, that place, and it's crowded, and you're still here in my sight and I worry.

Henrietta   I'll be doing math. Don't worry.

Margaret   Why not stay here and live with us and . . . teach?

Henrietta   No.

Margaret   Like every other girl with your temperament.

Henrietta   *I like my temperament* and I don't want it stuffed in a schoolhouse. I have questions, I have fundamental problems with the state of human knowledge! Who are we, why are we—where are we?!

Margaret   Wisconsin.

Henrietta   In the universe!

Margaret   Still Wisconsin.

Henrietta   *Margie*, I am not just curious I am charged and poised and you *know* that I'll just get more and more annoying until I go—You know this—You know this.

Margie *knows this. Pause.*

Margaret   One day there will be a word for you. Just—for me, for our father, who will only after much snorting approve of this—when you go? Take a Bible.

Henrietta   I think Harvard has those.

Margaret   You know what I mean. We look in the same direction—(*Points up.*) but our understanding is . . . distinct.

Henrietta   I love you. It's too cold for God.

Margaret   That's why we keep Him inside.

Henrietta   Margie, come with me.

Margaret   *I can't.*

Henrietta   Why not?

Margaret   Because Father counts on me, and if you leave I can't leave, and I don't want to leave and . . . Samuel proposed. (*Moment.*)

Henrietta   What.

Margaret   To marry.

Henrietta   Who?

Margaret   Henri.

Henrietta   I mean, "when."

Margaret   This morning, thank you for noticing.

Henrietta   Aha, jumpy.

Margaret   Yes. Other people's lives are also in progress.

Henrietta   Is he . . .?

Margaret   Inside looking very attentive until the service ends.

And I answer.

Henrietta   What's your answer?

Margaret   Of course I will.

Henrietta   To Samuel?

Margaret   Well I wanted to talk to you first.

Henrietta   You'd leave me for Samuel?

Margaret   You just said you're leaving me!

Henrietta   Not for Samuel!

Margaret   He is very good and . . . (*Small pause.*)

Henrietta   Yes. He is.

Margaret   He is. And I'm happy.

Henrietta   Then . . . I am too. (*They hug—marriage! Yay!*) Come with me.

Margaret   Just . . . come back. (*Squeezes* **Henri***'s hand and runs inside.*)

Henrietta   And so. I go. (*Preps herself as . . . The Harvard Observatory falls into place around her . . . We hear* **Margaret** *singing "For the Beauty of the Earth."*)

Margaret

> *For the beauty of the Earth,*
> *For the glory of the skies;*
> *For the love which from our birth,*
> *Over and around us lies;*
>
> *Lord of all, to Thee we raise*
> *This, our hymn of grateful praise.*

Margaret *fades away. Transition . . .*

Scene Two

Henrietta *stands in the vacant room of the Harvard Observatory—A small wooden room like an attic—desks, file drawers, and boxes fill the room.*

Peter—*unintentionally handsome, a bit bumbling—enters briskly, a pencil behind his ear, charts, papers.*

Henrietta   Excuse me, is this the Observatory office?

Peter   Oh—yes—Hello. You must be my ten o'clock. Miss Leavitt. You are Miss Leavitt?

Henrietta   I am. Henrietta Leavitt and I'm thrilled to—

Peter   Good. We'll make this quick. It's not that complicated.

Henrietta   May I just say how pleased I am to meet you,

Dr. Pickering. I am so honored—

Peter   No.

Henrietta   I'm not?

Peter   *I'm* not.

Henrietta   You're not Dr. Pickering?

Peter   I am.

Henrietta   You *are* Dr. Pickering?

Peter   So sorry. My name is Peter Shaw. I work for Pickering.

Henrietta   Oh. Lovely. Mr. Shaw. Nice to meet you. Colleagues then.

Peter *snorts.*

Peter   You actually work *for* me. And I work for him. So.

Henrietta   So we're still colleagues it would seem.

Peter   Technically yes but—

Henrietta   And here I thought Harvard was such a technical place.

Peter   No, I just mean that—I mean of course it is it's just—You see I'm Dr. Pickering's apprentice—Junior Fellow in Astronomical Research, summa cum laude, Mathematics *and* Physics.

Henrietta   And if you spot me I'll swoon.

Peter   What?

Henrietta   It's a technical term. Now, Mr. Shaw I've come a long way and I'm quite anxious to get started. (*He's staring a bit too long at her.*) May I?

Peter   Hm?

Henrietta   Get started. Or just point me to the telescope and

I'll be fine.

Peter   The telescope?

Henrietta (*looking out a window*)   Is that it? The Great Refractor.

Peter   Yes, but—

Henrietta   One of the largest in the world.

Peter   I am very aware. Quite a point of pride for us. But. *This* is the workroom for you girls . . . to work. In here.

Henrietta   A short orientation then.

Peter   We bring the Girls' Department photographic plates from the telescope—latest technology.

Henrietta   Yes. Good. Question. Why all women?

Peter   Oh. This is great. Pickering got fed up with the boys he was sent and said—really said this—that his housekeeper could do better, so he hired her. And she did better. Now it's quite a women's . . . world . . . up here.

Henrietta   I was expecting the usual world.

Peter   Oh I make regular rounds.

Henrietta   Rounds?

Peter   I come around.

Henrietta   To what end?

Peter (*snort-laughs*)   Evaluation. Of course.

Henrietta   Mr. Shaw, I also graduated summa cum laude, from Radcliffe, which is basically Harvard in skirts and lucky for us the universe doesn't much care what you wear, so my expertise and yours might just complement each other's if we can get past this encroachingly unpleasant first impression. (*Re: her hearing-aid.*) Or I could take this out, and you could keep . . . orienting.

Peter   Well. You'll fit right in the harem.

Henrietta   The WHAT?

Peter   Oh—no—nono—it's just a name—a joke—"Pickering's harem." It's a compliment.

Henrietta   If you're a concubine.

Peter   He picks the best is what we mean. We could just call you that—"Pickering's Best." "Pickering's Picks"—That's got a ring. (*Glances quickly at her hand—*) You don't.

Henrietta *looks too, hides her hand. Pause. Awkward.*

Henrietta   I was supposed to meet Dr. Pickering at ten.

Peter   Yes. Yes. And he sends his warmest welcome through me. He was detained. More important—not "important," *pressing*.

More pressing matters. I'll show you around.

Henrietta   I'll come back.

Peter   There's no need for that.

Henrietta   I'd prefer to speak directly to the Head of the Department.

Peter   Miss Leavitt—

Henrietta   Mr. Shaw. I don't mean to be brisk—maybe a little if that would drive home the point that I'm *finally* here. After a long time not being anywhere. And I'd really like to get started, and all you've thus far conveyed is that I'm in some kind of *math harem* waiting to be *picked*—and that doesn't sound right at *all*.

Peter   I am so sorry. And Dr. Pickering is thrilled to have you here. And I'd get in a lot of trouble with him if I ran you off on your first day. So. Please stay. We'd very much like you to stay. (*Pause.*)

Henrietta   You don't sound very excited about all this work.

Peter   Well, it is *work*.

Henrietta   It's not your—how best to make you uncomfortable—*passion*?

Peter   That's a bit excessive for physics.

Henrietta   Is it? I find the very notion of this work to be a thrill—a bracing excitement. And it's just something you *do*?

Peter   Well I enjoy the work, of course I do. It's interesting and reasoned and sound and my father pulled a lot of strings to—WhyDidYouSay"Passion"?

Henrietta   Unlike for some people, following this curiosity was not easy. I had to insist, which requires a dedicated desire unmatched by reason, which is called passion. You should try it. (*Tiny pause.*)

Peter (*blurting this out*)   I sing. Gilbert and Sullivan—I wanted to be an actor—Dad thought not—But—I still sing—On occasion—With enthusiasm. Does that count?

Henrietta   Technically. (*Slightly embarrassed, he picks up a glass star plate. Back to orienting.*)

Peter   Well. Here you go. One of the plates you'll be working with. A slice of heaven.

Henrietta   Beautiful. I should take one to my father.

Peter   *Excuse me.*

Henrietta   He's a pastor.

Peter   These never leave the premises.

Henrietta   You said "heaven," I was joking.

Peter   Harvard property—

Henrietta   Of course—

Peter   Very expensive—

Henrietta   And if you don't mention the attempted larceny and I won't mention the musicals. (*She extends her hand, he takes it, shakes it.*)

Peter   You're . . . curious.

Henrietta   In every way. (*A bustle outside—women coming back from break.*)

Peter   Oh, they're back. Watch out for Miss Fleming—Scottish stock. Swift and angry.

Henrietta   Oh my.

Peter   And Miss Cannon—don't get in her way, her name is Dickensian.

Henrietta   But I'd like to ask about—

Peter   What else can I tell you—Penmanship—key. Delicacy with the plates, they crack.

Henrietta   Mr. Shaw—

Peter   Twenty-five cents an hour.

Henrietta   I would love a chance to pursue—

Peter   It's good money for women's work.

Henrietta   It's volunteering.

Peter   What are you asking, Miss Leavitt?

Annie *and* **Williamina** *enter, unnoticed.*

Henrietta   That I might more fully engage in the ideas here?

Peter   Other than doing the work you've been hired to do?

Henrietta   Other than, pardon me, *do your math*. Now when may I use the telescope?

Peter (*flustered, not dismissive*)   Well. You can't.

Henrietta *is too shocked to answer.* **Annie** *clears her throat.*

Annie   I'll take over, Mr. Shaw.

Peter   Yes—very good—Started to brief her.

Williamina   Then I'd be brief.

Peter   Yes—well—Good day, ladies. (*To* **Henrietta**.) I'll see you . . . around. (*He leaves. They look at* **Henrietta**.)

Williamina   Welcome, Miss Leavitt.

Henrietta   Thank you. Hello. I was so excited to be here that I fear I might've scared him.

Williamina   Easy to do. Williamina Fleming. I like you.

Henrietta   Thank you.

Annie   Annie Cannon. I haven't decided.

Henrietta   Oh. Miss Cannon. I know that I probably shouldn't have gone on like that with him.

Annie   No you shouldn't.

Henrietta   And I'm sorry if I made a poor impression—

Annie   Harvard Observatory is the pinnacle of the astronomical community. The academic world looks to us.

Henrietta   To "bookkeep the stars," if you talk to Mr. Shaw.

Annie   Which is why we try not to talk to Mr. Shaw. We are mapping the sky, Miss Leavitt. If doing what has never been done before sounds unimportant to you, uninspired? I'd leave before you are asked to. Otherwise, show some respect.

Henrietta   Of course. And I would never—

Annie   Respect is a *quiet* thing, Miss Leavitt. Practice this.

Henrietta   Yes, Miss Cannon.

Annie   Practice now.

Henrietta *nods. Pause.* **Will** *holds up one of the photographic star plates.*

Williamina   Let me show you what we do here, Miss Leavitt. This is the latest technology. A photograph of the stars. And we chart every point of light on every one.

Annie   Every single one.

Williamina   Every scattered sneeze of them.

Annie   *Will*, don't be crude

Williamina   They look like ground pepper till you get the hang of it.

Annie   Williamina is our best photometer, from whom you'll learn much if she doesn't get herself fired.

Williamina *smiles,* **Annie** *glares.*

Williamina   I used to be her boss.

Annie   You still *are*. We share leadership of this department—

Williamina   She outdid me with those letters.

Annie   I did no such thing—

Williamina   The star classifications were her idea.

Annie   A *collective* effort, I assure you.

Henrietta   Star classifications? That's your work?

Williamina   Oh yes indeed, the sky was a riot until Miss Cannon coded it. *I* wanted to give every star a number based on colour—but *she* insisted on labeling stars with *letters* based on *temperature*—

Annie   Ladies—

Williamina	**Henrietta**
OBAFGKM.	OBAFGKM—
Yes.	

Henrietta   You created a . . . standard, Miss Cannon. My goodness. I'm so honored. I'm sure you'd laugh, but my professors made us memorize your letters using this ridiculous phrase—

Williamina   She also made up that ridiculous phrase.

Annie   But I didn't mean for it to find its way into textbooks.

Henrietta   "Oh Be A Fine Girl, Kiss Me." You did that too?

Williamina   She had a muse.

Annie   *Miss Fleming.*

Williamina   She thought it would be best for the boys.

That's all they think about anyway.

Annie   Let's get back to work please.

Williamina (*to* **Henrietta**—*whispering*)   Because she's the boss.

Annie   *I wouldn't have to be if you'd take this seriously, which is a ridiculous request of a woman who started the department.* (*To* **Henrietta**.) You know Will was the first woman to ever hold the title "curator" in astronomy? And the Draper Catalogue is *all* her work—She discovered stars, and nebulae, novae—She's the reason that I'm here, and even if she has far too much fun I am the first to admit that she is fundamental to this institution.

Williamina (*to* **Henrietta**)   And that, new friend, is how you introduce yourself without boasting.

Annie   I quit.

Williamina (*to* **Annie**)   "Oh Be A Fine Grandma."

Henrietta   It's a great phrase.

Annie   We have WORK. TO DO. And Dr. Pickering is a very particular man.

Williamina   He calls us his *harem*.

Annie   He's joking.

Williamina   He's not. He measures a project in "girl hours."

Annie   He's joking.

Williamina   He's not. Sometimes "kilo-girl hours."

Annie   The point is, we're busy because we're essential.

Williamina   We're the dirt.

Annie *glares. Correcting . . .*

From which mighty oaks grow.

Henrietta   And do we have a title of some sort?

Williamina   We do indeed. Congratulations, Miss Leavitt, you are now a computer.

Henrietta   What's a computer?

Annie   One who computes.

Williamina   Notate the plates, transfer the data, input the data, process, record, next star.

Henrietta   And the plates. How do I read them?

Williamina   Star Spanking.

Annie *reveals a wire-and-glass paddle like a small fly-swatter.* **Annie** *places the spanker over the plate.*

Annie   Align the spanker with a star. The matching dot indicates how bright that star is. Record magnitude, position, date, and repeat until you fill up the logbook.

Williamina   Or go slightly crazy.

Henrietta   And what about working on our own ideas?

Using the telescope for our own work?

Annie   You don't.

Henrietta   Oh. But I thought this was—?

Annie   We collect, report, and maintain the largest stellar archive in the world. And we resist the temptation to analyze it.

Henrietta   But you just said how much you discovered here—both of you.

Williamina   Resisting doesn't always work.

Annie   Can you do this job, Miss Leavitt?

Henrietta   Of course I can.

Annie   I need the consistent, not the creative.

Williamina   She can do it, Annie. She understands.

Annie   Good. Please show Miss Leavitt to her station.

Williamina   Will do, Mr. President.

Annie   You make me crazy and you know you make me crazy.

Williamina   Balance of power, darling.

(**Annie** *exits.*) Alright, you. More questions?

Henrietta   Is she mean or just to me?

Williamina   Oh nono. She's just meticulous. And blunt.

And she sings.

Henrietta   Sings what?

Williamina   Like a crow, but still. Shows her humanity—atonal though it may be. You want her on your side. She's always on the right one.

Henrietta   Good. Because I have some pressing issues with . . . science.

Williamina   The whole of it?

Henrietta   A lot of it. As far as I can tell we do not appear to know where we are. Astronomically. Which is shocking. This is the modern age. We've been looking *up* for millennia and we don't know how far away those stars are? We don't know if the Milky Way is the universe? That's just unacceptable.

Williamina   You're fun. But here's some perspective. I was Pickering's housekeeper before he brought me here. So we're a lot of things, but at present we are cleaning up the universe for the men. And making fun of them behind their backs. It's worked for centuries.

Annie *enters with more plates.*

Annie   Working isn't talking.

Here we like to say: **Williamina**

The sky's the limit.   The sky's the limit.

Williamina   And there's so damn much of it.

Annie   And so we work. (*She deposits the plates. The women sit down at their desks and work. As they label each star—a single bright star pops into being in their spare sky, accompanied by a musical note. Rote.*) Star Name—

Henrietta   Star Name—

Williamina   Star Name—

Henrietta   Alpha Leonis 3982.

Annie   Beta Orionis 1713.

Williamina   Ninety-five degrees declination.

Annie   Seventy-three degrees—

Henrietta   Fifty degrees.

Williamina   Spectral Class B.

Annie   Spectral Class B.

Henrietta *takes out her hearing device—The sound of the room softens, dulls.* **Henrietta** *and* **Margaret** *are normal volume.*

Williamina   Magnitude: one-point-two-five.

Annie   Magnitude: point-six-five.

Margaret *appears in a letter.*

Margaret   Henrietta! We miss you.

Henrietta   Star Name—

Margaret   And I can't stand the conversation since you left.

Henrietta   Alpha Andromedae 15.

Margaret   Everyone is so sensible.

Henrietta   Eighty degrees declination.

Margaret   Please write back.

Henrietta   Uh-huh. Thirty-three right ascension.

Peter *enters.*

Peter   Morning, ladies.

Williamina   Correct on both counts, Mr. Shaw.

Annie   Good morning, Mr. Shaw. Back again?

Williamina   And so soon.

Peter   Just passing by—Dropping these off—Picking these up.

Henrietta   Spectral Class A.

Peter   Hello, Miss Leavitt.

Henrietta   Magnitude: two-point—What? Oh. Hello, Mr. Shaw. How are you today?

Peter   Good . . . (*Lovely, awkward pause, during which he finds nothing else to say, except.*) Bye. (*He leaves quickly, embarrassed again.*)

Henrietta   He's an odd one.

Williamina   And getting odder.

Annie   Star Name—

Henrietta   Star Name—

Williamina   Star Name—(*Time is passing as the sky fills up in swatches. Another letter.*)

Margaret   Henri! Wish you'd be here for Thanksgiving. Daddy's planning a marvelous sermon on *family*.

Henrietta   Uh-huh. Magnitude: two-point-eight.

Margaret   You missed the news . . .

Henrietta   Star Name.

Margaret   I'm pregnant!

Henrietta (*finally stopping*)   Oh Margie. Oh my goodness.

Margaret   I think Daddy is happier that I am. And think of it, you're going to be an aunt.

Henrietta   I'm going to be an aunt. And you. A mother? Congratulations, Margie, that's such

(**Annie** *coughs at* **Henrietta. Henrietta** *hides the letter.*) Star Name: Alpha Cygnus. Spectral Class A. (*Time is passing as the sky fills up in swatches.* **Peter** *enters again . . .*)

Peter   Hellohello. Here I come. Coming around.

Williamina   A lot nowadays.

Henrietta (*putting in her hearing-aid*)   What's going on?

Peter   Just want to make sure she's—everyone's oriented.

Williamina   It's been half a year now. I think she can find the bathroom.

Henrietta   Am I doing something wrong, Mr. Shaw?

Peter   Nono. Of course not. I'm just . . . curious.

Williamina   Uh-huh.

Peter   About the . . . data.

Williamina (*to* **Annie**)   Oh yes, he's dreaming about the "data."

Annie   We're a bit busy today, Mr. Shaw. Unless you have a message for the room?

Peter   Oh—yes—Dr. Pickering and I wanted Miss Leavitt's opinion on something of great interest. If I may steal a moment.

Annie   You may borrow Miss Leavitt, not steal her.

Peter   Of course. Just an expression.

Williamina   Was it?

Henrietta   I'm so glad Dr. Pickering values my opinion. I didn't know he noticed me at all.

Peter   He did. And does. (*He holds a star plate and points to a spot, but this is obviously just a reason to get close to her.*) I was—*We* were wondering if you could explain what sort of phenomena this might be? I haven't seen anything like it on the other plates and thought of you—*that you* might offer some clarity. (*She looks. She knows.*)

Henrietta   Well, Mr. Shaw. That's definitely a scratch.

Peter   Is it?

Henrietta   I'm guessing someone's pocketwatch or perhaps a belt buckle?

Peter   A scratch.

Williamina   We can name it after you if you'd like?

Peter   No need. Glad that's cleared up. Time to go.

Annie   Yes indeed.

Henrietta (*something in her warms to him*)   Thank you. For asking, Mr. Shaw. We're always here if you need us.

Peter *deeply appreciates* **Henrietta** *in this moment. He smiles and leaves just as— Time is passing as the sky fills up in swatches. Another letter.*

Margaret   Henrietta.

Annie   Thirty-two degrees.

Margaret   Will we see you for Easter?

Williamina   Magnitude: six-point-two.

Margaret   Daddy's asking for you,

Henrietta   Spectral Class B.

Margaret   And I'd love to have you home—

Henrietta   Forty-five—

Margaret   Henrietta, it's—

Henrietta   Magnitude—

Margaret   *Henrietta.*

Henrietta   What? Yes. What?

Margaret   I have a son.

Henrietta   Oh. Oh, Margie.

Margaret   His name is Michael.

Henrietta   You have a son.

Margaret   You should meet him.

Henrietta   I should—I *will*—How did this happen already?

Margaret   It's April.

Henrietta   Oh my. Is it? It is.

Margaret   Henrietta, let me tell you, babies are remarkable.

Henrietta   I'm sure but I'm sorry—I'm just so busy.

Margaret   Too busy for me?

Henrietta   Too busy for *me* at the moment.

Margaret   Can't you come home?

Henrietta   There are a lot of stars out there.

Margaret   But you'd be so proud. I've found my calling!

Henrietta   Uh-huh.

Margaret   I will compose!

Henrietta   Music? How nice.

Margaret   When the baby's down and everything's clean it's just me and the piano.

Henrietta   That's great.

Margaret   It's not a hobby.

Henrietta   I have to work.

Margaret   It's very exciting.

Henrietta   It is. And I'm sorry I can't come home and I'm sure I'm letting you down, but I've got this work, and you've got yours, and I can't play house with you right now.

Margaret   I don't like this mood.

Henrietta   I promise I'll come home.

Margaret   *You won't.* You're hardening in some urban office and it's making you flinty.

Henrietta   Margie, stop.

Margaret   I know that there's more to life than that.

Henrietta   Than nature?

Margaret   Than math. There's more out there—

Henrietta   *Then why do you stay so close to home?* Why do you excel at every ordinary thing and then chastise *me* about what else is "out there." I specialize in what's "out there"—and let me tell you that "out there" does not happen *on a farm.* (*Beat.*)

Margaret (*cold to her*)   Check the post. Father sent a book.

Henrietta   Oh no. A Bible?

Margaret   If it were a Bible I would've said "Bible"—

It's a book.

Henrietta   On what?

Annie   Miss Leavitt?

Margaret   I don't know, Henrietta. I've got this life, you've got yours.

Margaret *vanishes.* **Peter** *reenters, approaches* **Henrietta**—*total, sweetheart nervous.*

Peter   Round and round we go.

Annie   Mr. Shaw.

Peter   Ladies of the Logbook.

Annie   By God you'd better have a supernova on those plates.

Williamina (*to* **Henrietta** *softly*)   You know he's here for you.

Henrietta (*to* **Will**)   *What.*

Peter   Nothing that exciting. I was just hoping to speak to Miss Leavitt.

Henrietta (*to* **Will**)   Mr. Shaw?

Peter   The work she's—*you're all* doing is just—well I find it *bracing.*

Annie   And I find it hard to work with such interruptions, if you don't mind—

Peter (*to* **Annie**)   I'm sorry, I can come back later—

Annie	**Williamina**
NO.	NO.

Peter   On my rounds.

Annie (*exploding*)   MR. SHAW. There is an inverse relationship between time lost on your rounds and the life of my overqualified staff, any one of whom you may speak to *after* work, so come in or stay out but you *must have reason to be here or cease. Coming. Around.* (*Pause.* **Peter** *looks to* **Henrietta**, *then back to* **Annie**.)

Peter (*breath, cheerily*)   See you tomorrow. (*Smiles at* **Henrietta**, *then leaves.*)

Annie   Sweet boy—I'm going to shoot him.

Williamina (*to* **Henrietta**)   You see what I mean about him. He never thought we were "bracing" before.

Henrietta   Can we talk about *anything* else, please. Miss Cannon, help.

Williamina   Just so we're all clear: *He fancies you.*

Henrietta   I don't care. I barely know him. I *don't* know him.

We just—we work. He comes around.

Williamina   Like a hungry cat.

Henrietta   Who's the cat? Am I the cat?

Annie   *You're* not the cat.

Henrietta   I better not be. I mean, my goodness, I wouldn't even know where to begin.

Williamina   He'd be happy to help you with that.

Annie   Work, ladies.

Williamina   I don't know, I kinda like him. He wouldn't be bad to marry.

Henrietta   Then *you* marry him.

Williamina (*to* **Annie**)   Oh, he's not my type.

Henrietta   Whomever's type he is, I couldn't work if I were married, and that is not an option, so my husband would have to be quite the advanced creature to handle that and I'm not sure our Mr. Shaw fits that bill.

Annie   Agreed.

Henrietta (*lost in her thoughts*)   Although I do admire his persistence. And gait. He has a nice gait.

Williamina   Meow meow.

Annie (*to* **Will**)   *Would you heel.*

Henrietta (*snapping out of it*)   The point is that, like you, my work is my life. And that's just fine with me. And excuse me for saying this Miss Cannon, but—these Mr. Shaws, they all come around, they need this work, they need *you*. Why don't you demand a faculty position?

Annie   Because I don't need a title to do the work.

Henrietta   But the boys need your work to keep their titles.

And eventually one of us *has* to be a . . . what was it?

Williamina   Mighty oak.

Henrietta   Mighty oak! You deserve it.

Annie   Neither of you are getting a raise and that's final.

Henrietta   I don't want a raise.

Williamina   I do.

Henrietta   I want a model. Miss Cannon, if they won't give *you* what you deserve, they're never going to give it to any of us.

Annie   What do you want them to give you?

Henrietta   A *chance*. To show them what we can do.

Annie   Which means what?

Henrietta (*breath*)   I'm seeing things.

Annie   Which *means what*?

Henrietta   I'm spotting more and more of the blinking stars, the variables? I'm working on the Small Magellanic Clouds and I'm tracking these stars that pulse.

Annie   Cepheid stars?

Henrietta   I think so. Some of them blink once a week, some take a month.

Annie   The fact that Cepheids pulse is not new.

Henrietta   I know. It's the amount of them. The large amount I'm finding.

Annie   Actually they're quite rare to find.

Henrietta   Not if you're doing it right. (*She looks for approval.*)

Annie   Continue.

Henrietta   I put together a simple comparative that lets me analyze the plates *quickly*. The *same* star field at different times—and you can see that some of the stars are much brighter. And I'm seeing them in most of the plates. Now if these are true Cepheids, and if there're as many of them as I'm starting to see, it could be a big clue.

Annie   To what?

Henrietta   I don't know. But it's got to be important.

Annie   No it doesn't.

Henrietta   But my instincts are telling me that—

Annie   Dr. Pickering does not pay for those instincts.

Henrietta   He doesn't really pay me at all.

Annie   Then do the work you're assigned or don't work.

Williamina *throws a paper ball at* **Annie**. **Annie** *concedes, turns back to* **Henrietta**.

Annie   You may, however, stay *after* hours if you'd like, Miss Leavitt.

Henrietta   What.

Annie   If you're quiet.

Henrietta   *Really? REALLY?!*

Annie   Only rule was "quiet."

Henrietta   Understood. Thank you. (*She does a little silent cheer.* **Annie** *thinks this is stupid and walks past* **Williamina**—*who grabs her and kisses her cheek.* **Annie** *exits.* **Williamina** *too.* **Margaret** *appears in a letter. Still annoyed.*)

Margaret   Henrietta, Daddy was wondering if you'd received the book. Or if you'll come home for Christmas? Write back.

Henrietta (*in a letter light*)   Dear, Margie. Sorry we fought. Here's a book for Michael from his favorite aunt. Could you send sweaters? Love, H.

Margaret *gives up, folds some sweaters during the transition . . .*

Margaret (*singing*)

> *For the joy of human love,*
> *Brother, sister, parent, child . . .*
> *Friends on earth and friends above . . .*
> *For all gentle thoughts and mild.*
>
> *Lord of all to Thee we raise*
> *This our hymn of grateful praise . . .*

Scene Three

Morning. **Henrietta** *is asleep at her desk. About 1905.* **Peter** *and* **Williamina** *enter.*

Peter   Oh my. Is she—?

Williamina   Dusting. *Aren't you Miss Leavitt?* (**Will** *pokes* **Henrietta** *awake; she grabs her hearing-aid.*)

Henrietta   What. Yes. Sorry. Up.

Peter   Miss Leavitt, are you ill?

Henrietta   Nope. Just. Here. Hello.

Peter   Is she under an influence?

Henrietta   Ha. That would be—

Williamina   Ridiculous.

Henrietta Delightful, but no.

Peter You slept here?

Henrietta Nono—very little sleeping. These stars, the Cepheids?
The pulsating ones?

Peter I know what they are.

Henrietta There's a shocking amount in the Magellanic Clouds. I've become quite intimate with the Magellanic Clouds.

Peter I'll let the boys know we'll need to add a few to the register.

Henrietta Two hundred. (*Pause.*)

Peter Two—?

Henrietta Hundred.

Peter Last—?

Henrietta Night. Yes.

Peter Oh. (*Pause.*)

Henrietta So.

Peter *and* **Henrietta** *are looking at each other. She breaks.*

Henrietta Why don't I make a habit of this.

Peter Why don't you.

Henrietta I'm going to take a nap.

Williamina Why don't you. (*Gives a thumbs up.* **Henrietta** *smiles, starts to exit.*)

Peter Very good work, Miss Leavitt. It's really very good.

Henrietta (*smiles at him*)   Thank you. (*She exits one way,* **Peter** *exits another.* **Annie** *enters—***Williamina** *preemptively shushes her.*)

Annie Where on earth is she going?

Williamina She's taking a nap in the file room. And we'll let her.

Annie She *has* an apartment?

Williamina You'll want to hear what she's finding.

Annie Then wake her up.

Peter *reenters, flustered, excited, confused.*

Peter (*an announcement*)   There is a lot. Going on. In the world. (*Pause.*)

Williamina Uh-huh.

Peter We are in an age of defiance—I mean defying and upturning it all—all the ideas we held, all the things we knew for certain. Fundamentals even. Distance, light, time—

Williamina   You read that paper, didn't you.

Peter   You've read it?

Annie   Relativity.

Peter   Relativity! It's impossible. Except that it isn't. Time is elastic, space is part of time. It's ridiculous.

Williamina   Doesn't make it wrong.

Peter   Nonono. The idea that there could be galaxies as big as ours? *Outside* of ours? That the universe is *that* large? No!

Annie   The theory seems to suggest it.

Peter   But it makes it all undone, untethered. In the history of human thought there was a steady progression of ideas—

Williamina   Unless you're Catholic.

Peter   Standing on the shoulders of giants is what I mean.

Williamina   I dunno, there's a lot of stupid giants.

Peter   But we're *modern*. The modern age—building up, building on top of other stately ideas—

Williamina   Sensible!

Peter   *Yes.*

Williamina (*totally kidding*)   Physics was about wrapped up!

Peter   *Yes.*

Williamina   But then that fuzzyheaded man blew up your stately foundation.

Peter   You're not supposed to do that to Isaac Newton.

Will *makes the sound of Einstein blowing up Newton.*

Peter   What do we grasp?

And how? And until what point when it all shifts anyway?

Annie   I'm not sure what you're looking to hear, Mr. Shaw.

Peter (*re:* **Henrietta**)   She found something—*is* finding—uncovering, discovering—and I . . . don't know what that's like. Which makes me think I'm not very good at this. And things might just be too . . . strange.

Williamina   You don't usually talk this much when you come up here.

Peter   I don't? I do. Rounds. I come around.

Williamina   Oh yes, the life affirming *rounds*.

Peter   I'm just doing my job. Trying to.

Williamina   And you know why she's got something? Because she's *not just* doing hers. Because she knows she's not getting anything handed to her except the corner of someone else's chance. Because we can't use that apparently hyper-sexed telescope you boys get to, but the mind is sexless and so is the sky—Are you made nervous by how many times I've said the word *sex*?

Peter   Somewhat.

Williamina   Oh good.

Peter   Just. I admire . . . what you all do. It's . . . precision.

Annie   Thank you.

Peter *leaves.* **Henrietta** *walks in grinning—she heard it all.*

Henrietta   What. Was that?

Williamina   Wonder meeting competence.

Annie   You see why we keep him around.

Williamina   Is it wrong that I like him a wee bit more because of that? 'Cause I quite enjoyed that little fluster. Speaking of, has he proposed yet?

Henrietta   What? *What?*

Annie   Williamina.

Henrietta   To me? No. What? No.

Williamina   He always seems like he's going to.

Annie   That face he makes.

Williamina   Pinchy.

Henrietta   Pinchy? Who's pinchy? No. We've talked about this. Marry? You're not married. You're not married. Nobody's married.

Why is this an issue.

Annie   It's not an issue.

Williamina   Not unless you admit it, prove me right, and live happily ever after.

Henrietta   Oh God.

Annie (*to* **Henrietta**)   Our only power is ignoring her.

Williamina   I'm not laughing at you. I'm not. Love makes us all look a bit stupid.

Annie   Pinchy.

Henrietta   *Is pinchy good or bad?*

Annie   It's all terribly relative.

Annie *and* **Will** *burst into laughter.* **Henrietta** *gets up to go.*

Williamina   Oh Henrietta. It's just life. Ridiculous and miraculous and often not funny at all. But better when you're laughing. Especially husbands.

Annie   She had one.

Henrietta　You did?

Williamina　I did. Abandoned me as soon as we docked in Boston. I was twenty-one, pregnant, poor, and Scottish. So I laughed. Found my way to Dr. Pickering, worked his house as a maid, he brought me here, and here I sit. So I laugh, because that seemed to work.

Peter *enters, stops—All three ladies are staring at him. He tries to understand—starts to say something—decides it's best to just back away slowly . . .* **Peter** *exits.*
Henrietta *keeps staring.*

Williamina　Time to breathe.

Henrietta *lets out a held breath. Transition . . .*

Scene Four

Henrietta *is working alone at night, no hearing-aid.* **Annie** *enters quietly;* **Henrietta** *doesn't notice.* **Henrietta** *stops looking down at her pages and cries.*

Annie *tries to leave but bumps into a desk.* **Henrietta** *turns, scrambles for her hearing-aid.*

Henrietta　Miss Cannon. I'm so sorry.

Annie　Nono. I'm sorry.

Henrietta　I take it out when I work.

Annie　Of course. Carry on. Forgot my gloves.

Henrietta　Oh no, I was leaving.

Annie　No, I'm leaving. I just came for my hat.

Henrietta　Your gloves.

Annie　My gloves. (*Small pause.*)

Henrietta　Please don't think I sit here all night crying.

Annie　May I *see* what you sit here all night doing?

Henrietta (*hands* **Annie** *her notebook.* **Annie** *reads. Nothing.*)　The Cepheids. Of course.

Annie　You certainly have a knack for finding them.

Henrietta　But I'm finding that *finding* them isn't really worth much if they don't mean anything. And right now they don't.

Annie　They might.

Henrietta　I'm going on two thousand of them. And I'm starting to think it's like counting grass. You can count it, but why?

Annie　I *do* know the feeling. Show me what you've found.

Henrietta (*showing the ledger.* **Annie** *keeps reading. Nothing.*)   The left side is a list of Cepheids arranged by fastest period of brightness. The middle column is their spectral class but I think I need to change it to luminosity because I'm not coming up with anything. There's no pattern.

Annie   No there's not.

Henrietta   I've wasted so much time on this.

Annie   Miss Leavitt—

Henrietta   I really thought I could sense something in the numbers. Really feel there was something important we weren't connecting, but no—

Annie   Miss Leavitt.

Henrietta   *Twelve* notebooks packed, staring at me, loose ends all loose and nothing to show and no meaning and nothing, *nothing* makes any damn sense.

Annie   Henrietta.

Henrietta   Excuse my language.

Annie   You're close. Keep working. Think about how you're thinking. It's in there.

Henrietta   Should I ask Dr. Pickering?

Annie   No.

Henrietta   Mr. Shaw.

Annie   Oh no. This one's yours.

Henrietta   Thank you.

Annie   Miss Leavitt, I think you're in the middle of it.

Henrietta   Of what?

Annie   That chance. (*She pulls out gloves from her coat pocket and puts them on.* **Annie** *leaves.* **Henrietta** *smiles, breathes. She takes out a spanker and does some kind of celebratory dance thing.* **Peter** *enters.*)

Henrietta   Oh my God.

Peter   Oh my God. Not to worry.

Henrietta   This is just—

Peter   Imposition, so sorry.

Henrietta   This is—

Peter   My fault completely.

Henrietta   This is *so* exciting! She's right, I push through it, charge through it, matter of time—I know the answer is there—I just keep going. Right? Yes! Hi. (*Lovely awkward pause.*)

Peter　Hello. I just came by for my . . . hat.

Henrietta　Oh.

Peter　My gloves—left my gloves—and I saw the light and I thought, "Well I wonder how all the spanking is going."

Henrietta　Might we all agree to another name for that?

Peter　I think that's for the best.

Henrietta　Mr. Shaw, I know I shouldn't be here this late.

Peter　Actually I'd prefer it—much prefer it if you called me by my given name. Peter. Would be—nicer, nice.

Henrietta　Oh. Henrietta.

Peter　Good. (*Takes his gloves out of his pocket.*) Found them. (*Starts to go but doesn't—*) Miss—Henrietta—I—I don't know anything about you really and—and that's a shame. So. Might I know something about you? Now. Would be nice.

Henrietta　Oh. I grew up in Lancaster, family in Wisconsin, my hearing's not great, and I used my dowry to get here, which is why I'm a bit zealous about all this.

Peter　Ah.

Henrietta　And I play the clarinet. Not well.

Peter　I play also. Also not well.

Henrietta　Then we could be terrible together! I mean—that's not what I mean. I have a habit of blurting.

Peter　And I have a Dachshund. Named Carl. Which is fun. (*He smiles, she smiles. He wants to say . . . but doesn't.*) Carl awaits.

Peter *leaves, forgetting his hat.* **Henrietta** *smiles. Picks up his hat. Flips it and puts it on her head.* **Peter** *returns.*

Peter　Sorry. Hat.

Henrietta *hands him the hat. He touches her hand.*

Peter　I think that . . . you might be quite . . . marvelous. I think that. Often. (*Silence. He leaves.*)

Henrietta　Oh that is not standard. (*She smiles.*)

Peter *enters again. This is an outpouring of pent-up romantic enthusiasm in nearly one breath.*

Peter　There's an ocean liner leaving tomorrow—You should be on it—I'll be on it—I'm saying come with me—to Europe—For a month—or two? You don't have to decide now—but close to now because the liner leaves tomorrow—I said that—Pack warmly—cold at night—We might stop in Spain—And there's dancing and lobster and water and moonlight and bobbing around and that's romantic—or sickening—Either way there'll be an eclipse. Which is fun.

Henrietta   I . . . oh my . . . yes, that sounds . . . very interesting.

Peter   Interesting?

Henrietta   Incredible.

Peter   Oh good.

Henrietta   If it weren't on a boat.

Peter   You don't like boats? I didn't think of that.

Henrietta   No, I just can't leave my work. I'm very close to something and—

Peter   The ladies can't manage?

Henrietta   Not *this* work, no. It's my findings and I've worked so hard and—

Peter   You don't have to leave it. I can pack them. You and me *and* work.

Henrietta   They crack.

Peter   So they'll be here when we get back.

Henrietta   I'm too close to leave—I'm so close.

Peter   But we could meet astronomers all over Europe. Talk about your ideas. See the world!

Henrietta   That sounds marvelous but why don't we just go to dinner?

Peter   Because you're always up here!

Henrietta   Then I can't go to Europe!

Peter   Henrietta.

Henrietta   Peter.

Peter   This is a rather large moment for me so I just want to be clear because it took me three years to get this far. So. Your mind and spirit . . . I quite adore . . . those things . . . about you. And I don't expect you to reciprocate immediately or at all, but I feared combusting if I didn't tell you that you've been the brightest object in my day since we met. And we work with stars. And I know I haven't been the most emotive suitor but I have been a thoughtful one, and I hope that counts for something. And I also hope I do not offend you by expressing how very deeply I . . . admire you.

Henrietta   Well. I think it's an accurate statement to say that I . . . approve.

Peter   You do? That's just tremendous. And a bit shocking, I thought I might have ruined it with that first impression. Or the second. Or this one.

Henrietta   Fortune favors the unashamed. But. My work is very important to me and if there is any resistance to that then you might reconsider your adoration promptly.

Peter   I couldn't reconsider if I tried. I know you and I know your work and . . . if you can't go with me, I'll stay. Because I cannot walk away from this.

Henrietta   What *is* this exactly?

Peter   Well it's—it's love right?

Henrietta   I don't know. Is it?

Peter   It's got to be. My heart's beating like a train. That's your fault.

Henrietta   *My* fault?! It's *your* fault.

Peter   Yes! See? Love!

Henrietta   How, God, *how* do you know that?

Peter   Comparative analysis. Before you: content. After you? Passionate, confident . . . idiot. Rounds? Please. An ocean liner? Just to be with you in the widest world. And finally I tell you. And finally you hear. And finally . . . (*Eyes connect.* **Peter** *takes her hands . . . As the Harvard Observatory falls away into . . . The deck of an ocean liner—night. Stars ablaze overhead. A band plays somewhere. He spins her into a dance . . . Suddenly—***Margaret** *appears in a telegram—*)

Margaret   Sister—stop. Come home—stop. Father stroke—stop.

Henrietta *stops. The stars go dark. The dream shatters. The Observatory—***Peter** *and* **Henrietta** *alone.*

Henrietta   Oh god. Peter, I'm sorry. I have to go.

Peter   Go? Where? What's wrong?

Henrietta   My family needs me. My father. Oh god.

Peter   I can help. I can come with you. Whatever you need.

Henrietta   My father is sick, my sister's alone.

Peter   I'm coming.

Henrietta   You don't need to do that.

Peter   I can help. I want to help.

Henrietta   Thank you and I'm sorry but I have to go home and you have to go to dinner in Europe.

Peter   No.

Henrietta   Go, Peter.

Peter   No.

Henrietta   I don't want you to miss this because of me. So go. And write me. And come back.

Peter   Alright. Yes. But—

Henrietta   Go. We go, we come back. And then we . . .

Peter   Continue the great experiment of our mutual compatibility.

Henrietta   And weather the storm of Williamina's laughter at our expense.

Peter   I imagine it will be thunderous.

Henrietta   I'm certain of it.

Peter   So. You leave for a while, and I leave for a while.

Henrietta   It's just space.

Peter   And time.

Henrietta   Which leaves us . . .?

Peter   Afar. But not apart.

Henrietta   Afar. But not apart. I like that.

Henrietta *kisses him sweetly on the cheek. Then* **Peter** *kisses her gorgeously, passionately. Wow. But* **Peter** *and the Harvard Observatory are swept away from her as the Leavitt home takes its place.*

Scene Five

Leavitt home—no stars. **Henrietta** *comes to a stop in front of a waiting* **Margaret**. *A box or two of glass star plates sit next to her.*

Henrietta   Hello. Margie, I'm here.

Margaret   Henri. Come in. Hello. Come in. Everything's a wreck. Glad you're here.

Henrietta   How can I help? What can I do?

Margaret   Everything. Nothing. It's been a mess since last Sunday.

Henrietta   Last Sunday?

Margaret   We couldn't get ahold of you.

Henrietta   I would've come sooner. I didn't know. What happened?

Margaret   He just fell over. Couldn't talk. Couldn't move.

Henrietta   Is there anything I can—?

Margaret   I don't know where to start. He can't do anything. I'm at my wits' end.

Henrietta   Where's Sam?

Margaret   Trying to organize for Sunday. When the town preacher can't preach— And with Sam hurt, his leg, he fell—it's just so much. It'll be fine. I'll play so at least it'll sound good.

Henrietta   They couldn't find someone else to play on Sunday?

Margaret   *I can play. (Pause.)*

Henrietta   I'm so sorry you've had to do this on your own.

Margaret   Well. There it is.

Margaret (*sits. She's exhausted. Sees the boxes of plates*)   What's that?

Henrietta   Work. A little.

Margaret   You don't think this might be the time to put the work down.

Henrietta   It's important.

Margaret   And this is not?

Henrietta   No. I mean Yes. I mean I'm here. I'm right here.

Margaret   I just wonder why you exceed expectation in everything except this family. Even so, Daddy is so proud. You think he isn't. You think he resents your "great escape," and because you never wrote or came home, you wouldn't know. You also wouldn't know that I made you up for him. I wrote letters for you, "from you," brought them in the house every week—So happy—thrilled!—Read them to the whole family—"Look what we got from Henrietta today!" "Oh Daddy, she says hello, she says she loves you, thank you." On and on. Such a comforting fiction.

Henrietta   You didn't have to do that.

Margaret   I did. So that you could have a home to come back to. (*She goes.*)

Henrietta   Margie, please—

Margaret   I am so busy. He'll need to be fed, the doctor's coming in an hour. This is suddenly a lot of work and I am quite sure you'll be leaving any minute so I better not get comfortable.

Henrietta   Margie, please stop. (*Touches her. Connects with her.*)

Margaret (*asking what she never asks*)   Please. Help me.

Henrietta   I am not leaving. However long you need me. I will not go.

Margaret   But your work.

Henrietta   Is portable. They can send more and I can stay here.

I want to. I do. I do.

Margaret *stops. Breath. Then scared, letting it go.*

Margaret   It's been so much. Too much.

Henrietta   I see that and I'm so sorry.

Margaret   He was fine and then not and now . . .

Everything changes. Why does *everything* change?

Henrietta (*tentatively*)   Not changes, just changes form.

Margaret   What?

Henrietta   There's a new theory. A German physicist—

Margaret   Oh God.

Henrietta   Wait, he says that mass and energy are just different forms of the same thing. They shift back and forth forever. So nothing's gone. It just shifts. (*Beat.*) Why don't you practice for Sunday. I'll find Sam, and see if I can help.

Margaret *nods. Goes to her piano. Plays "For the Beauty of the Earth."* **Annie** *and* **Will** *appear faraway, together looking up. A letter.*

Henrietta   Dear Dr. Pickering, Miss Fleming, Miss Cannon . . .

Peter *appears faraway, looking at* **Henrietta**.

Henrietta   Due to family needs, I must remain here. Send more sky.

Henrietta *looks out over us as time passes . . . Letters . . .* **Peter** *on a ship.* **Henri** *at home.*

Henrietta   Dear Peter, I imagine you on the sea, night brilliant with stars. Instead, I spend the nights just as I did as a child—alone in the yard, looking up, dreaming of another life. Yours,

Peter   Dear Henrietta,   **Henrietta**   Henrietta.

Landed in England. Eclipse was stunning. You are . . . everywhere. Afar but not apart,

Henrietta   Peter,   **Peter**   Peter.

It's hard not to feel like I've gone backwards. But it's good that I'm here. Father's not improving and Margie is so glad to have me. But I do miss . . . everything.

Peter   Henrietta,   **Henrietta**   Henrietta.

Met the most brilliant men at Oxford, everyone discussing relativity.

Paris was great, Zurich was cold. How are things at Harvard?

Henrietta   Peter,   **Peter**   Peter.

I haven't yet returned. But once I help Margie I intend to make my

way back to my perfectly creaky desk. And your "rounds."

Peter   Henrietta,   **Henrietta**   Henrietta.

I just arrived in Cambridge and I have so much to tell you. When will you return?

Henrietta   Peter,   **Peter**   Peter.

I promise I'm coming as soon as I can.

Peter   But when will that be? We need you here.

Henrietta   Please send more plates.

Peter   I don't care about the plates. Where are you?

Henrietta   The same place: Afar but . . . (*Perhaps she expects him to complete her sentence . . .*) not apart? (*No response from* **Peter**. *An offering.*) Peter? (*No response from* **Peter**.) Father's funeral was brief but full of friends. Which was good for the family. (*No response from* **Peter**.) It's been so long since I've heard from you. I fear my letters have gotten lost. Or you have.

Peter   Miss Leavitt,   **Henrietta**   Henrietta.

I am very sorry to hear of your father's passing. (*Different, formal now.*)
Harvard's very busy. Dr. Pickering is sending more plates for analysis. If you can
manage.

Henrietta   Of course I can manage. And I'll be coming back soon.

Peter (*not a letter, a crack into his heart, which doesn't know what to say . . .*)   Of
course you will. I just wish . . . (*Lights dim, transition to . . .*)

Scene Six

Henrietta *sits at a table trying to look at the star plates, but there's not enough light,
she doesn't have the equipment . . .* **Margaret** *plays . . .*

Margaret (*sings*)
    For the wonder of each hour
    Of the day and of the night
    Hill and vale and tree and flower

While working **Henrietta** *sings, almost unconsciously, with* **Margaret** *on the last
verse . . .*

Margaret and **Henrietta**
    Sun and moon and stars of light . . .

Beat. **Margaret** *stops playing, approaches.*

Margaret   I think it's time we built you a study for all these boxes.

Henrietta   I'm sorry.

Margaret   Or a ranch.

Henrietta   I can move them. I know it's a lot. They've been sending more and more.
Which is good, I want to work, I *need* to work.

Margaret   And now that things are calm. You should think about going back.
(**Henrietta** *looks up—thrilled.*) Don't look so excited—I'm not being nice—I just
can't stand all these boxes in my house. And Daddy would've wanted you to go.

Henrietta   Why are you so good to me?

Margaret   Because I'm a saint, and you're easy to pity.

Henrietta   I accept that. Can I take your son with me—he knows three whole
constellations.

Margaret   Yes, boys and glassware is a good idea. (*Picks up a star plate.*) It amazes
me that the entire sky fits on these little windowpanes. And how shockingly full it all
is. It doesn't look that full from the back yard. But every one of them is just bursting
with stars.

Henrietta   And nebulae. (*Showing her on a plate.*) There and . . . there.

Margaret   My goodness. It's a whole other world up there.

Henrietta   Or worlds. You know they call me a *fiend*.

Margaret   Who calls you a fiend?

Henrietta   "A star-finding fiend." One of the most prominent astronomers at Princeton said that about me.

Margaret   You're important to them?

Henrietta   I am actually.

Margaret   They're not taking advantage of you?

Henrietta   Oh they're surely are. But it's a compliment.

Margaret   A love letter is a compliment.

Henrietta   We've talked about this.

Margaret   Sitting at Harvard and you can't find a gentleman?

Henrietta   My department is all women.

Margaret   Well, get out.

Henrietta   It's complicated.

Margaret   Wouldn't be romance without. Is it?

Henrietta   What?

Margaret   Romance?

Henrietta   *No.* Not . . . yet.

Margaret   And who is this "not yet"?

Henrietta   What about your music?

Margaret   What about your secret fancy?

Henrietta   Margie. It's nothing. It's a boring story with a boring ending.

Margaret   Why?

Henrietta   Because it ended. Or . . . didn't really start. It's unclear.

Margaret   I'm sorry.

Henrietta   That was never in my plan anyway.

Margaret   Maybe it's your plan that's boring.

Henrietta   Oh just play something would you.

Margaret   You can't distract me with my own music.

Henrietta   It's not a distraction, it's a celebration.

Margaret   That you're leaving me? Again?

Henrietta   I've been hearing bits and pieces for months now. I want to hear the whole of it before I go.

Margaret   Well. I have been working on something—tiny—just a sketch.

Henrietta   A hymn?

Margaret   Concerto.

Henrietta   Really?

Margaret   I'm working on a symphony.

Henrietta   My goodness. I guess I thought—to write a whole symphony I thought you had to be—

Margaret   Male.

Henrietta   European and angry.

Margaret   Upsetting tradition might just run in the family. (*Pause. Grin.* **Margaret** *plays a simple, lovely piece on the piano.* **Henrietta** *takes it in.* **Henrietta** *notices the stars above her starting to shine again . . . They appear in time with* **Margaret***'s music . . .* **Margaret** *stops playing—the stars stop blinking.*) What's wrong?

Henrietta   Keep going—keep—yes, *please play.*

Margaret *plays—the stars blink to her music* **Henrietta** *grabs her logbook—scanning it wildly—*

Henrietta   Oh my God.

Margaret   What?

Henrietta   It's—it's tonal.

Margaret   It's what? (*Stops playing.*)

Henrietta   *Play.*

Margaret *plays. A letter light on* **Annie** *and* **Will**—*this is the slight future.*

Williamina   Henrietta's written another letter!

Annie   That's not a letter, that's a book.

Williamina   She's found something.

Henrietta   It's—the whole thing—it's like music.

Margaret   My music?

Henrietta   The stars are music.

Margaret   *My* music?

Henrietta   The pattern. The numbers—When you put them in the right order—they're—Oh my God the blinking is music—so simple—Right there!

Margaret   What's right there?! (*The letter.*)

Annie   She found a pattern in the Cepheids.

Williamina   Look at that. The pulsing isn't random—

Henrietta   The pulsing isn't random. There *is* a pattern. (*Her big idea.*) The brightest stars take the longest to blink.

Annie   It's so simple.

Williamina   I love it when it's simple.

Margaret   I don't understand, how does a pattern help?

Henrietta (*while* **Margaret** *plays*)   *A pattern is a standard*! And if we have a standard we can *compare* stars all over the sky. Right now if we see two stars that look equally bright, we can't tell which one is the *brighter star*, and which one is the *closer* star. But the pulsing can tell us which is which. *The pulsing is the answer.*

Margaret   And somehow musical?

Henrietta   Yes. If you think of the notes as the star's brightness. If *this* is the dimmest the star gets—(*she hits a low note*) and *this* is the brightest. (*Hits a high note.*) Then the time it takes to get from here—(*Low note, then every note in between until.*) to here—(*High note.*) could tell us *how bright it actually is,* which we could compare to how it *appears,* which could tell us how far away it is, which we could compare to other stars, (*She plays various chromatic scales—some short, some longer.*) which could tell us how far away *they* are, and if we know *that* we can— We can skip star to star across the deepest space until we know . . . (*Music—Stars—Music!*)

Margaret   What.

Henrietta   Exactly where we are. (*This is the peak of the music.* **Henrietta** *looks to the stars, drops her hearing-aid.* **Margaret** *sees the stars too.* **Annie** *and* **Will** *are celebrating back in Boston! And* **Peter,** *alone, reading Henri's letter, proud of her. Blackout but for stars.*)

End of Act One.

Act Two

Scene One

December 1910. Ocean liner—at night. **Henrietta** *on the deck, looking up at the sky, no hearing-aid.* **Peter** *enters next to her.*

Peter   Gorgeous night, Miss Leavitt.

Henrietta   It really is, isn't it?

Peter (*re: the stars*)   Checking on the children?

Henrietta   Tucked in but wide awake.

Peter   Tell me more.

Henrietta   Are you tempting me with astronomy?

Peter   That is my greatest asset.

Henrietta   Then you would remember from school—

Peter   Your cheek, your neck—

Henrietta   Pay attention, young man. Stars are classified by their heat—

Peter   Your eyes, my God.

Henrietta   And given one of the letters

Obafgkm—

Peter   And how will I ever remember—I wish there was some phrase—perhaps one with an irresistible directive.

Henrietta   "Oh Be A Fine Girl, Kiss—" (*He kisses her.*)

Peter   Now I remember.

Henrietta   Let's stay here forever.

Peter   Adrift?

Henrietta   Afloat.

Peter   In the sea?

Henrietta   In the sky. Always the sky.

Peter *strangely shifts into an echo of himself as . . . The ocean liner dissolves around them quickly—*

Peter   Always.

Henrietta   Yes.

Peter   The sky.

Henrietta   Yes.

Peter   Send more sky. (*Then* **Peter** *is gone.* **Henrietta** *is alone.*)

Henrietta   What? Peter? (*She retrieves her hearing-aid as her dream fades completely into Harvard Observatory.* **Peter** *has changed too—cold, formal.*) Peter.

Peter   Yes? Oh. Miss Leavitt. Hello.

Henrietta   Hello.

Peter   You're here.

Henrietta   I am. Very here.

Peter   Yes. Well. Welcome back. And I'm . . . so glad to read about your work. The pattern. It's very good. Work.

Henrietta   It took long enough to find, but in the end it's a compliment to all of us.

Peter   It's kind of you to share credit, but I seem to recall *you* working all those nights alone.

Henrietta (*immediate embarrassment*)   Usually, yes.

Peter   I'm sorry, I should be going. Welcome back. We'll need your next batch soon.

Henrietta   Batch of . . .?

Peter   Those little Cepheids. You're the fiend.

Henrietta   Oh. Well yes but—

Peter   Pickering will be glad to have our best computer back in house. Good day.

Henrietta   Wait.

Peter   I really can't talk, Miss Leavitt.

Henrietta   But I haven't seen the publication yet. And I was hoping to move past computing to real research—

Peter   I'll let you discuss that with Dr. Pickering, excuse me, I have a class.

Henrietta   You're teaching? How nice.

Peter   It is a university.

Henrietta   Peter.

Peter   Miss Leavitt. (*She steps to him.*) Please don't.

Henrietta   Don't what?

Peter   I can't, I'm sorry.

Henrietta   I thought we could—

Peter   Miss Leavitt. I cannot talk right now. I'm sorry.

Henrietta   I know it's been so long.

Peter   *It has.*

Henrietta   I couldn't come back right away, I tried, I did, but there were complications.

Peter (*letting it out*)   *Years of complications?* (*Stuffing it back in.*) I'm sorry. We shouldn't be—I should go.

Henrietta   Peter.

Peter   Excuse me.

Henrietta   *You* stopped writing to *me*.

Peter   Well. There were complications.

Henrietta   And space and time—yes, I know—But when I saw the truth in those numbers, when I finally felt that thing I've always wanted to feel, I thought of you. Because you understand. I thought.

Peter *steps towards her—God, he loves her. Beat—almost speaks—She does too—but then . . .*

Williamina (*bursts in, handing her the journal*)   You know, there should be mandatory exclamation points with this sorta thing. I saw you coming up the path and about bit my fist I was so pleased. (*Hugs her hard.*) Hello, darling. Here ya go. (*Reading aloud.*) '"The Period-Luminosity Relation' by Miss Henrietta Leavitt." Blah blah blah—ah!—"There is a simple relation between the brightness of the Cepheid stars and their time periods." Ha! Published and triumphant you stand. (*Pause.*) In case those were worry lines. (*To* **Peter**.) Why don't you tell her it's brilliant.

Peter   It is an achievement. Especially now that Pickering and the lot have their hands on it.

Williamina   "The lot" have nothing to do with it.

Peter   I'm saying that when others have a chance to apply it—progress, indeed.

Williamina   You wouldn't know progress if it swam up and bit your ear.

Peter   Excuse me.

Williamina   I don't blame you for being jealous—

Peter   I'm not *jealous*.

Williamina   And *I'm* not standing right in front of you.

Henrietta   I'd like to ask Dr. Pickering if I might continue working on this now that I'm back. Perhaps start a project just for the Cepheids—

Peter   We already started one.

Henrietta   You what? But I want to participate.

Peter   You're not an astronomer.

Henrietta   Of course I am.

Peter   Not without a degree.

Henrietta   Then I'll get one.

Peter   And who will do your work?

Henrietta   This *is* my work.

Peter   It's not.

Henrietta   My work!

Peter   Not any more.

Henrietta   *Peter.*

Peter   *Miss Leavitt.* You've done a good job. Let's let that be that.

Henrietta   No! The impact of this could—it could change the very—

Peter   *It's just a pattern, Miss Leavitt, it's not a revolution.* (*Calming down, apologizing.*) Though we, of course, thank you for your contribution. (*Tension. Pause.*)

Williamina   You are a giant ass.

Peter   I'm sorry I raised my voice

Williamina   Why don't you GET OUT.

Peter   I will not.

Williamina   DO NOT PRESS ME.

Peter   After all I've put up with from this department—

Where is Miss Cannon? Hm? Gone *again*.

Williamina   She's sick. Of you.

Peter   We all know where she is—She's out—*Making trouble for this institution.*

Williamina   And if you ever made as many *contributions* as she makes *trouble* in *one* day? *Any one* of us would care what *you* think about *any one of us*.

Peter   I'll go.

Henrietta   Home to your Dachshund?

Peter   To my wife.

Henrietta *drops a glass plate—it cracks. Silence.*

Peter   That's ruined.

Peter *starts to go—stops—wants to apologize—doesn't. Exits. Silence. As they clean up the glass plate.*

Williamina   Dr. Pickering is finally getting us new chairs.

Henrietta   That's . . . that's very . . .

Williamina   Darling. We are in the business of perspective. *You* know it's fundamentally hard to tell if something is big and bright or . . . just close by.

Henrietta   I don't know what you mean.

Williamina   And if hearts were stars we'd all connect the damned dots.

Henrietta   Oh nothing ever . . . materialized.

Williamina   Not saying it did. Just . . . Hearts and stars. Can be blinding.
(*A moment.*)

Henrietta (*is she talking about* **Peter** *or the Cepheids?*)   How do we know that any of this matters? How does anyone know that? I want to know that.

Williamina   You can't. Which is why you must never doubt or you'll drown. Now. Annie'll be so happy to see you. She's on her way back from a protest. Very exciting these days. And they gave her a sash. She loves that sash. Both of them are off to change the nation. (*Pause.* **Annie** *enters.*) Speaking of . . . (*To* **Annie**.) Look who's back, Annie.

Annie   Miss Leavitt.

Henrietta   Miss Cannon.

Annie   Here you are. Welcome.

Henrietta   It's so good to see you. (*She hugs* **Annie**. *A little much.* **Annie** *awkwardly pats her on the back, pries herself off.*)

Annie   And you, my dear. The responses to your finding have been numerous.

Henrietta   It was in there. You were right.

Annie   Then let's all never doubt me again, shall we?

Williamina (*to* **Henri**)   See? (*To* **Annie**.) How goes the march?

I defended your honor.

Annie   It was profound and pointless as these things tend to be.

Williamina   And the sash?

Annie   Patriot thread. (*Reveals her suffragette sash—"Votes for Women!"*) So you're back for good, I hope. Can we start you on something new then? How do feel about supernovae?

Henrietta   Miss Cannon. I'd much rather continue with the Cepheids, keep working with them, follow it through.

Annie   Through to where?

Henrietta   To some . . . true . . . *place.*

Williamina   Put a big red X on it if you find it.

Henrietta   *If we're not finding the largest truth then what have we spent our lives doing? What's the point of all this?*

The Observatory falls away as **Henrietta** *watches the following in another space . . .* **Peter** *appears in a spot. He's giving a lecture . . .*

Peter   The cosmic question of our age—

Henrietta   What is "the point"?

Peter   What is "the universe"? The question itself admits a singularity of size—We are stuck—

Henrietta   We are stuck—

Peter   On this planet.

Henrietta   In this life. And our perspective is—

Peter   Our perspective is—

Henrietta   Intimate.

Peter   Imperfect.

Henrietta   Which means that I might have forgotten—

Peter   However—

Henrietta   To live.

Peter   Because we lack the measurements, we are left wondering: How big is everything? Which leads to the central question—Is everything contained within our Milky Way or not?

Henrietta   Are we contained or not?

Peter   Is all that we see—

Henrietta   Is all that we see—

Peter   The extent of the universe?

Henrietta   The extent? No. *No.*

Peter   Absolutely.

Henrietta *is shocked by this. She is now watching his lecture from the back of the room.*

Peter   It is my judgment that the universe is exactly the same thing as the Milky Way Galaxy. There is nothing greater and nowhere else. How could there be? To even consider that would mean that these stars are thousands of light years away. And nothing is thousands of light years away. The universe is simply not that vast. Nor need it be to inspire the deepest human wonder. Thank you.

Henrietta *walks right up to* **Peter**.

Henrietta   Professor Shaw.

Peter   Miss Leavitt. You were watching?

Henrietta   How could you say that the universe "isn't that vast." How could you say that?

Peter   Because the majority of astronomers agree.

Henrietta   No they don't.

Peter   The ones that matter do.

Henrietta   The ones who gave you this job do.

Peter   If you look at the literature—

Henrietta   Which I have, Mr. Shaw. Which is where *my finding* is now quite at home.

Peter   Then you'd see, Miss Leavitt, that there is simply no other way to think.

Henrietta   Well it's a good thing the universe doesn't care what you think. Or me. Or Newton, or Kepler. It just marches on.

And waits for the blind to catch up. That would be you. (*Starts to leave. Comes back.*) That would be you.

Peter   Henrietta.

Henrietta   *I'm sorry but I have to go—I always have to go—*

Peter   Henrietta please.

Henrietta   *What.*

Peter *stops her, checks to make sure they're alone.*

Peter   When I came back from Europe my father decided that it was time. And that she was a good match. And I barely knew what happened, and I barely knew her. And I don't know why I acted that way. Yes I do. Seeing you is . . . Very hard.

Henrietta   I am so sorry that this has been so hard. For you.

Peter   That's not what I meant. Perhaps we could talk.

Henrietta   We can't.

Peter   Why?

Henrietta   Because. There's a boat that leaves tomorrow. For Europe. And I just decided that I'll be on it. Because I've heard that seeing the stars from the sea is not to be missed. And I don't want to miss anything else. And apparently there's lobster.

Peter   That's . . . that's . . . good for you. But—wait. I need to say—I should say . . . that your findings *are* very important and I am *very* proud of . . . you.

Henrietta   Thank you. (*After a moment of looking . . . A transition sweeps* **Peter** *off and sweeps into . . .*)

Scene Two

Henrietta *on that ocean liner at night. She is alone. Noise of people around her though. The sounds of a ship. She is so thoroughly happy. This is real . . . not a dream. She looks up. A letter to* **Margaret** . . .

Margaret   "Dear Margie," (*But faraway,* **Peter** *reads a letter from* **Henrietta** *as well.*)

Peter   "Dear Mr. Shaw,"

Henrietta   I would like to say that I wish I could send you an image of this sky tonight. But I hope we never invent pictures that perfect—that would miss the point.

Peter   '"Which is what?' I think staring out to sea."

Henrietta   I used to think that to *be truly alive* I needed answers. I needed to *know.* But all this does not in fact *need* to be known, does it? *We* do.

Peter   "*We* do."

Henrietta   Because the real point . . . is seeing something bigger. And knowing we're a small part of it, if we're lucky. In the end that is a life well-lived.

Peter   "Please tell Miss Cannon that when I come back . . . I have work to do."

Henrietta   Because thank God there's a lot out there bigger than me. See you soon.

Peter *and the ocean liner fade into time and distance . . . as* **Henrietta** *returns home on a huge ship greeted by* **Margaret** *with a huge wave . . .*

Margaret   Henrietta!   **Henrietta**   Henrietta.

The sisters hug a long hug.

Henrietta   Margie! I missed you so much. Welcome to Boston.

Margaret   And the same to you. Welcome back. Now tell me everything.

Henrietta   Well Paris *is* as perfect as you'd like to think and London is just—

Henrietta *staggers, sits, then cringes as a pain sweeps over her abdomen.*

Margaret   Henri. *Henri.*

Henrietta   I'm fine.

Margaret   You're not fine. What is this?

Henrietta   It's nothing. It passes.

Margaret   It's not nothing. You should have come home *immediately.*

Henrietta   There were only a few bad days.

Margaret   Henrietta, they've invented doctors.

Henrietta   I saw one in London.

Margaret   And you're seeing another one right now.

Henrietta   Margie, no—

Margaret   The luggage can wait.

Henrietta   I'm going straight to Harvard—

Margaret   You're coming back to Wisconsin with me—you're resting and—

Henrietta   I'm going to work—I want to work—

Margaret   I don't care. There's time for all that—

Henrietta   *There's not.* (*Pause. Her look tells* **Margie** *it's serious.*)

Williamina   Wait now, there she is! Henri!

Annie   Henrietta! There she is.

Williamina   That's what I said. I said that was her. Henrietta, dear!

Henrietta   Oh my goodness, what are you doing here?

Annie   What are we doing here? Your sister told us you were finally coming back.

Williamina   And you have to save us from each other.

Annie   You really do. Now, we have a mountain of work to get through.

Williamina (*to* **Margaret**)   Hello, you, I'm Williamina.

Margaret   I'm Margaret. Hello.

Henrietta   Oh, this is my sister Margie. I thought you'd met.

Margaret   Not yet, but I've heard so much—

Annie *gives* **Margaret** *an uncharacteristically large hug.*

Annie   You're the sister! We've heard of you!

Margaret   Oh my.

Williamina   You're scaring the poor thing, Annie.

Annie   Unfortunately common.

Williamina   Didn't Henrietta say you have a son?

Margaret   I do. As tall as his father, and twice the charmer.

Williamina   Oh dear.

Margaret   Let's just say that I do not fear a lack of grandchildren.

Williamina   Send him to me, I'll straighten him out.

Annie   Alright, ladies. The early graphs from Princeton are in and we need your eyes on them.

Henrietta   I can do that.

Margaret   Henri, wait—(*To* **Annie.**) She was just saying she's been a bit poorly these days.

Henrietta   I'm fine and I'm so looking forward to being back.

Annie   You're sick?

Henrietta   No.

Margaret   *Yes.* She nearly fainted just now—She's not well—and I really must insist—

Henrietta   *I'm* insisting, Margie. My work is here. And my life, and every chance I've ever had. Is here. (*Pause.*)

Margaret   Then so am I. You can't get rid of me.

Williamina   Me neither.

Annie   And you can work from home when you like, so there's not a single reason we can't all go about our business as usual.

Henrietta   Thank you. Lunatic women. (*She braves a small pain again. She leans on* **Margie.**)

Williamina (*helping her . . .*)   Here we go, darlin'.

Annie   I'll get the bags.

Margaret   We've got you, Henri. We're right here. (*Helping* **Henrietta** *walk off. Transition . . .*)

Scene Three

Annie *is in the office gathering plates.* **Peter** *enters.*

Peter   Excuse me. Miss Cannon.

Annie   Not today, Mr. Shaw.

Peter   I heard about Henrietta—Miss Leavitt. I heard she's sick? How sick? How is she?

Annie   Well she's making do. Working from home just down the street. I think you know that nothing is going to keep her down for long.

Peter   Nothing short of an earthquake.

Annie   That sounds about right. (*Pause.*)

Peter (*handing her a letter*)   Would you please give her this? I took the liberty of inquiring to a family physician and he said he'd be happy to see her. She would never ask, but . . . If you would tell her to please accept his services as a favor to me.

Annie (*the first time they've ever really connected*)   I will. Thank you, Mr. Shaw. That's very . . . Thank you. (*She takes his hand, shakes it. They are equals, for a moment at least. Transition to . . .*)

Scene Four

Years later. Around 1918. **Henrietta** *is at her small home in Cambridge with* **Margaret***. She sits in a chair, covered by a blanket.*

Margaret   We got the census today. I started to fill it out but I didn't know what to put under your profession?

Henrietta   Astronomer is my profession.

Margaret   Alright.

Henrietta   *Astronomer.*

Margaret   With a capital "A." And how are we doing today?

Henrietta   You know the worst part of this? Sitting still.

Margaret   For you, I'm sure it is. How's the pain?

Henrietta   Not bad today.

Margaret   But relaxing bothers you?

Henrietta   You can't order someone to relax and have it be relaxing.

Margaret   Would you like to read some news?

Henrietta   I can't take any more war news. Did they send another astronomy circular?

Margaret   You'd think a world war would make the stars seem trivial.

Henrietta   You'd think stars would make war seem trivial. I have never felt so helpless.

Margaret   You're not helpless.

Henrietta   I write all these letters and no one answers. These men, colleagues, all using my work, but they won't let me near it.

Useless. Helpless.

Margaret   You're getting upset.

Henrietta   *Life* is about getting appropriately upset. And all I want to know is what's true—what *else* is true. And how long is that list. And I know I won't know. And what does all the knowing of the not knowing do to a sane person? What does *that* mean?

Margaret   It could mean that we're all helpless. And alone. And because you can't connect everything yourself that nothing's connected. Or. It could mean that you may not know how you might matter to people right now, and you cannot know how you will matter in the future. But you are *already* connected—and you *already* matter. Because what you do outlasts you. Sometimes. Am I helping or hurting?

Henrietta   I can't tell. But thank you. And . . . I want to explain.

Margaret   Oh, you've tried explaining it and I'm just too thick.

Henrietta   Not stars. Something like . . . souls.

Margaret   Henri . . .

Henrietta   I just know that you worry about those things. And I don't want you to think that I don't believe in anything. I do, just a different kind of . . . Faith in . . . Grand Observation.

Margaret   Which is comforting?

Henrietta   Which is . . . nimble. And that is comforting. *My* heaven? Is a cosmos deep in a gorgeous void.

Margaret   A void?

Henrietta   Full darkness—

Margaret   Not *all* darkness—

Henrietta   Mottled with immaculate combustion—

Margaret   But the stars are—

Henrietta   Hot gas in a lonely—

Margaret   Not lonely—

Henrietta   Broad, airless—

Margaret   Don't say airless—

Henrietta   Deep, vast, dark—

Margaret   Stop it just *StopIt*. Alright. I know we don't speak plainly about this but . . . Where does *my* heaven go?

Henrietta   Maybe it doesn't.

Margaret   Henri.

Henrietta   I'm going first, I'll tell you who's right. (*Pause. Tense.* **Margaret** *leaves. Comes back.*)

Margaret   You cannot say that. Not to me.

Henrietta   I've made peace with that part.

Margaret   I haven't. And what other part is there?

Henrietta   The part of meaning something.

Margaret   You mean everything to me.

Henrietta   But you have your babies, your music, you . . . like church.

Margaret   You can't compare us.

Henrietta   You have a life.

Margaret   And you have a legacy.

Henrietta   Work that I can't finish!

Margaret   That's what a legacy *is*. The way I see it, and this is just how I see it. You asked God a question and He answered. That's the meaning of meaning for most of us. (*Doorbell.*) Now. *Relax before I drug you.*

Margaret *leaves.* **Henrietta** *sits a moment.* **Margaret** *returns.*

Margaret   How about some mail?

Henrietta   Fine.

Margaret *reveals—***Annie** *and* **Williamina**. **Annie** *wears pants—which* **Margaret** *notices.*

Margaret   And messengers.

Annie   Henrietta.

Williamina   Darling.

Annie   Margaret dear! Thank you again for keeping Henri so comfortable and close by. To have her just blocks away with all these new girls and their temperaments and their outfits—

Margaret (*looking at those pants*)   Uh-huh.

Annie   You would not believe their shoes.

Margaret   Probably not.

Williamina   How are you feeling today?

Henrietta   Fine. Bored. Angry.

Williamina   Not for long you're not.

Margaret   Alright, you ladies chat. I've got dinner for us.
You'll both stay. I insist.

Williamina   Wait now, you should hear this.

Henrietta   Hear what?

Annie   We have news.

Williamina   Great news.

Henrietta   What news, Annie, *tell me.*

Annie   Head of Stellar Photometry. It's yours. Pickering sent me to make the offer.

Henrietta   Oh my goodness.

Margaret   Henri!

Annie   And a raise.

Williamina   Of a quarter.

Henrietta (*to* **Annie**)   Head of Photometry? But that's *your* job.

Annie   Now I'm Head Curator. Everyone's moving up.

Williamina   Like mighty oaks!

Margaret   Oh that's wonderful. Congratulations.

Annie   It's a great honor, Henrietta.

Williamina   Like magma from the depths of men's minds, a nice hot compliment erupts.

Annie   A change in the system is what it is. A model. For the future.

Williamina   Oh Lord.

Annie   And if we use things like this and take a *real* stand—

Williamina   She's about to give you a pamphlet.

Annie   We can make a larger difference. (*Handing them pamphlets.*)

Henrietta   What's all this?

Annie   We need a vote, girls. It's about equality—and it's about time!

Williamina   "And it's about time!"

Williamina   I know all the slogans.

Margaret   Oh. I'm not really—

Annie   If we can organize the sky, we can organize our minds to choose our own future.

Williamina   She heard a speech a year ago and—

Annie   Is this a democracy or not?

Williamina   Now she's a patriot.

Annie   A *true* patriot, yes I am. Does it say "We the People" or doesn't it?

Williamina   It does.

Annie   It does! And we're marching in D.C. next month. You should join us. Both of you. (*Pause.*)

Margaret   I'll read the pamphlet.

Williamina   It's a great pamphlet.

Margaret   Glazed ham for dinner. I should get it ready.

Henrietta   Thank you, Margie.

Williamina   Why don't I come and get in the way.

Margaret *and* **Williamina** *exit.*

Annie   So. We have new computers. You should come by the office.

Henrietta   Trust me, how much I wish I could.

Annie   What can I do?

Henrietta   I need more work—anyone's, whoever's working on this. I've been keeping up with the circulars. I've been writing everyone I can think of. I need to know what they're seeing. If I can't do the work myself—even the tiniest pinch of information—I'm fine with being tiny—I just need to know.

Annie   Of course you do. I'll have some girls take time and investigate.

Henrietta   Thank you. All I have is time and all I haven't is time.

Annie   Time is . . . persistent.

Henrietta   Yes.

Annie   But light, its speed, is a constant—one of the few in the universe. Just so you know. I choose to measure you in light. (*Pause. She grabs* **Henrietta***'s hand. Pause.*)

Williamina (*offstage*)   *Annie.* Ham needs your help.

Annie   What on earth? I'll go get your sister. (*Exits.* **Henrietta** *reaches for a star plate. Can't get to it without too much pain.* **Peter** *enters—out of breath—thrilled, overjoyed, we've haven't seen him like this since his ocean liner proposal.*)

Peter   Miss Leavitt—Hello—

Henrietta   Mr. Shaw?

Peter   I'mHere—Iknow—It's odd—but I had to see you.

Henrietta   *Why? What's going on?*

Peter   *There's a new finding.* And I don't think I'm overstating—it changes everything. And you had to be the first to know—

Henrietta   Mr. Shaw, please tell me what you're talking about, and why you're here, and be aware that they're likely pressed ear-tograin against that door.

Peter   Well. I didn't know exactly where you lived so it starts with me following them.

Williamina (*offstage*)   *He followed us? I will smack his—(A scuffle behind the door as* **Will** *is dragged away.*)

Peter   That doesn't matter. What matters is that today I received a—well, *you* received, but it all comes to my office now—

Henrietta   What comes?

Peter   Letters from colleagues to you.

Henrietta   To me?

Peter   I thought they were copied.

Henrietta   *They weren't.* I live blocks away! I've been trying to find out what's going on for ages!

Peter   Sorry.

Henrietta   Ages!

Peter   The point is. This morning, Hertzsprung—The Danish one?

Henrietta   Big beard.

Peter   Right. He used your work to measure the distance to those Cepheids. (*Pause.*)

Henrietta   *My* Cepheids?

Peter   In the Small Magellanic Cloud, yes.

Henrietta   He calibrated . . . *actual* distance to my Cepheids?

Peter   This could be the first measurement of anything outside our galaxy.

Henrietta   Which means there *are things* outside of our galaxy.

Peter (*showing her the letter*)   Yes. Proof. That the universe *is* vast.

Henrietta   How did he do it?

Peter   He used statistical parallax for the zero-point against the sun, then plugged in *your* data for the slope and . . . there you have it.

Henrietta   That makes it sound so easy.

Peter   But without your work it was impossible. Your work made the leap—for us all. Now we have a standard measurement—for the rest of time we have a standard. Oh. And another man keeps writing. Hudgins?

Henrietta   Hudgins. Hubble?

Peter (*A ha!*)   *Hubble.* Yes.

Henrietta   Peter. How far away are my stars?

Peter   Thousands and thousands of light years away.

Henrietta   Oh my God.

Peter   Incredible.

Henrietta   Which means our galaxy *could be* one of many.

Peter   Perhaps one of many . . . billions. (*Beat. Thrilled.*)

Henrietta   I knew it.

Peter   You did.

Henrietta   You were perfectly wrong.

Peter   I was. Ha! (*Pause. Turning to her, a different energy. This is his version of "I have always loved you."*) I am so proud to know you. (*Handing her a wrapped* *package.*) And. This was under your desk. A new girl found it. I thought you'd like it back.

Henrietta   This. Is the book my father sent me.

Peter   You never opened it?

Henrietta   I was too busy. And then too . . . ashamed, I think.

She opens it—it's a book.

Collected poems.

Peter   Really? (*She shares it with him.*) Whitman.

Henrietta   My father sent me poems?

Peter   This one's marked.

Margaret *enters, unseen.*

Peter

"When I heard the learn'd astronomer,
When the proofs, the figures, were ranged in columns
    before me,
When I was shown the charts and the diagrams, to add,
    divide, and measure them,
When I sitting heard the astronomer where he lectured with
    much applause in the lecture-room,
How soon, unaccountable, I became tired and sick,
Till rising and gliding out I wander'd off by myself,
In the mystical moist night-air, and from time to time,
Look'd up in perfect silence at the stars."

Beat.

Margaret   So he's not a marauder, then? Williamina had me worried.

Henrietta   Margie, this is Mr. Peter Shaw.

Margaret   *The* Peter Shaw?

Peter   A pleasure to meet you.

Margaret   You'll stay for dinner?

Peter   Oh no, I shouldn't—

Margaret   And yet you will. We have much to discuss, Famous Mr. Shaw.

Henrietta   And Margie is a wonderful musician. Maybe you and Annie can sing for us.

Margaret   Oh yes!

Peter   Oh God.

Henrietta   Margie knows musicals.

Peter   I couldn't.

Henrietta   You're singing.

Margaret   How nice!

Peter   I've learned just not to argue with women.

Margaret   That's correct. Dinner is on the table. We'll be there in just a moment.

Henrietta   And you must tell Will and Annie immediately.

Margaret   About what?

Peter   Henrietta just became the first person to measure the universe. (*He smiles and exits. Beat.*)

Henrietta   You knew about him.

Margaret   I did.

Henrietta   You knew about him the whole time.

Margaret   I did. That many letters? (*Pause.*)

Henrietta   Sisters are strange friends.

Margaret *smiles.* **Henrietta** *takes her hand. Beat.* **Annie** *bursts in, followed by* **Peter** *and* **Will***, reading the letter from Hertzprung.*

Annie   WHAT DID HE JUST TELL ME?

Peter   It's real. I couldn't believe it.

Williamina   Of course he couldn't.

Peter   *Would you be nice to me?*

Annie   Henrietta was right!

Williamina   You were right! Look at this.

Annie   Oh my goodness, look at this!

Williamina   That's what I said! Look at this! The whole world should be looking at this!

Annie   Henrietta.

Henrietta   I know.

Annie   This is . . . This is just . . .

Williamina   It's everything.

Annie   It is. Everything. (*A moment for the size of this discovery to sink in . . .* **Annie** *whispers something to* **Will***.*)

Margaret   How do you celebrate measuring the universe?

Peter   I have no idea.

Margaret   I have cookies?

Williamina (*to* **Annie**)   That's brilliant. (*To* **Henri**.) Alright. Come on. We're celebrating. (*Whispers something to* **Peter**.)

Henrietta   We already are celebrating.

Annie   Not enough. And you deserve it.

Henrietta   Thank you all but—

Peter (*to* **Will**)   That's perfect! Let's do it. Let's do it right now.

Henrietta   Do what right now?

Margaret   What are we doing?

Annie (*to* **Margaret**) You're coming too.

Margaret   Me what? Wait.

Henrietta   No. I can't go anywhere.

Margaret   She's really not supposed to.

Peter   You have to.

Annie   You deserve this, Henrietta.

Henrietta   It doesn't matter if I can't.

Annie *whispers the plan to* **Margaret** *aside . . .*

Williamina   It's not that far.

Peter   Only a few blocks away.

Williamina   Just up the hill!

Henrietta   It's freezing! I *can't*. Cannot. Go anywhere. So thank you. But let's just sit down, have a nice dinner—

Margaret *gets it, springs into action.*

Margaret   Leave the ham, get the car.

Henrietta   For a few blocks?

Williamina   Now we're talking!

Henrietta   *Margie.*

Margaret   Henri. Relax. (*The room falls away as they run off. Perhaps* **Annie** *and* **Peter** *sing into—*)

Scene Five

BOOM. Faraway we hear "For the Beauty of the Earth."

Henrietta (*to us*)   On top of a hill . . . Just blocks away . . . Across the courtyard from my old desk . . . where it stood offlimits . . . I see. The Great Refractor Telescope. To which we happily break in that night. And taking Margie's hand. I lean close. Hold my breath. And see . . . (*She gasps.*) My heaven. (*BOOM. Stars everywhere—more than ever—***Peter***, ***Will***, ***Annie***, and ***Margie*** *fade as* ***Henrietta*** *takes out her hearing-aid. Tosses it.*) Some time from now I gather myself. And sneak outside—and look up. In perfect silence. And I know—that distance is only space and time, and for some of us . . . light. I am out of time. But light has never let me down. And so. I shift. (*She points up. The ocean liner takes over—***Henrietta*** *stands tall on the deck, breathes deep.*) The next year . . . Annie gets a vote. (*Faraway.* ***Annie*** *and* ***Williamina*** *put ballots in a box.*) The next year, a man named Hubble uses my work to prove that our most unique galaxy is in fact one of billions . . . upon billions. (*Faraway,* ***Peter*** *hears this—wow.*) Then a man from Sweden calls wondering if I might like . . . a Nobel Prize. It's too late for me, but I take the compliment. (*Faraway* ***Annie***, ***Will***, ***Peter***, ***Margaret*** *look up.*) Another few years and Will dies in Boston, Annie by her side.

Williamina *joins* ***Henrietta*** *on the ocean liner.*

Henrietta   Another year and another war takes over the world. Then Annie dies.

Annie *joins* ***Henrietta*** *and* ***Will*** *on the ocean liner.*

Henrietta   Then Peter.

Peter *joins them.*

Henrietta   Then my sister, kissed by twelve grandchildren, a symphony on the radio. (*Her symphony crackles through a radio as* ***Margaret*** *joins them on the ocean liner.*) Then we harness the atom, then orbit the Earth, then stand on the moon. (*Shocking human achievements.*) Then a *telescope* named Hubble, with wings set for space, shows us how vast and beautiful it all is . . . (*Pictures from Hubble Telescope projected everywhere. The music stops. Silence. True sound of space. The stars begin to take over—the ship, the women, the audience. Spots of light powdering every surface.*) Because wonder will always get us there . . . Those of us who insist that there is much more beyond ourselves. And I do. (*A pulsing light surrounds and becomes* ***Henrietta***. *She is now a blinking star.*) And there's a reason we measure it all in light. (*Blackout—but for stars everywhere.*)

End of Play.

Natural Shocks

Thanks

Thank you to Christina Wallace who had the idea to launch this play across the country with a series of free readings to raise funds and awareness for gun violence prevention; to the team of producers—including Leah Hamos, Corinne Hayoun, Erica Rotstein, Audible and WP Theatre—who pulled it off and brought it to New York; to Kathy Najimy who first read it with such heart and humor; and to all the women and men behind the more than 100 readings in forty-eight states that raised money for gun violence prevention and domestic violence prevention in April of 2018.

Character

Angela, *a woman. Probably 40 years old, maybe younger, maybe older. She's funny, she is smart, she thinks fast, she rambles, she is self deprecating. She is feeling everything as it happens. She is trying not to lie but she always does. She is trying to survive. Resilient, hopeful, optimistic, not sorry for herself. She can be any race, from any region, with any accent. She might wear things that would make your local audience pre-judge her (a frumpy sweatshirt with a big sports logo, or gaudy earrings, or too much eyeliner, or no makeup and camo shorts). They should come to empathize with her even if they first assume they wouldn't.*

Setting

A half-finished basement in a normal house in America right now.

Notes

The wind will grow as the play goes on.

It's a comedy . . . until it's not.

The Play

Angela *runs into her basement, locks the door.*

Angela   Shit. I think this is real. This might be really happening. God it happens so quickly. Turns so quickly. Shit.

OK. The things you need to know are: This is the basement. This is where you're supposed to be. It's way safer down here. I think? Right? Right. What else. The door is locked. It's a good lock. Of course what's a lock really gonna do against a natural disaster heading this way at two hundred miles an hour? That's why we're underground. We'll be fine.

Jesus I can't believe this is happening. How is this happening?

But everyone always says that don't they. "How is this happening? Not here! Not me!" Well it seems it's here and it's me and it's getting very windy out there.

Or maybe it's a dream? No. *I want only fun and sexy dreams please, fun and/or sexy and* basements are neither.

Wind outside.

OK. You have questions, good for you, we're gonna answer everything. So! The tiny little window will tell you it's dusk, which it is. It's a beautiful sunset actually, but that's a lie because there's bad weather coming and it's coming fast. Like real fast, like—shit. Wifi's out. Does anyone have a signal down here? By the window you can usually get one.

Actually don't. You can't get help until *after* things like this. You're just gonna get more people hurt if you call for help now.

Did I mention this is a tornado?

Yeah. Sorry. I do that. I rush ahead. You're like: "You said disaster but didn't specify. What is the dress code?"

Tornado is the dress code. Tornado, like *right out there.* I want to run. Don't run. Stay here. Shit.

You know my mom saw one when she was a kid. She grew up a county over. She was five or six when it touched down across the street, and *man* does that burn a vision into your tiny kid brain. You believe in fairies and monsters at that age and then you wake up and see a mammoth storm outside your window, like the kind from *Wizard of Oz.* You know what she did? She named it. She stared at that funnel and her little mind went . . . "Oliver." Because of course Oliver is a man, a woman would never make that much of a mess— and Oliver is drilling the ground, grinding the earth below and he is coming for you.

Yeah. Her bedtime stories used to scare the shit out of me. Obviously they still do.

My mom. Poor woman. She did not deserve the bullshit she got handed in her life.

And yet the song she sang while washing dishes every day? That song by Judy Garland where she's singing about being so happy and having no cares and hallelujah and suddenly she's all like, "And here comes Judgment Day."

And if I was anywhere nearby she'd kinda side-eye me on "Judgment Day . . . *Angela.*"

We were not friends. But I still make her black-walnut pound cake. I don't eat it because it's so crumbly and dry and what *is* a black walnut? I can't make it right, or it just *can't* be made right. But I still make it. But that recipe is the only thing I have in her handwriting.

I wish I knew more of her secrets. I wish she knew mine.

(*Listening outside . . .*) Wind's down. Even looks clear out there, like every other sunset. Nature is such a liar.

Actually I have no problem with lying. Sometimes it makes things easier. What am I saying, it *always makes things easier*.

Sometimes I'll just say something—very confidently, very factual you know—and then a second later I'll realize, "No, Angela, that is absolutely not true what you just said, You did not go to high school with the guy who plays the cowboy on that HBO show." I don't know why I do it. Little lies. Harmless.

So yeah, OK: door locked, window closed, stay away from the window, bunch of blankets down here, bottled water for sure, gun in the closet, I'm rereading *Sense and Sensibility* so that's in here in case I get bored (bored in a tornado, Jesus), there's a— what's this? Oh of course: a really old copy of *Field & Stream* because he won't throw anything away because we're definitely going to need to reference an article about duck calls from 2001.

Y'all got wigged out when I said there's a gun in here didn't you.

You're not those kinda people are you. I get that. I respect that. I don't really like guns myself, I just grew up around them and you gotta be able to protect yourself. This is a messed up world. I have a right to a gun, you have a right to think I'm nuts. That's all we need to say about it.

Pause.

It's in a safe under my snow boots. It's not gonna bite you.

Though I should definitely make sure it's not going to go off if a goddamned tornado hits this house. That's all I need. A pistol in a tornado.

Anyway I'm sorry we had to meet like this. Not that I had a choice but just so you know I'd rather this have been a nice ice-cream social or a super boozy cocktail party. Not too late for that one actually. We could all wait this thing out by getting super drunk and honest. Actually I think we're more honest when we're facing the worst. Forget the niceties, show me your crisis management. The worst brings out our best.

Anyway. I'm Angela. This is my basement. My new year's resolution to work out is going well, thanks for asking. How's yours? Of course it's totally OK if we're all getting fatter and weirder. That's actual physics. That's real entropy. Get older, eat more chocolate, say weirder and weirder shit about death and technology—

Oh. Maybe if I switch out the walnuts for chocolate my mom's pound cake would be edible. I should try that.

See. This is when I wish I was more like my mom. She would have had a way better plan for this kinda thing than I obviously do. She would have had snacks. She would have had that radio with the hand crank that NPR always tries to give me during pledge week. She would have had a plan. She always had a plan.

But plans take planning and this just came out of the blue. I was just thinking, "Ooh. Maybe I'll go to Chick-fil-A." And then—"no, no I will not go to Chick-fil-A, tell those people to drop the chicken, there's a tornado coming."

But here? Things like this don't really happen here. What are the chances?

Actually I know the chances.

Because I'm an insurance agent.

"Yay!" you're thinking, "I'm stuck in a basement during a natural disaster with *an insurance agent, oh my god this just got serious* GET HELP NOW!"

Don't worry, I'm sure you're covered. And because this is not a professional setting I can be as glib and morbidly humorous as my dog knows I am.

I'm kidding, I don't have a dog. If I had a dog he would be in here with me because what kind of monster leaves their dog loose in a tornado. I would love a dog. If I survive this I'm getting a dog. They're supposed to make you happier right? Or stupider—do you know how much money Americans spend on Halloween costumes *for their pets*?

I can't get a dog. I work too much. I don't want to get a dog just to make it wait for me all day. My husband would hate it. Or maybe he'd finally be happier . . . or stupider. This is not the time to worry about a fictional pet, Angela.

But I love worrying. I'm a professional worrier.

As a Homeowners Insurance Specialist I spend pretty much every day thinking about various forms of peril, which is what we actually call these scenarios because we take our shit *seriously*. Now there are basic covered perils which I'll run through rapidly right now just to make you realize how much shit can happen to a person. We've got: (*A well-memorized stream of perils.*) Fire, Lightning, Wind or hail, Explosion, Vehicle collision (including aircraft—yikes), Smoke, Vandalism, and lastly Riot or Civil commotion. That's basic coverage.

Then there are "named perils" designed to cover the most common forms of property damage. Those are aggravating and chilling but not usually mortal: Burglary, Falling objects, Freezing of plumbing, Accidental water damage, and Artificially generated electricity.

Then there's the really wild stuff. We call it the "special perils" and these bad boys are: Earthquake, Flood, Power failure, Neglect, War, Nuclear hazard, and Intentional acts. Now I'm not saying those last few perils are more necessary now than in the recent past but—you know—I can leave you some brochures.

My boss has this chestnut on a poster in his office: "Needing insurance is like needing a parachute. If it isn't there the first time, chances are you won't be needing it again." This is one of the least groan-inducing jokes you'll hear at every conference of insurance agents. Every one. All of them.

But truly. What I find so thrilling about insurance is the math. I mean actuarial science? The math of the future? Come on! What a rush!

I know, we're so annoying. It's endless. Here's another terrible joke:

God looked at His newly created world and saw that all its chaos needed order, so He created actuaries. Then the actuaries looked at God and His creation and all its chaos and said, "We think that You're the problem."

HA.

It's not that funny. Especially if you're my mom. You *cannot* joke about God with my mom. Nope. I'm serious. Don't do it.

My mom never laughed at one of my jokes. That's not true. There was one.

"What's the difference between a man and his life insurance policy? At least the insurance policy matures."

HA. She liked that one a lot. She liked a terrible joke better than she liked my husband. That should have told me something right there.

Wind again.

God for a second I literally forgot about the tornado. Isn't that crazy. Just—"Oh, *what* imminent threat to my personhood and property? Oh this one? This one right here?"

Eesh, I just can't tell what's happening out there, where it is, which way it's moving. Hurricanes you can track, but tornadoes? Too small, too quick. I mean not when they're on top of you. Then it's *way too big* and I imagine not quick enough.

That's called perspective.

Truly though, it's all chance. All of this. Which city you're in on which day under which roof next to which power line, distracted by whatever it was that made you flinch for the second it took to change everything and get you smashed by a falling—I don't know— chandelier. That's a complex image I just painted. Sorry. The point is: chance.

She retrieves a pair of dice.

Here.

I always have dice. I love dice. So compact and shiny and . . . swallowable if you're a toddler. I used to get them in every colour. So weird, I know. But people collect anything you can imagine. I collect dice.

Roll them and meet your fate . . .

She rolls a pair of dice.

A six. Beautiful. A four and a two. Of course games of chance can be understood through probability, which I obviously love. I get way too hyped for the mathematics of probability and statistics, y'all. I mean I'm *all in*. It's like magic. It's witchcraft. It knows the future.

Quick reminder from undergrad: Statistics analyzes data from the *past*, probability analyzes models for the *future*. One looks back, one looks ahead. Are you obsessed yet?

See. I should've been an actuary. I know that. I was intimidated by the exams. I was being such a *girl* about it. I knew I was good enough, I was better than the g uys. *Ugh.* Self doubt is so cruel. Anyway. Now I'm a backseat actuary, a Monday-morning actuary. I know how to read the signs and tell you what's coming, just no one believes me.

OK I rolled a six. There are five ways of coming up with a six using two six-sided die. Divide five by the total possible combinations, 36, and you get 13.89 percent probability of doing what I 100 percent just did.

Life is just a Game of Chance.

I mean it's Chance that we're here right now, isn't it?

It all makes me think of Hamlet. I know that's not what you were expecting. This lady's gonna go for Hamlet right now? But really. When I get into the thick of what I do—decoding peril—I think of Hamlet. The big speech, the one everyone thinks they know but don't really. "To Be or Not to Be." I had to memorize it in high school and it never left me. The consideration of suicide. I mean I never thought Hamlet was actually going to kill himself, that's not the point of that monologue. It's a logic exercise, right? He's a very logical, calculating guy, Hamlet. He's my people. And he's like, "But no really, what *are* our choices here? To live or not. In that binary, we do have a choice. Not a good one. Not like— *fish or chicken? Hmmm.*" No, but the exercise of considering one's existential options is profound. No one comes out of life unscathed. Everyone's life gets hard. You *could* just wrap things up early and ditch the misery.

> *"to die, to sleep*
> *No more; and by a sleep, to say we end the heartache, and the thousand natural*
>   *shocks*
> *that Flesh is heir to"*

"The thousand natural shocks."

It makes me cry just saying it out loud.

If I ever have a shitty band, that's gonna be our name: The Natural Shocks.

"For who would bear the Whips and Scorns of time," Another good band name.

"The Oppressor's wrong, the proud man's Contumely," I never knew what contumely was but, OK.

"The pangs of despised Love,"

I definitely know what *that* is.

> *"The Law's delay,*
> *the insolence of Office, and the spurns that patient merit of the unworthy takes"*

Yeah. That's a lot for one person to deal with. We don't have coverage for most of those. Why don't we just get out while we can?

> *"But that the dread of something after death,*
> *the undiscover'd country . . . makes us rather bear those ills we have,*
> *than fly to others that we know not of"* Yep.

That sums up humanity pretty well I think.

We're just scared shitless. All the time.

I am. Sitting in this underground shelter I am scared into quivering breathlessness thinking of what's to come.

Pause. Breath. A creaking of trees outside in the wind?

Help me, Hamlet.

And those thousand shocks? That's my entire life's work. Planning for them, knowing them, outsmarting them. And yet here I am. In the middle of one.

But I will survive this. I always do. This shock will not take me down. Plus I've got a solid-gold insurance policy. I've got insurance coming out of my insurance.

Because people just don't get risk. What's actually worth being afraid of.

Everyone's afraid of planes but they're totally fine with cars, which kill millions more people each year. You know *why* they kill people? Because *cars* don't kill people, their drivers do. Human fallibility is our primary feature. We fuck up. We don't pay attention. We lose it.

This is why I'm totally down with driverless cars. That way my neighbor's kid never drives a car in his life. God what a relief. Computers don't lose their freaking minds when their team loses the playoffs. Computers don't get text messages. Or do they? Whatever, they don't drink. Let *them* drive for god's sake.

Like, people *choose to smoke cigarettes*. They still choose that. It's the number-one killer worldwide and people are like, "Yeah that's fine, light that bundle of chemicals on fire and put it in my mouth." Because people are fine with terrible perils as long as they control them. That's why people hate planes, they're not in control. That's why people already hate driverless cars. "But who's steering?!" "Not you! That's the point! That's the genius of it! That's what's going to save your goddamn life!"

See. If we were all taught Risk in school the world would be so much saner. Risk Literacy. That's what the world needs. "Don't be an idiot, kids: Comprehend Risk!" I should write a book on risk literacy—a coloring book! Start 'em young.

I'm telling you. Risk literacy is the science of survival. And I know this because I was at an insurance conference in Denver last month. I know. Super sexy. But then I swear to you I met a member of the actual Illuminati. I did. You wanna know who? I'm gonna tell you.

Have you ever heard of RE-insurers? I didn't even really know what those were until I ended up at the only breakout session that I wasn't too tipsy to go to and it was on reinsurance and it changed my life.

Reinsurers are the people who insure the insurers.

Listen, these people are *not* like you and me. They don't think on the level of the individual. They think on the level of the planet. It's not *one* flood, one drought, one outbreak, it's all of them. Because think about it. OK. If a natural disaster is so bad that too many people activate their claims at the same time . . . there is a chance that an entire insurance company could just seize up. I mean it'd have to be a massive event that would do that, like A Thousand Year Event (that's what they actually call these end-of-the-world kinda things), but it's possible. Like if everyone covered by State Farm activates a claim at once. It'd break the system. Everyone would be screwed. No one gets payouts, everyone suffers.

So. Reinsurers insure against that kind of institutional failure by transferring the risk from one massive company and diversifying it. If something titanically destructive happens, reinsurers will save us all.

Are you as excited about this as I am? Don't answer. I'm excited enough for all of us.

Again, I had no idea about any of this until I hear this lady's session and—OK there were only like four of us in the breakout session so it was basically a personal TED Talk—and I'm smitten. This is amazing. My mind is on fire thinking about this. And the one word that this lady kept using was "overwhelm." Not "overwhelming." She used it as a noun: "an overwhelm, this overwhelm." What a great word. *And* a great band name: *The Overwhelm*. Oh my god The Overwhelm's music would be so terrible. We can all agree on that. Just awful.

And maybe you're not as pumped by reinsurance as I am. I get that. It's frankly too big of a thought—no offense. What kind of disaster would defeat an entire insurance system? Synchronized terrorism? Plague? Asteroid. Definitely asteroid.

I sound like I'm pitching a summer blockbuster but these are not impossible events. *Improbable* yes,—I mean plague is absolutely probable, that's happened before and it's going to happen again, superflu, count on it. I mean it's all possible. So says the Reinsurance Lady in the Blue Suit with the PowerPoint in Denver.

I'm telling you. Insurance is the ultimate Game of Chance. Reinsurance, life insurance, pet insurance if you're one of those people. And once I get my dog I will obviously be one of those people. What will I name him? Him. I automatically think all dogs are boys. Isn't that dumb? But yes he will be a boy dog and of course I will name him Hamlet. And I will buy him a stupid costume for Halloween. And he will save my life.

Wind makes the walls rattle.

It's all statistics until it's happening to you. Then it's happening 100 percent.

Have you seen that footage? From inside a house while a tornado rips through it? Oh my god, y'all. It's . . . well, pretty soon you might have some comparable experience but it's pretty chilling.

This guy is pointing his phone at a big-ass twister. Like it's big, dark, churning and it's not that far away, like it's half a block away, and just like that . . . you see the thing change its mind. Just—"Nope, now I'm coming for *you*." And the guy behind the camera starts freaking out. "Josie!" or "Sheila" or whatever the hell her name is, "*in the basement! Go! Now!*" And of course I'm thinking, "Why the hell aren't you already in the damn basement?" So the screen goes black when the guy goes underground right. But the camera's still on. And I'm thinking, "Why is the camera on? You're gonna tape your own death?!" But then it's like, "Of course. He wants to be seen. He wants *us* to see." And then it comes. You hear them screaming, and she's just saying over and over "oh my god, oh my god" and then—and this is the creepiest moment—the sound gets all wiggy. It's the air pressure. The tornado is sitting on top of them at this point. And the air is being sucked out of every crevice. But then it passes in seconds—literally seconds!—and the guy—the camera's still going, god bless him—gets up and opens the door from the basement to his living room and he sees . . . that his goddamned house is gone. And he's like, "Josie, Sheila," whatever, "it's gone. Everything's gone." And Josie or Sheila Whatever is losing it, and her husband points the camera at the wreckage of his front lawn and just goes, real easy and breezy, just goes, "Oh look. A car." And we see spinning slowly on his driveway, someone's red sedan, upside down, tires to the sky, grinding to a crunching stop.

And I think . . . whose car is that? Are they OK? And how the hell could everything be destroyed in seconds? Chance is how. Hope you had insurance.

Yeah. See I've had to be the one to tell you that your coverage was not adequate and you are not getting money for your upside-down red sedan. I've had to do that. That sucks. I know it sucks *more* for them than for me but I'm not heartless. I'm just dedicated to paperwork. That's why people hate insurance agents. And I have to be the asshole that says, "I mean we did *talk* about getting flood insurance . . ."

I really do try to help. Help find some sense in all the . . . overwhelm. Some reason in the madness.

Then again tornadoes can't be reasoned with. It can't change its mind, it doesn't have one. A true force of nature isn't evil, it can't be. That's why only humans are evil. We know better. We're supposed to.

Although people can take that to an extreme, can't they? The idea that nature is perfect, that "natural" means "good." These are the Whole Foods people, the kombucha people, the people that really truly believe that nature is pure and kind and organic.

That's called "the naturalistic fallacy."

Cancer is "all natural" too, you know. Nature isn't evil but it isn't kind either. It's nature. It's rough, it's competitive. It doesn't stop and it doesn't care and nothing is terrible or beautiful, it just *is*.

My mom died of cancer.

Two years ago. Or three. God, how is it three years already?

That was such an awful time. We'd never had a great relationship. We would definitely not have chosen each other if God had been like: "Cool. Now you get to pick your family! Remember these are the people you will spend the majority of your time with and never truly escape. Choose wisely!" But as a kid she was there for me in a tough-love kinda way. And as soon as she got the diagnosis I was there for her. "We haven't spent much time together in the last fifteen years but screw it, I'm going." You know? My dad left when I was eight so it really was just me and her for most of our lives. Although, oh my god. He sent her flowers in the hospital. Yeah. The first time they'd made contact in *decades* and it's a bouquet of cheap get-well flowers that his new wife obviously thought would be gracious to send. Mom literally bit one of the carnations off its stem and spit it out.

She did not want to die. She was not Hamlet. She was like, "I don't need to have an existential monologue about this, give me the goddamned cure, and let me live!" There was no cure.

Nature was not cruel to her, but it felt like it.

An urgent prayer to her mother:

Dear Mom, I wish you peace. I wish you the deepest peace because you worked too damn hard to be busy in Heaven. And spite is not fun, so drop it. Don't be a bitter angel, Mom. It's not worth it. Be free. Listen to that damn song you sang every damn day and be happy!

Because that is the great lie of my life . . . telling myself, my mother, and the rest of the world that I am happy with him.

But I'm not. And now I'm going to leave him.

Because he makes me very sad.

I think he hates me a little too. I think I hate him. More than a little.

Sometimes I think those BBC nature specials are the only way I'm going to see the wide world if I don't leave now. That and the country pavilions at Epcot. "I'm not going to Norway but I rode that log ride and ate a salmon sandwich so I guess that's good enough for one life." No. I can do better.

Without him I can do a whole lot better.

I've thought about leaving him in the middle of the night. In my mind I've packed the bag. What do I take, what do I leave? I almost did it one night when I thought, "All I need is my purse, phone and charger. That's it." Two a.m. one night, I had my keys in my hand, purse, phone, charger, and . . . I froze. I couldn't open the door. I even wanted too, I was talking to myself, "Go, go, this is it, go." But I didn't.

Hamlet again. To go or not to go. Indecision. Inability to act. Me and Hamlet.

I told myself it was because of my mom's china. It would be too loud and heavy to abscond with it at two a.m., and I couldn't leave it, she was so proud of that china, she bought it for her damn self, and I loved that china, and I couldn't stand the idea of leaving it with him. He'd smash it. I know he would. It would be in sharp chunks all over the driveway if I left. I couldn't let that happen.

I couldn't go.

So I stopped thinking about it after that. Tried to. But I served dinner that next night on my mom's china. It was a vegetarian lasagna. He hated it. *"Where's the fucking meat?"* I said it's healthy. He made two ham sandwiches and ate them in front of the TV.

What a dick.

Just. OK. Don't get weirded out. It's not like *that* . . . He doesn't— like—smack me or anything. He's just a dick. I didn't know he was a dick when we met. I mean he wasn't a dick. He was all sweet and nice. I think. How are we supposed to know this stuff when we're young? Young people are idiots! I was!

We met at a casino. I know. This was years ago. My god, so many years ago. I actually was the roulette croupier, the dealer, you know. The lady running the table. I told you I like odds. What better game of chance is there than roulette! Roulette is literally nothing but chance. I'm telling you it all goes back to insurance! Probability! Anyway, I was just starting out, needed a job, hadn't decided on insurance just yet. I looked good in the stupid little uniform. It made sense at the time.

And I loved running the math in my head with every bet:

There's the complicated math and then the easy math.

The easy math is just one over 36 plus n. I'd run the numbers as quick as I could and place a silent bet on who was going to win at my table. And yes I was usually right.

Anyway. He comes in with some friends. Lands at my table. Bets, bets, bets. Loses a lot, but still has this smile on his face. I ask him why, he says, "You." God, romance is so dumb.

He was cute and liked to show me off to his friends. He bought me pretty things and we went on dates. We had fun. Went to the beach, to the mountains. I purposefully withheld him meeting my mother because she was very distrustful of men and I didn't want her ruining this for me. Which she did.

My mom said: "Nope. He's a dipshit." She actually said dipshit! I was so mad.

"I can't do *anything* right can I?"

"You can *not* marry him, that'd be right."

"He's sweet! He's cute! Good job. He wants to marry me!"

"Angela." Whenever she said it like that it was deadly. "Angela. No." He wasn't soulful. He didn't inspire. I was like: so, he's not a soulful guy. Can we forgive him that he's not Oprah?

"Angela. No."

"WHY, Mom, WHY?"

"He's not funny."

Well that sounded like the dumbest reason not to marry a nice guy. So we eloped and I didn't tell her until later.

He just gets less and less funny.

Look it hasn't been . . . that bad. It's been many years and most of it's been OK. Just lately. You know. Things fall apart. That's what they do.

Maybe we should go back to Epcot. Hard to be depressed at the Norway Pavilion. Or is it? I don't know. I heard they took down the old ride—what was it called—the Tempest or—*Maelstrom!* Yeah. That's what it used to be. The Maelstrom. Oh man I used to get so scared of that ride. The gnomes or elves or whatever they were. But I loved it.

The first time I went was when my mom took me after my dad left us. She was like, "Our life sucks now, let's go to Disney World!" What a good mom. I should have told her that. Holding her hand, walking through the park, both of us in new sunglasses and Minnie Mouse ears, on our own, doing our thing, screw him. That was the time of my life. Until we rode the Maelstrom and I barfed on my dress.

She bought me a new one. It was great. We went every year until I got angsty as a teenager. "It's all fake, Mom. I'm not about being fake." Ugh. Gross. Teenagers are gross. Who cares if it's all fake. For once in your life you can literally buy happiness.

Pause. Sad. To her mom:

You were a good mom, Mom. I'm sorry I was so angsty in high school. I'm sorry I dated jerks. I'm sorry I married somebody you didn't like and that pushed us apart. I'm sorry you died mad at the world. I do not want to be mad at the world. I will not be like you and I hope you will come to see that as part of a compliment. The other part is that, of course I'm like you and thank god I am. Strong and caring and resilient and determined to perfect that goddamned black-walnut pound cake. When life gives you lemons, go to goddamned Disney World and get you some goddamned lemonade and get goddamned happy.

She recovers.

You know now the Maelstrom is a *Frozen* ride. Like the movie. They added princesses. Of course they did.

Fucking Disney.

Actually I wouldn't mind being a princess. A princess with a gun in her closet.

I said it again. I know it makes you nervous when you remember it's there. It's OK. I promise. He locks them all up. There's a cabinet for them upstairs.

I said "all of them." Yeah. Sorry. There's more than one. More than ten. I collect dice, he has his guns. It's his thing. He also collects coins if that makes you feel better.

Maybe just forget about it.

But we can't, can we? Once we know what's real we can't unknow it . . . like a three-year-old in a Best Buy—let me explain.

I saw that exact thing happen. To a three-year-old in a Best Buy. His mom's busy with a phone or something and this kid ends up standing in front of this huge wall of TVs. And I see him crunch his little brow and he says, "Not very nice," to the TV. He was watching some cop show and the murderer is wild-eyed and yelling and waving his gun. And this little dude gets really upset and screams at the wall of TVs: "Not very nice! *Not very nice!*"

I bet you money that kid had never seen violence before. I bet he'd seen nothing but *Sesame Street* up to that point. And to go from dancing numbers to full murderous rage?

And then he starts bawling. He thought it was real. And he thought we were all fine with it. Looking at all of us like, "Are you going to do something about this? There is a mad scary man and no one seems horrified but me!" What a revelation for a three-year-old in a Best Buy. His mom grabbed him and ran out of the store totally embarrassed.

But he's right. We were fine with it. We *are*. Why do we find mayhem so seductive?

Natural disasters, war, massacres, plane crashes. It's all captivating. Why? Horror makes us lean closer, not look away. Why?

Because we want to see how bad things can really get. Because of our inner insurance agent. We want to see it for ourselves, we have to *see* it to *believe* it. So we can learn. Can't protect yourself from something you don't understand. We're all just trying to understand.

But sometimes you do everything right, and you just can't stop the overwhelm, the flood, the wind, or the man with the wild eyes.

It's all a game of chance.

A sudden prayer:

Dear God, please protect me, God protect my neighbors, God protect us all, God I can do better. I can do everything better. I can give more and help more and donate and . . . buy way more Girl Scout Cookies, I don't know, is that helpful? Seems like a win–win but—anyway, please God please. Forgive me. And let me—I don't know— help.

Fuck. I did not want to do this. I did not want to get heavy and real right now, not in a basement.

OK. I mean . . . God knows this already. But you don't. So.

I had an affair.

I mean I'm still having it. If I weren't in this room right now I'd be texting him, or emailing, or with him. I know it's not a thing people should do. It's not. It's just gonna end badly. All the movies end badly. You always get caught. I know.

But it's . . . everything to me. Right now, it really is. God that sounds so awful. I'm a better person than that. I'm a good person, I just hate my husband and cheat on him all the time.

OK. Wait. I'm gonna ground this in some reality because I'm making it sound crazy. My marriage has been rocky for a few years now. When I realized it wasn't getting better, I doubled down on work. Work I love. Save me, Statistics! And it did, for a while. I was giving my all to my clients and it got me noticed. I'm a star agent now—thank you. I have the respect of my entire office, my entire branch! They gave me plaques and raises and bonuses. I got a billboard! And of course: the conferences.

Oh yeah. I was invited to a national conference. On a panel. Yes that's right. I have been empaneled.

And that's where it began.

We met at an insurance conference. In Denver. I know. He was in the breakout session on—I know—reinsurance.

We were so excited and inspired and liberated and—yes—quite drunk. I really did not listen to the people warning me about the altitude in Denver. Jesus those drinks are like missiles. Two tequilas and I was—OK five tequilas, what can I say, I was in love.

And she was so beautiful and so smart and she said that I was so beautiful and so smart and—

OK yeah I lied. Yeah. Not a guy. The lady who gave the talk on reinsurance, blue suit, PowerPoint. It's her. I don't know why I said that it was a guy. I don't know you. You might hate me. I don't like the idea of being hated.

And gay is new to me too. Sort of. Not really. College.

What is new to me is . . . real love. Comfort is new. Being understood.

Linda is new and I am new. And I am . . . happy.

I think my mom would be too.

So yeah. Linda, Denver, reinsurance, tequila. It was the most exhilarating thing I've ever done in my life. And her hotel room was so fancy too. A view of the snowy mountains, a big old bathroom with a jacuzzi tub! We stayed there for twenty-four hours solid. She even stayed an extra day. For me. And we went on an actual *date*. Across town so none of our colleagues would see and we could get all handsy. We ordered champagne and dessert. We talked about traveling together. She said Paris, I said Norway, she said sure! It was like meeting someone you should've known your whole life.

She knows I'm married. She got divorced a long time ago. She has a son in college. And a little dog named Ophelia—I'm kidding. She calls it Winkie or Binkie or something stupid. We'll work on that. But you know—dog!

She was worried when I told her about him. She's the first person I told about him. She said it was shocking that I'd live with him for so long. That his behavior was not OK. That I was in . . . denial.

When I got on the plane home I thought it was a dream. Was that real? Why would she ever want me? I still don't know.

But I know I'm meeting her tonight. Tonight's going to be the beginning.

Half of you are all swept up in the romance, and half of you are like, "What a terrible person." And probably a few of you are like, "Are we still in a tornado warning? 'Cause that seems to be the main issue at hand." Yes, you have not missed the tornado. It will not be subtle.

And I know. I really do get it. And I'm going to get a divorce. Whether I can actually be with her or not—I already know I can't stay with him. I know this. Look at me telling you with such glee about how much I hate him.

And. Look. Shocker: I lied before. He . . . he did hit me. He does. You don't have to believe me but he does. Not always in the face, but emotional stuff, you know. Anger. Threat. Overwhelm.

God I should have left him so long ago. Why didn't I? It was too hard.

Bank accounts, mortgages, divorce and lawyers and bills and—Jesus—I just froze. *Why is my life worth less than my mortgage? Get out, get out, get out Angela!*

I used to think I deserved it, that's how bad it was, that's how normal it was. I deserved whatever bullshit mini rage he cooked up.

Well I don't deserve it.

I didn't deserve it when he threw a jug of milk at my head. I almost called the cops on him but what, get him arrested for milk? It was a *gallon* of milk though. I had a bruise on my cheek and a neck I couldn't turn for a month. I'd called the cops before. Didn't help.

But still. I didn't deserve it when he threw me against the wall of our living room after the Super Bowl. I didn't deserve it when he smacked the veggie lasagna out of my goddamned hands.

I don't even deserve the look he gets in his eye when I can tell he's trying to decide whether I deserve it or not. That look. Wild. Lids flung open. Pupils wide like a coin. Jaw tense like it's cracking a nut, breathing through his nose like a bull.

I'm living with a wild animal and that animal is a man.

He pointed a gun at me once.

He pointed a gun at himself once.

Yesterday.

He makes me sad and scared and I think he might be dangerous.

So tonight I leave.

My mother would be thrilled.

Liberating anger and defiance as she practices what she'll say to him. It's like she is *saying it to him.*

"HEY.

I'm leaving you.

Right now.

Because I can't do this anymore.

But more importantly . . . *you cannot do this to me anymore.*

You're angry, you snap, you yell and *you hurt me.*

For years, you did this and half the time you seemed to really enjoy it.

Well. *You do not get that pleasure any more.*

I'm leaving you and I *cannot wait.*

You make me so sick. I'm sick thinking of how long I lived with this. How many times I went to bed with a bruise; how many times you broke my things; how many times I ducked and flinched and thought, 'I wonder if he'll kill me.'

Did you ever think that? No. You have no idea what that thought is like. You lived next to a flower, I lived next to a bomb.

So. Do not call me, do not email, do not force me to look at you ever again so I can start to forget *the decades of my life I wasted on you.*"

The wind really picks up now.

I said that to him. About an hour ago. Every bit of it.

He got pretty mad.

A different kind of mad than I'd ever seen before. This frozen kind of mad, like someone paused him. Like a calm before a . . . yeah. The air felt instantly noxious. I just started to back away from him.

"Get your keys, purse, charger—"

Then he said, "No. I go first." And he stormed out. And I thought, "Oh. Is that it? Maybe that's it. Maybe I'll leave my husband and go get Chick-fil-A for dinner."

Then the storm started. Because No. No, that's not *it.* Of course it's not.

I have lived with him for long enough to know . . .

That this was coming. What kind of complicity, what kind of brainwash is that, holding that knowledge and doing nothing?

If he is who I am fast realizing he is. . . then who does that make me? Someone who lies to the whole world to make it all easier. *A loud jolt from upstairs, something banged, something heavy dropped.*

I heard him let loose a yell from the other room. A yell like a shot moose, like a bear with a broken leg, like a creature dying. A raging moan, a train, a horn, a howl.

That's when I came down here.

My gun's down here.

He doesn't know I have a gun, I bought it a month ago.

Little lies. Harmless.

Why would I tell him? Have to protect myself. What are the chances?

A racket sound from upstairs— is it the tornado smashing things or a madman?

She gets her gun from the closet safe. Ready to protect herself. She never points it at the audience though.

She starts a rapid recitation—more calm than panic. It's a runaway train of facts and truths and statistics and story. She starts to find a rhythm, an unstoppable recognition of her true situation. She is repeating some earlier lines in a new context now. She is telling the whole truth now. It's coming, he's coming.

And now the storm is here.

And statistically, domestic abuse victims are five times more likely to die if there are guns in the house.

And now the storm is here.

And women are three-point-six times more likely to be killed by their partners when trying to leave.

And now the storm is here.

And the thousand natural shocks that flesh is heir to.

And nature is not nice.

And man is the only evil animal.

And a woman is killed by a man she knows every sixteen hours in this country.

And Shit. I think this is real. This might be really happening. And the things you need to know are: This is the basement. Gun in the closet.

And does anyone have a signal down here?

And you can't get help until *after* things like this. You're just gonna get more people hurt if you call for help now.

And I didn't deserve it.

And I don't deserve it.

And I'm leaving.

And it's the judgment day.

And I tried to leave him

And I froze, I couldn't go GO GO

And of course it's a man, a woman would never make a mess like that.

And the gun in the closet, and the guns in his closet.

And I roll the dice

And a game of chance

And isn't that life.

And it's all statistics until it's happening to you. Then it's happening 100 percent.

And a pistol in a tornado.

And the pistol is the tornado.

And the tornado is the man.

And the man is upstairs.

And he's coming, and he's coming and he's here

And the storm is here

And the judgment day

And he has a gun and knows now that I'm in the basement And "while perpetrators of domestic violence account for only 10 percent of all gun violence, they accounted for 54 percent of mass shootings."

And the thousand natural shocks

And the thousand natural shocks

And sitting in this underground shelter I am scared into quivering breathlessness thinking of what's to come. And what's to come is not a force of nature but a force of man.

A sobering pause. Slowing down. Connecting with us. Wanting to be very very clear now.

And the things you need to know are:

I lied.

There is no storm.

There is only him.

And this is the judgment day, which makes you the judges. And I tell you this . . . *all* of this tonight because . . . I do not want to be known only as his victim.

She tells us the truth.

After he shoots me in the heart with my own weapon, he will leave me to bleed.

And he will do what he's planned.

And he will drive to a place he knows well.

And he will unpack his weapons.

And he will fire on a crowd.

And he doesn't care who's in it.

And you might be in it. There's a chance it will be you. Roll the dice.

Because it's chance that we're here right now, isn't it?

And tonight is 100 percent happening to us.

Because I was a warning sign that no one ever saw.

And they will find me some hours from now. Once they name him. "He's married. Find her. What can she tell us?" That is the question.

"To be or . . ."

> *She breathes as*
> *The wind howls and howls and howls.*
> *The tornado is upon us.*
> *It rips the house apart. The lights plunge out.*

> *They flicker on for a moment and perhaps we see her on the ground or standing*
> *staring back at us, bleeding from a gunshot wound in her chest.*
> *She can't speak any more.*
> *"See me," she wishes she could say to you. See me.*

End of Play.